Finding Blossoms
in the Darkness

Published on behalf of The Zhubin Foundation
by Cultureshock Media
www.cultureshockmedia.co.uk

Author: Simin Sarikhani
Editor: Alison Sturgeon
Design: Luke Smith and Alfonso Iacurci
Production: Nicola Vanstone

Illustration: © Lesley Buckingham,
Central Illustration Agency

Printed by Pureprint Group Limited

© The Zhubin Foundation 2018

All rights reserved. No part of this publication may be reproduced, copied or transmitted in any form without permission from The Zhubin Foundation.

ISBN 978-0-9954546-4-4

Finding Blossoms in the Darkness

A mother's journey
through deepest loss to hope

Simin Sarikhani

Table of Contents

Words of Gratitude — 1

PROLOGUE
In My Garden — 5
Where is My Son? — 10

PART 1 – DUSK: A MEANINGFUL LIFE
Born in Turbulent Times — 14
Childhood — 19
Return to Iran — 25
A Lesson in Loss — 31
An Ending and a Beginning — 35
Onset of Darkness — 38
Sleep Like the Dead — 44
Young Wisdom — 47
Shock — 49
Keeping Hope Alive — 51
The News — 55

PART 2 – NIGHT: DARKNESS FALLS
The Missed Lunch — 60
Zhubin's Going — 62
Burial — 66
The First Touch — 67
Agony — 72
Was It My Fault? — 73
Darkness — 76
The First Gift — 78
The Passage of Pain — 79
A Circle of Loss — 82
Brothers — 90
My Confidante — 92
My Winding Road — 95
Where Do They Go? — 97
The Tombstone — 100
Feeling the Bond — 102
Blessings From a Broken Heart — 104
Remembering the Promise — 108

PART 3 – DAWN: THE FIRST SHOOTS

Mya	112
What Kind of Bird is a Dove?	114
Healing Through Helping	117
Letting in the Light	120
Cemetery	122
Self-mastery	126
The Glove	127
Spiritual Mysteries	131
Learning to Live Again	134
The Happy Learner	136
Finding Blossoms in the Darkness	138

PART 4 – RAYS OF LIGHT: MESSAGES AND SIGNS

Ladybugs From Joo-Joo	147
Garden of the Heart	150
My Lucky Number	155
A Chance Encounter	157
Jarred	161
A Gift Deferred	164
The Red Fox	167
A Hand-stitched Message	170
Daisy	172
What Do Signs Mean to Me?	175

PART 5 – SUNSHINE: A PEACEFUL HEART

The Biggest Show Ever	180
Back in My Garden	181

PART 6 – WINGS OF WORDS

Who Was Zhubin?	186
The Master Plan	188

PART 7 – A PARTING GIFT

Farewell	232
A Letter to Mothers: Heart to Heart	236
Au revoir	239
A Letter to Zhubin	265

Words of Gratitude

The creation of this book was a journey that confirmed my belief that the Universe is the perfect organizer. Everyone who played an essential role in bringing it to life generously contributed their unique talents – each person appearing at the right time and for the right purpose. They dedicated long hours, showing immeasurable patience with my limitations, and the pages that follow bear the indelible trace of their spirit. I am convinced that it was fully intended for these individuals to join me as instruments to breathe life into this book.

Knowing what I would have to face, and the help that I would need, the Universe placed me beside Jill Martis, my dear friend and neighbour of the past 20 years. A breath of fresh air in my many dark days, she has been with me since the very conception of this book. The endless hours of work she has devoted to it made me understand the true meaning of a "labour of love", as she called it.

When I told my brother Ali Sarikhani that I needed to find a publisher, without any hesitation or question as to the book's nature he replied, "Come to London with it and I will take you to the right person." That person turned out to be Jane Lawson, a director of the Victoria and Albert Museum. Even though she too knew nothing of my early draft manuscript, she offered not only to help me find the right publisher, but to follow the project's progress to its completion.

That publisher turned out to be Phil Allison of Cultureshock Media, who believed in this book and agreed to take it on, even though its subject matter was unfamiliar. When I asked him to explain his surprise acceptance, he replied: "I look at it as art."

Handpicked by Phil, Alison Sturgeon has been so much more than a mere editor – taking me under her wing, her vast knowledge and experience were invaluable in guiding me to polish and improve every aspect of this book. Her gentle patience will never be forgotten.

Phil and Alison then introduced me to Luke Smith, my talented young designer whose sensitive touches and ideas helped elevate the book to a plane that we could not have hoped to reach without him.

Together with Alison and Luke we then persuaded my gifted artist Lesley Buckingham to help. Her delicate illustrations spiritually bind this book.

Finally, the base of this book and pillar of my life is my husband Zygmunt Marcinski, whose commitment and support has never wavered.

That this book came to pass is a living example of Zhubin's words: *"Togetherness is multidimensional."* I am grateful to all from the bottom of my heart.

"Make flowers bloom wherever you go."

– Zhubin Moshir

Prologue

In My Garden

I speak to you simply as a mother. I am not a writer nor a storyteller, and English is not my first language. I must find the strength to tell my story, despite not knowing where to start, what to say, or how to say it. I am neither trying to impress nor preach.

This is not a book about loss, grief, sadness or pain, although, when my only child ended his life at the age of 21, I was forced to face all of these beyond imagining. This is not a story about either myself or my son, and it is not an attempt to make a hero of him or a victim of myself. Instead, it is a tale of faith, hope, and finding inner peace and contentment – a belief that "all is well". It is about becoming whole again.

I do not know who will read this book, or how many hearts, if any, it may touch. All I wish is to share with you my journey, that of a mother who lost her child yet became open to the world, and so received miracles as small as the spots on the back of a ladybug and as big as the all-encompassing love of God, who, for me, is found not in any one religion and is known by many names. He is the unknowable force that unifies us all in the end. I believe that all paths to God lead to one source: love.

My deepest and most sincere desire in sharing my story is to open a door for parents who are suffering because, like me, they have lost a child. Should this book help just one mother, then my work is done. When, in chance conversations, emails and phone calls, I shared my experience of loss with grieving mothers, I felt their desperation to find a way to survive the pain that they were in. Each mother asked these two questions: "How is it possible?" and "How did you do it?"

This book is my answer.

In telling this story it is not my wish either to sadden you or to seek pity for me and my son Zhubin, but it is the only way that I can show the beauty of pain: first I must describe the horror of the darkness we each endured before I can reveal to you the light I discovered, hidden deep inside what had seemed a bottomless pit of loss.

When I held a pen to write this story I was often paralyzed by memories of grief, the streams of tears pouring down a testament to the enormity of my loss. How can a mother go through life without her child? How can a mother witness her child's burial, yet survive and go forward? Some of the words that found their way onto my paper flowed easily, while others barely trickled. They are the words of a once shattered, now healed, heart. Losing a child is a searing agony, one that breaks you into shards that cut like glass. You then must try to put the pieces back together and find a way to live again. I know that now, but it has been a hard lesson to learn.

Zhubin's suffering and death brought many gifts – for himself, for me, and many others. The greatest of these was given to me: I saw that I had long been asleep and that it was time to wake up. I discovered a dormant longing in me to be pure and free, to learn and to seek. The more I learned, the more I realized that I knew nothing, yet the wonder was in the thirst I had to better understand – while I still had time here.

After years of holding my breath waiting for the worst, I now take deep breaths and every day feel my son around me – not so much as a benevolent spirit but as a presence in the air I breathe, the flowers I tend, and most of all in helping others. As I write these lines, I feel so grateful – what a blessed mother I am! Even as I still miss Zhubin so very much, the feeling of joy and peace in my heart is overwhelming and inexplicable.

Looking back, only God knows how hard, painful and lonely the road was; how many times I lost the path and was unable to find it; how many times I fell, again and again. And yet, over and over, I felt the abundant help God was giving me. Each and every time, at the right moment, I remembered words from Zhubin's writings that helped me persevere. In the course of his short and turbulent life, Zhubin wrote down his many thoughts about life and its meaning for him, and it was his wish that I share these with others.

"Be my voice and spread my words. The beauty of it is that it is self-sowing. You will never see the end or how many hearts you will have touched."

It is a privilege to include in this book his words, written due to and in spite of his suffering. Extracts are threaded throughout this book, both embedded in the text and at the end of many chapters, while the full collection appears in the final pages. Their essence is a simple wisdom offering tender guidance that touched my heart and soul.

Because these words are all I have left of him, it has not been an easy decision to share with you this part of my son: I had wanted to keep for myself his words and so Zhubin. Afraid to lose my connection with him, I had not wanted to talk about his writings – even with loving family and friends. Oh, I had been so desperate and broken!

More than ten years passed before I felt ready to undertake this project. In addition to my desire to hold onto both our story and his words, I asked myself repeatedly: "Who am I to write about my journey? Every life has its own unique purpose and wonder." At first softly, and then louder and louder, my heart heard the same answer: "Share the story – it could help others. It is not only about you."

I hope that this book and Zhubin's words inspire grieving parents with some hope and comfort. It seems as if we will never get used to the agony of loss, never be free of it, and can never deny it. To the end of our days, every cell in our bodies burns with longing to have our lost children back again, even if only in a dream: just a little hug for a moment; just to hear their voices for one second.

It is my earnest wish that every one of us finds a path through to the beauty and blessings that surround us, no matter how obscure this pain of grieving makes them. What I eventually learned from Zhubin, guiding me to and keeping me on the steps of my path, was a belief in a higher truth of the Universe.

This book attempts to fulfil my promise to Zhubin, who asked me: *"Mom, share your learning and be touched in return. Share our story, our journey."* Having told this story I now have the peace of mind to continue the rest of my journey.

In my tiny garden, where today I write these lines and where so much of this book was written, it is quiet, fresh and inviting. I take pleasure in sharing this sanctuary with many different and exquisite creatures: cardinals, chipmunks, honeybees, butterflies and even hummingbirds. Zhubin loved nature, believing that it was a pure giver, not only through its loveliness but also in its hidden lessons. Here in my garden, at this very moment, I hear him saying: *"Life is a living garden and one has to celebrate life always. Add colourful flowers and enjoy them. This way you are painting the canvas of your life. Celebrate your life, mine and all life."* And I reply silently: "Let us celebrate together." Knowing that he is helping and guiding me with this book gives me boundless joy: we are doing it together.

Sitting on my garden bench, amid all my papers and with a mug of fresh coffee that smells so good, the past unfolds. Isn't it interesting how the mind categorizes memories as "happy", "funny", "sad", or "unbearable"? I now embrace to my heart all my memories – even the ones that had been unendurable, stemming from the darkest times. The happy ones brought joy, but it was the hard ones that each carried a lesson for me to learn. I could not and did not understand this for many years following Zhubin's death.

Two nights ago, I had one of my most serene moments of connection with the Divine. With all my being I was talking to God, giving thanks for all the gifts He gave to Zhubin and me. Very early the next morning, I heard Zhubin's voice speaking to me. I don't know if I was dreaming, or if I really heard him saying once again: *"Mom, go ahead with pride in your heart."* At that moment, I knew the time had come to start the work, to open a new chapter in my life and pass on his words. I remember him telling me: *"Mom, you can do it. It is your mission and your responsibility. Remember, I talked to you about courage and vision? Go ahead, open doors for others. Help others. You are not alone."*

With unconditional love, I wish you a peaceful journey.

Simin

"We cannot plan out everything. What is inescapable is destiny. Just take it and go forward. But what we can plan to do is to make the right choices – whether we do or not, that's up to us. Coming here to this life is like signing a contract with the Universe: when the work is done, we go back home."

The bench in my garden where this book was born and I spent countless hours writing.

Where is My Son?

When the police came, we were not at home.

It was a brisk Saturday morning in May, the day before Mother's Day – a day of flowers, gifts and brunches. Had we planned something? A lunch with family, I think, although we had not decided on a specific restaurant. The previous evening I'd asked Zhubin to pick a place – he had a talent for coming up with fun ideas.

Zhubin had appeared calm, smiling and joking before he went downstairs to prepare for bed. As I had done every evening for months now that he was so frail, I went with him to his bedroom to help him get ready and to say goodnight. Looking back, I believe that I sensed an air of peace about him.

"*Simin, would you wake me up tomorrow at 7.15?*" he asked me. Zhubin didn't call me "Mom" – or "Mâmân", as I called my own mother in Persian. Ever since he had spoken his first words, he had addressed me as "Simin", as if we were equals and friends, and not just mother and son.

"Are you sure?" I asked, startled. Usually, I roused him an hour later.

"*Yes,*" he replied with certainty.

"It is much too early," I insisted.

"*No, Simin, promise.*"

"Then of course, my love. I promise."

As I turned to leave the room, he stood up, hugged me hard and asked: "*Mom, Mom, do you really love me?*"

I was surprised by the question – as if he didn't know? – and even more so by his calling me "Mom." Holding him tight, I kissed him and replied: "More than anything and anyone in my life." Although we hugged often, I remember that this time the embrace was longer, deeper and tighter than usual. As I left his room, still feeling his arms around me, I prayed that for once he would have a good sleep, a deep sleep from which he would rise rested and ready to face another day.

Of course, I was fooling myself. Sleep is not an accurate word to describe what Zhubin did. Every evening around 10pm he would collapse into unconsciousness, as if in a coma whose onset was sudden, like fainting – a broken body falling to the floor. Unlike true sleep, his was neither restful nor restorative, but instead left him as if he were dead, unmoving. Every night I would return downstairs to check if he was still breathing – standing over his inert body and praying for a miracle. It was a simple plea, as on that Friday night: Please, God, let my son have a good night's sleep.

It had been too difficult to organize a Mother's Day celebration for that Sunday, so instead we had planned our lunch for Saturday. I rose early that morning and, as I made my way downstairs, I wondered once again why Zhubin had asked me to wake him an hour before the usual 8.15am – it was hard enough to rouse him even then. Maybe he wanted us to spend some time together before the lunch scheduled with my dear mother-in-law, Mila? To my surprise, when I entered his bedroom I saw that his bed was already made up, his pyjamas folded and neatly placed on the bedcover, and his slippers arranged on the floor. There was no Zhubin. How strange, I thought, not yet alarmed.

As if in a trance, I turned back to check in his bathroom – but he was not there either. Nor had I seen him already upstairs in the kitchen or outside sitting in the garden, wrapped in a blanket against the chill. I returned to his bedroom. Had I missed him? That's when I saw the bedroom window was ajar, a stepladder outside propped against the cement wall of the light shaft that led up to the garden. A small post-it note was stuck to the window pane:

"Simin, do not keep me alive if I am comatose. Promise me that. Zhubin XO"

Part 1

Dusk: A Meaningful Life

Born in Turbulent Times

Zhubin came into the world at a time of great upheaval, in a country far from the place I had called my home: I was born in 1952 in Persia, now Iran, an ancient land of philosophers and poets. I had enjoyed a happy childhood, growing up in Tehran surrounded by my brothers and sisters. As my parents considered education to be of the utmost importance, they managed to send all their children abroad to complete their studies. It was while I was briefly studying in London that I met Zhubin's father, Shervin, who had come to England from Iran several years earlier on a scholarship to attend university. Overcome with homesickness, I returned to Tehran after just nine months. Once Shervin completed his degree a few months later, he too returned home and we were married in Tehran soon after.

Four years later, Shervin and I were still living in Tehran, settled in the modest but cozy house we had built two years previously. Close to my parents' residence at the very top of a hilly section of the city, our home was fortunate to have both a spectacular mountain view and the intoxicating scent of jasmine flowers. We enjoyed an active social life enriched by an extended family with whom we shared lively gatherings and conversations.

Then the Islamic Revolution of 1979 to 1980 turned my world upside down.

For a while there had been dissatisfaction with the government in Iran, leading to rising popular support for the exiled religious leader Ayatollah Khomeini. This eventually erupted into street protests and turmoil across the country. Every day, increasingly violent and dangerous riots moved closer and closer to our neighbourhood. It was a frightening time, but we never imagined that things would go as far and as quickly as they did. Soon the city was ruled by revolutionaries and Ayatollah Khomeini took power, completely changing the face of Iranian society.

As a result of the many dangers, we decided that we had no choice but to run away leaving everything behind: our home, all our belongings, and – most important of all – my parents, Shervin's beloved mother and his two sisters. We planned to fly to London to join my brother Ali, who had left Iran several months earlier in a hurry: not only had it been dangerous for him to stay any longer, but his seven months' pregnant wife and two young children were already anxiously waiting for him alone in England. During Ali's rushed departure my father had reassured him: "They may confiscate everything, but they cannot rob you of your brain." He would be proven right when Ali went on to become one of the most successful Iranian émigrés.

Then it was our turn to flee Iran. Arriving at the airport at 4am, fully 12 hours prior to our scheduled flight departure time, all that Shervin and I had with us were our pre-Islamic Iranian passports stamped with still-valid UK tourist visas, one suitcase each and US$2,000 in cash, the maximum permitted to be taken out of the country. The terminal teemed with revolutionary guards armed with machine guns. Frightened, we could see many travellers not only being denied exit permission, but also having both their possessions and passports seized. I held my breath, watching Shervin's hand shake as he handed over our passports and documents to the border official. After what seemed an eternity, we were given permission to leave.

In London, my brother Ali awaited us. He and his wife Sabine had also left everything behind and were now scratching to make a new life for themselves and their young family. Sharing with us what little they had, Ali and Sabine took us under their wing. I have never forgotten their kindness and love during those particularly trying days.

When we fled Tehran in 1980, I was already two months pregnant with Zhubin. Every one of us who left was convinced at that time that it would be but a temporary displacement, and so I kept telling myself that we'd be back home as soon as my child was born. How wrong we all were – so terribly wrong!

Shervin and I were among the very lucky ones who left Iran before the revolutionary authority shut down the airport, which had become an absolute madhouse. After its closure, many people, including several close friends, risked everything to make the dangerous trek out of Iran by traversing high mountains on foot and on horseback in order to cross the border into Turkey.

One of the few possessions I had brought with me from Iran was a burnished copper bowl, a keepsake given to us the night before our departure by my parents' beloved housekeeper Bibi, who had been like a family member since my childhood. Bibi came to mind several months later in London, when I was near the end of my pregnancy. We were living in a tiny walk-up flat, sleeping on rolled-up blankets on the hard floor, with hardly any money and little food, wondering how we would survive: "Oh my God Bibi, you were a widowed mother of four, cooking and cleaning for us so that you could go home and support your children; you came to our house every day, witnessing the comfort of our lives, and yet had no expectations for yourself." Great teachers are those who teach essential lessons in quiet and humble ways. With her generous heart and her constant smile, Bibi was one of my great teachers – one whose lessons I carry with me to this day.

At this time there was great uncertainty about the future, to say nothing of the trauma of losing our home, our country, and the comfort of family and friends. While in London, I could not stop thinking of Tehran – all the wonderful times and joyful memories – and how different things would have been had there been no revolution: what I could have shared with my mother as I became a mother myself; the new home left behind in Tehran; and the nursery I had planned for our child. London was a nightmare.

As time marched on, Shervin and I lost all hope of ever returning to Iran. We were also in a state of panic because our UK tourist visas were set to expire soon. Heavily pregnant, I visited the Home Office to request an extension of our visa until our child was born. Although we were granted an additional three months, the questions remained: What would happen to us? Where could we go? The answer to these concerns came just in time. Ali came home one evening accompanied by a close mutual friend from Iran. I could not believe it and was thrilled to see our friend again after all this time, hugging him tight – he even smelled of home! It was a very happy reunion. The concerned friend, who knew of our situation, told us that he was living with his parents in a Canadian city named Vancouver and suggested that we apply for Canadian residency. We did so and received our Canadian long-term-stay visas – miraculously, it seemed – within only two months. How happy we were, relieved and so very grateful to Canada for agreeing to take us in!

The difficulties we found ourselves in during my last days of pregnancy were all the more distressing due to the outbreak of war between Iran and Iraq. Naturally we worried about our friends and family back home, with whom communication was haphazard as telephone contact was often disrupted.

Late one evening, as I was sitting with Ali and Sabine in their tiny flat, I began to feel some twinges. When I had attended an appointment that morning with my obstetrician he had informed me that I was not due for delivery for another three weeks, so I dismissed my pain, putting it down to fatigue from the very long walk to and from the doctor's office. I noticed, however, that Sabine, by then a veteran of three deliveries, was looking at me intently and holding a watch in her hand. A short while later, she insisted that we go straight away to the hospital, overriding my protests that I wasn't due for another three weeks. As we left the flat, I could hear Ali's laughter as he joked about how foolishly Sabine was behaving. But only a few minutes later, while in the car on the seemingly interminable drive to the hospital, the pain turned much worse. I was admitted immediately upon arrival and after a brief examination confirming that birth was imminent I was escorted directly to the delivery room. Within two hours Zhubin was born on September 26th, 1980, with the sole assistance of two very young nurses as no doctor had been available late at night.

I was left overnight in pain, but the next morning my visible discomfort was met with hostility by the female Iraqi doctor on duty: she brusquely informed me that my suffering was trivial compared with the sacrifices of the women fighting and dying in the Iran-Iraq war.

Due to complications following Zhubin's birth I didn't leave the hospital until 13 days later. Thinking about it afterwards, I do not know how much more serious my condition would have been had Sabine not been watching so keenly. She had been there for me when Mâmân couldn't be, and we had grown to be like sisters: not only had we been constantly together in Iran for the past ten years, but now in exile in London, where we were both young, homesick and desperately worried, we loved and supported each other unconditionally, sharing what little we had.

Soon after Zhubin's birth, Shervin left for Vancouver, where he had landed a job, in order to make arrangements for our arrival. The happiness of knowing that there was going to be a safe place waiting for us to live was tempered by the sad realization that I was going to be somewhere so very far from the ones I loved. I remember asking a friend where Vancouver was – at that time I had no idea! He replied: "If you were to dig a hole straight down from Iran on this side of the world, you would reach Vancouver on the other side." He was right: there is an 11.5-hour time difference between the two points. The last thing I did before leaving for Canada was to telephone my parents. Because of the war with Iraq, it was not at all easy to get a connection and it was also very expensive. But it didn't matter to me that the money for that call could have bought us a week's worth of food: I desperately needed to talk to them. Because we were embarking on a journey to "the opposite side of the world", I had no idea what was going to happen to us or when I would see my parents again, if ever. I did not want to lose what might have been my last chance to speak to them. Mâmân's voice was worried for us and especially for Zhubin, the grandchild she had not yet seen or held. Anxious about the distance to Canada and its cold weather, she advised me on how to keep the baby warm and asked why we were going so far away instead of somewhere closer to Iran – closer to them. Her love and concern were overwhelming and we both wept. My strong and wise father, whom we called Baba, tried so hard to give me comfort and courage. While he did his best to hide his emotions, I could hear the sadness in his worried voice.

More than 35 years on, that phone call remains an unforgettable and precious memory in my life. I remember very clearly their words of encouragement and love, and then how Sabine and I hugged one another, crying as we said our goodbyes. It was heart-wrenching to part from my nephews and niece – I loved them like my own. But we had to go.

Cradling two-month-old Zhubin in my arms, I set out for Canada. There I found myself far away from friends and family in an unfamiliar place, caring for a baby who was often ill and unsettled. A constant concern for us during this time was Zhubin's crying. We could not have known then, but his difficulty in sleeping was not that of an ordinary baby. Life in Vancouver proved hard, with many challenges to meet. We were on a roller coaster, but life went on and so did we.

"Life has its ups and downs. Ride them like waves."

Childhood

From the start, Zhubin was a fussy baby. He took his time to develop: slow to walk and then slow to talk. But when he finally did speak, it was in full sentences. In no time at all, he mastered the English alphabet. Zhubin was an observer, a curious boy, quiet and patient. He loved puzzles, playing with Lego and building things with blocks. He quickly grew to be both an eager reader and a lover of nature, connecting with creatures of any description.

From a very young age, everyone could sense Zhubin's gentle soul. Whenever he saw a living creature for the very first time, he became so excited and wonderstruck that he did not know what to do. This is what occurred when, as a toddler, he first saw a fluffy yellow and black caterpillar, pointing it out to me with his little finger and just standing, immobile, looking intently. Later Zhubin would take an empty shoebox, line it with tissue paper and paper towels, and every day go around the tiny garden gathering injured insects and putting them ever

Zhubin, not yet one year old, enjoying the beach at Stanley Park, Vancouver.

so carefully into the box, hoping for them to heal. Naturally I kept my eye on this box, secretly removing the dead. When Zhubin asked what had happened to the missing ones, I made him happy by explaining that they had gotten well and returned to their moms. It is no wonder that Zhubin's nickname became Joo-Joo, which in Farsi means "cute little bug".

Seeing a snail for the first time, he remarked: *"Look Simin, they are so cute: they carry their homes wherever they go!"* Zhubin's love for all creatures was a quality that those who met him would recall, even years later. On one summer night, while sitting talking with an old friend in the kitchen, I jumped to my feet to kill a mosquito between my clapped hands. A young child at the time, Zhubin looked at me and said: *"Simin, would you like a big giant to crush you between his hands? You cannot kill!"* Some 15 years later at Zhubin's memorial in Vancouver, the same dear friend who observed this scene would share with the gathering this memory. How much it must have touched him to remember it after all those years!

One afternoon, at Zhubin's insistence, Shervin and I took him on a visit to an animal shelter that was within walking distance of our home. He was so excited, wanting to take home all the dogs, but at that time we had not been prepared to have a pet of our own. I realized that we had made a big mistake in bringing him there, since it would be heartbreaking for him to leave without taking home even one dog. To bring peace, we promised him instead to return every afternoon to the shelter and volunteer to walk a dog for the allotted 45 minutes. He kept us to our word, and we developed a routine of going every afternoon to the shelter to walk Lucy, a toy poodle, lame and blind in one eye, who he insisted on as his choice: *"Simin, Lucy is blind and no one else will walk her."* One of the shelter's attendants would relate to us how excited Lucy would get as her time to be with Zhubin drew near. The two of them enjoyed many, many walks together.

In time Zhubin converted our home into a menagerie that included as its guests a dog, a cat, two rabbits and three turtles. He also cared for a raccoon he named Charlie, a frequent visitor to our kitchen who became almost a playmate for Zhubin. For many years Zhubin took care of him and his family. One day Charlie brought his two very young babies, along with his mate whom Zhubin had named Katie. *"Simin, Simin, come quickly!"* Zhubin had called. *"Charlie is here with the whole family, but don't come too close or they'll be scared off. You know what this means?"* he had added. *"More food! We need to buy bigger bags of food."* I understood that very well: if I failed to buy enough dog food for the raccoons, I would find the fridge empty the next day.

In general, Zhubin had his own way of doing things. When he was three years old, I enrolled him in the Grouse Mountain Ski School in North Vancouver. After a few weekends of lessons, the school called me to come and get him, as he had refused to do anything but sit in the snow. I told them to leave him be. The next year, I enrolled him again. Again, the ski school called – but this time utterly amazed: Zhubin was out skiing with his classmates, fearless, turning back and forth on the hill, sure of himself. I explained to his instructor: "You just have to give him time, that's all." His pattern was to watch, understand and wait until he was sure he could do something to the best of his ability, always aiming for perfection. *"My life,"* he often said, *"is about all or nothing. There is no in between."*

Because he was so gentle, as he grew older I often worried that Zhubin wouldn't be able to survive the harshness of life. One day he came home from school with several bruises. Upset, I asked him what had happened. Not answering me at first, he finally admitted to being bullied by an older boy who had wanted to take his fruit roll-ups. When I asked him, "Why didn't you fight back?" he replied that he hadn't wanted to do so lest he hurt the boy, adding, *"But Simin, he needs the fruit roll-ups more than me, because he comes to school without lunch."* After that, I made sure to put extra fruit roll-ups in Zhubin's lunch box for that boy – Zhubin even went on to invite him home after school so we could feed him. Zhubin had a small group of friends, but they were very close and he would keep these friendships throughout his life.

A very bright child, Zhubin was not only an "A" student for whom education was very important but was also quite athletic, participating in a variety of sports. Like his father, he became a collector – but, in his case, of hockey cards, comic books, old daggers, "Transformer" toys and a particularly beautiful collection of seashells, as well as semi-precious stones.

Zhubin loved to hear anecdotes about my childhood, especially those about growing up with more than 35 cousins more or less my age, all playing together and swimming in a pool filled with natural water in my grandparents' garden. Growing up in Vancouver, with only occasional visits from family scattered over the globe, he could not comprehend such an existence. He'd ask me to repeat them again and again, and each time would be amazed. Years later, when he was ill in Montreal and lying on his bed, he'd smile and tell me: *"Simin, I wish we were living in Iran; we wouldn't suffer this much – it would be much easier to have the family and cousins around."*

Fortunate to have had a father with many interests, Zhubin was introduced to the worlds of music, art, history and literature. Father and son had a close relationship. At times Shervin would play with his son as if he were a child himself. Their laughter would rise from Zhubin's bedroom while Shervin read Garfield books to him. In the summer, they would set up a tent in the backyard and picnic inside it. They both loved making up a bed, bringing a big flashlight and all kinds of snacks, books and games. I would overhear their excitement over board games and Shervin putting on a funny voice when reading scary stories to Zhubin, making them even more thrilling. Waking up covered in mosquito bites never stopped them from enjoying these overnight adventures.

As Shervin loved to listen to classical music and opera, Zhubin naturally developed an appreciation and love of music, ranging from rap and hip-hop to classical. It was Shervin who first made a good reader out of his son, then encouraged an interest in history, movies and art. In time, Zhubin and Shervin would discuss politics and other topics that much older children may not have understood.

Shervin was a sole-practitioner chartered accountant, and was particularly busy each spring, preparing clients' personal tax returns. Starting at the age of nine, Zhubin accompanied Shervin to his office during this hectic time to give him a helping hand under his guidance. When I asked him not to keep Zhubin too late at the office, Shervin would reply: "He is a good help and a good companion." Only now do I understand how much Shervin cherished those days with his son. He was a good father: the two enjoyed each other's company, and Zhubin retained fond memories of these times with his father.

Although Zhubin had always been both academic and athletic, by the time he was almost 19 the symptoms of his condition forced him to reluctantly suspend his studies and most activities – yet he never lost his zest for life. I was stunned witnessing the unassuming, quiet way with which he accepted his fate.

From early childhood, Zhubin showed considerable sensitivity and compassion towards others. The plight of the homeless, the poor and the needy, and of those who were handicapped and weak caused him much sorrow. He wanted to share with others what he had. He had kept a special place in his heart for the homeless since an early age, and as he grew older he made a point of talking to them and bringing them food and coffee, especially in cold weather. I often worried about his safety whenever he spent time with street people and once voiced my concerns, asking him to stop. I still remember the way he looked at me at that moment. Disappointed that I was so unaware of the difficulties faced by these people, he asked: *"Do you know what homeless means? It means they have no place to go and no family to go to. How can you not understand what is going on in their hearts and minds? They are in this pain all the time."* Looking at me with a gentle smile, he put his hand on my shoulder and said: *"Don't try to change me. I cannot help myself – even if I wanted to, I cannot. It gives me satisfaction."* How could he have gone to these people with all the pain he himself was experiencing?

The Stanley Park petting zoo, Vancouver, where Zhubin first showed a great connection to animals.

"Remember: give love, receive love, be love. You will receive shining stars."

Whenever he came back home and I saw that peaceful satisfaction on his face, I knew he had been with his homeless friends.

From a very young age, Zhubin had also been curious about God and life, what was destiny and what was not, and he seemed to have an innate understanding of it all. He always believed in a higher power and a Master Plan. He believed in a full life, in miracles, and talked constantly and passionately about the genius of the Universe and the spirit of life, exclaiming: *"Don't you love it all?"*

"Enjoy your life, really enjoy it, because life is a gift from God."

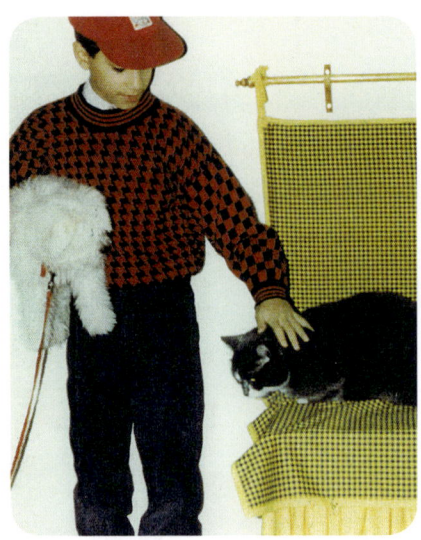

Zhubin with Rollie and Fluffy.

Zhubin, aged eight. He enjoyed his elementary school in West Vancouver and kept all the good friends he made there.

Return to Iran

One afternoon, when Zhubin was aged 20, he asked me: *"Simin, will you come to my room and stay for a while?"* I went and lay on his bed listening to the music he was playing – a CD by Leonard Cohen, whose music we had both come to love. He was feeling better that day and took advantage of the moment to work on his notes. As I was watching him, out of the blue he said: *"Simin, I remember Mâmân Shervin. She would bathe me in a sink. I wouldn't cry, but I didn't like it at all. The sink was too small for me."* I was stunned: Zhubin was referring to the time when, as a three-year-old, I had taken him with me on a trip to Iran to help my parents wind up their affairs and emigrate to Canada. Zhubin fondly recounted our extended stay with his paternal grandmother, whom he called Mâmân Shervin, recalling playing on the bed with her big black cat and being smothered by his grandmother's kisses as she bathed him. He wanted to know all about the reasons for that trip, so I told him the story.

Three years after arriving in Canada, Shervin and I had been thrilled to become Canadian citizens: this meant we could finally apply for permission for my parents to immigrate to Canada. Shervin wasted no time in getting started. We knew it would take a while, but never imagined how complicated it would become.

In 1979, Iranian students had occupied the US embassy in Tehran, holding a number of American diplomats hostage for over a year. With the assistance of the Canadian embassy, however, six American diplomats had managed to avoid this fate and eventually escaped Tehran. As a result of Canada's role in the hostage crisis the Canadian embassy in Tehran had been shuttered. Canadian immigration officials consequently informed us that my parents' file had been assigned to the embassy in Damascus, Syria, which we would have to contact to pursue the matter.

It was during this time that I received very disturbing news from my brother Ali: Mâmân had been hospitalised with a serious heart condition and might not survive. My three US-resident siblings had no access to an Iranian embassy and, in light of the circumstances of Ali's departure from Iran, it was dangerous for him to return – leaving me as the only option. Shervin immediately left to petition the Iranian consulate in Ottawa. I don't know how he managed it, but within 48 hours he had returned to Vancouver holding all the travel documents for Zhubin and me.

The very next evening three-year-old Zhubin and I boarded a plane, bound for Tehran. Waiting for us at the arrivals gate was my tall, handsome Baba. Shrieking with joy, I ran to hug him and, in my excitement, abandoned Zhubin in the luggage cart! After a kind passerby rescued a crying Zhubin, my father greeted his grandson for the first time, picking him up, smiling at him, and kissing him all over his cheeks and forehead. Wrapped in Baba's arms, Zhubin was immediately reassured. On the drive home from the airport, Baba explained that Mâmân had just been released from the hospital and that her medical condition required a calm environment. In short, I had to control my enthusiasm. Once home, with Zhubin on my lap, I sat beside Mâmân holding her hand, barely able to restrain myself from hugging her. She kept looking at Zhubin and, at last, very quietly asked me: "Your baby? My grandson?" Nodding yes, I kissed her hand as she reached out for him. I could not believe this scene: to be home beside Mâmân, with her cradling her grandson.

These were frightening and dangerous times in Iran, so the day after my arrival I telephoned the Canadian embassy in Damascus to explain our situation and ask for their assistance in getting my parents to Canada as soon as possible. The person I spoke with was most compassionate and helpful, and all the necessary Canadian documents were issued in short order. We immediately purchased our one-way plane tickets to Vancouver, scheduled to leave in only three weeks' time.

Then the work began: I had to help Baba sell the entire contents of my parents' home, including their valuable antique collection. In the end, they practically gave everything away. I remember Mâmân watching as her home melted away, Baba trying his best to comfort her: "Don't look so sad; think of where we're going. We'll be with our children and the grandchildren. That is worth more than anything." Of course, I knew very well that Baba was hurting too, but they both understood they were making the right decision.

Baba seemed excited at the prospect of moving to Canada. Watching him, I wondered whether he realized that they might never return to their beloved Iran. I like to believe that the joy of being with his children and grandchildren was stronger than any fear and doubt he may have felt. Both our large family and a wide circle of friends respected my father as a particularly wise man. Two years before the revolution Baba had, in all seriousness, counselled Ali, Shervin and me to sell whatever we had and move to the United States where my older brother Nader and sisters Soussan and Shirin (nicknamed Shishi) were already living. "This country is not a safe place to live anymore," he had warned, adding that if we followed his advice, then he and Mâmân would join us. "We'll all be together and safe." We hadn't taken his warnings seriously and instead teased him about what we thought was a silly idea. At the time Iran was booming and there was considerable inbound foreign investment. When Shervin and I started to build our home, Baba even tried to "bribe" Ali and me, telling us, "You're making a big mistake building a home here. Why won't you listen to what I am telling you?" and promising that, if we were to leave, he would buy a house in the US for each one of us. He had seen the warning signs before and he could feel a big storm coming. Armed with the certainty of youth, we thought we knew better. But he had been so right, and we had all been so terribly wrong!

Shervin's two sisters and niece were overjoyed to see Zhubin, while Shervin's mother was especially delighted with her only grandson. I decided to leave Zhubin with Shervin's family for some of the time while I concentrated on getting my parents ready for their departure. With the help of some friends and family, and in the short time available to us, we managed to complete the enormous task of uprooting them. Zhubin stayed at my mother-in-law's house, where he was happy, surrounded by a loving family who pampered him and filled his days with walks to the park and other fun activities. Meanwhile, my days were taken up with the stress of cutting through the Iranian bureaucratic red tape of getting us all out of country: endless forms regarding my parents' application for new Islamic Republic passports, medical check-ups, and interviews closely questioning what they were doing and why.

The day before our scheduled departure, Baba and I went to retrieve our Iranian passports: those who wished to leave Iran were obliged to submit their passports to the Iranian authorities for verification three days prior to their scheduled departure. Waiting for our turn was particularly nerve-wracking, as it was not unusual for people to be sent to jail and/or refused permission to leave the country for any number of reasons – one never knew who might be next.

At last our names were called. My parents' passports were returned to my father, but I was informed that I was not allowed to leave the country and instead given a slip of paper with the address of the office to which I was to report at 7am the following day for questioning. With no idea as to why permission to leave had been denied, I nearly collapsed, my thoughts immediately flying to Mâmân, Zhubin, and, of course, Shervin waiting for us in Vancouver. The time I had expected to stay in Iran for was now up. Everything had been in place for us to leave on the following day. Now I had no idea what was going to happen or how long it would take before I would be permitted to leave with my family. In the end, it would take four more months.

Glancing at Baba, I saw that he was really worried: we had heard many unbelievable stories about would-be émigrés being detained – but why me, and why now? I had never been involved with any political organization or with the pre-Islamic regime, nor had I done anything against the new regime. We also both knew that we could not let Mâmân find out what was going on.

Too disturbed to go home, at Baba's suggestion we first went to see one of his friends who was reputed to have some experience in helping resolve the kind of difficulty I suddenly found myself in. He was a friendly gentleman who comforted us and advised us not to panic: "They might be looking for someone with the same name as yours, or it could be that they want to ask you about your husband, or just ask how much money you took out of the country." He went on to instruct me to cover myself up with a hijab and act as if I were a devout Muslim. Whatever they asked, I should respond that I knew nothing about my husband's affairs, putting on the face of a good Muslim wife who just follows and obeys her husband. "Don't forget to mention how much your little boy misses his father," he added, then cautioned me: "Although it is not easy to deal with these fanatics, do your best to remain polite and calm at all times."

Heavy with uncertainty as to what was going to happen, and not knowing how to tell Mâmân, we went to my aunt's home where she was hosting a big farewell dinner party for my mother, her older sister. That evening we broke the news to my aunt, but told my mother only that some documents were missing and that we needed to wait for them to arrive from the Canadian embassy.

Wearing a hijab borrowed from Bibi the following day, I went to the place of interrogation, accompanied by Baba. But military security prevented him from entering and I had to continue alone. After examining my documents, a uniformed guard led me to a room at the back of the building where I was ordered to take a seat and wait for my name to be called. The room was empty, save for a young teenaged girl curled up against the wall. Before closing the door, the guard, wagging his finger, warned us not to talk to each other. The girl looked terribly frightened – a visibly shaking hand holding a boarding pass was trying to keep her hijab in place. Right away I realized she had been detained at the final airport security checkpoint prior to boarding her flight. Ever so quietly, I asked why she was there and my heart sank when she mouthed that she was Bahá'í: a very serious matter indeed due to religious persecution.

Over the next two months I was interrogated on four separate occasions, enduring extensive questioning about my husband, how much money he had taken from the country, his finances, his job, and so on. Each time, the officials finished by giving me another piece of paper with yet another appointment date for further questioning. When, each time, I asked, "Why do you prevent me from leaving? When will you allow me to leave?" the only reply I received was that it was not my place to ask such questions!

More than three months had elapsed since I had arrived in Iran. Shervin called us repeatedly, inquiring why we were not already back in Vancouver. Each time I had to lie, as we all knew that the phone lines were tapped and everyone had to be very cautious.

As Zhubin was under the loving care of his Mâmân Shervin and his aunts, I was not at all worried for him, but he was missing his father. Our predicament made me increasingly nervous, all the more so since we no longer had a proper place to live: my parents' house was by now a shell, emptied of most of its furnishings. Our desperation grew to the point that Baba began to consider making arrangements for Zhubin and me to be smuggled out of Iran, but these thoughts were stillborn when, as if by some miracle, we at last received a call advising that I was free to collect my passport – with no explanation given for withholding it. We left Iran immediately thereafter. Sitting on the plane next to my parents with Zhubin on my lap, I couldn't believe that – after all the madness we had been put through – I had actually succeeded in extricating my parents from Iran.

I am forever grateful to Shervin for enabling my parents to come to Canada. Through his efforts they could once again see their children and grandchildren on a regular basis, whether in Vancouver or visiting them wherever they happened to be living. Most important of all, my parents were not alone in their old age. Truly, it was a dream come true.

Adjusting to their new life in Canada was not easy for my parents: neither spoke English, they were no longer surrounded by their relatives and lifelong friends, and Canadian culture was completely different from anything they had experienced before. At times, they were like two birds trapped in a cage. After a lifetime of hard work devoted to raising their five children and facing so many trials along the way, they now ought to have been savouring the fruits of their labours in their homeland, surrounded by their children and grandchildren. But that was not to be.

My parents during their courtship, flanked on the far left by my 15-year-old uncle who chaperoned them.

Zhubin was a big comfort and joy to my parents. Not only was he the only grandchild living in Vancouver, but he had learned to speak Farsi fluently and could translate a word here and there for his grandparents. Baba and his grandson would go for long strolls around the neighbourhood, with Zhubin holding Baba's finger and racing to keep up with his grandfather's long stride. Zhubin was always excited whenever Baba asked him if he was ready to go for their walk, eagerly asking me for his shoes. What a heart-warming picture that was of handholding and bonding. On occasions, Mâmân joined them, doubling Zhubin's joy. I remember one afternoon, when all four of us went on a walk together – a breezy, sunny day and the air was fresh. Zhubin had been very busy choosing and collecting here and there little wild flowers for Mâmân, asking Baba if he would like to have some too. What a sweet feeling it must be to be a grandparent! Their love is a soft blanket wrapped around their grandchildren. I can only imagine that kind of unconditional love. I am so glad, or should I say blessed, to have witnessed this wonderful relationship after such a long separation.

But having Baba near did not last long: soon after arriving in Vancouver he was diagnosed with cancer.

"Take time for the family. It is holy on its own."

A Lesson in Loss

My father's given name was Habiballah, which means "God's beloved" or "Dear to God". Although never a practising Muslim, he was proud of his name, truly believing that he had been favoured with grace. A cultured man who loved art, music and poetry, his calligraphy was exquisite. My father loved his country – its landscape, culture, history and people.

Throughout the two-year ordeal of his terminal illness, Mâmân never left Baba's side. Their children and grandchildren would visit from Europe or America, doing their best to cheer Baba and provide

Mâmân with emotional support. We all wished our father could be with us for longer.

For the last two months of his life, Baba had to remain in hospital. Moving rooms after a few weeks, he was perfectly aware of why he had been transferred to the palliative care floor, understanding that his days were numbered. Baba was known as a man of great dignity: he did not want his friends to see him destroyed by cancer or to feel sorry for him, so at his request we hung a "No Visitors" sign on his hospital room door.

The cancer had spread into his bones, causing not only acute pain but also paralysis of his right arm. Shortly after the move to the new room, at his insistent request, he was at last administered a very strong, around-the-clock painkiller that brought his pain under control – that was all he wished for. The morning following the change in his medication found him feeling much better and he asked me to take him for a walk. Supporting himself with his left hand on a mobile IV drip while resting his paralyzed right arm on my shoulder, he managed to make his way down the length of the hospital corridor. During our walk he asked me to give him a bath in a room at the end of the hall that was equipped with a big walk-in tub. It was heartbreaking to see the toll that the cancer had taken on Baba's once strong body. Pouring warm water over him, I witnessed how much pleasure this simple act gave him as he expressed his heartfelt gratitude to God for the joy of the moment. He also told me that he was so thankful to Canada, being in this modern hospital, staffed with caring nurses, and his children around him. He knew it had not been easy for them to come and see him from afar. When he added, "I'm happy with all of you, and each one of you has my blessing", I felt he was saying that he was fortunate not to be dying alone. My wise father knew he was facing the end of his life and yet he appreciated each moment, as always able to find a blessing in everything.

The following evening, Baba slipped into a coma and, surrounded by all of his children, died shortly thereafter. He had been with us in Canada for less than five years.

Only years later, when I reflected on these final shared moments with Baba, did I understand how important they would prove to be. During my darkest days following Zhubin's death, I was able to draw strength from witnessing first-hand Baba's acceptance of his fate, as well as his joy in small pleasures, despite his condition. It was he who planted in my heart a seed of faith in the Universe. His wisdom and advice remained within me and helped me through the painful years I was to experience.

Mâmân's given name was Houri – a most suitable one as it means "angel". She was a mother to all, not just to her own children, but also to all her younger siblings, in-laws, nieces and nephews. To this day, she is remembered by all who knew her with deep admiration for her selflessness, generosity of spirit, and compassion for everyone around her.

Mâmân would remain a widow for 22 years. At the time of her passing, she too was surrounded by all five of her children, as well as several grandchildren. Drawing on my later experience witnessing many deaths in the course of volunteer work at a geriatric centre, it comforts me to know that Mâmân had one of the most peaceful passings I have ever seen.

My parents gave a lot and asked for nothing in return. With their strong faith in God and their gratitude to Him, together they were able to go through thick and thin. Most importantly, they lived life to the fullest.

"One brick at a time builds a house. Life is not an event. You just dedicate the first brick towards the completion of the house, so you can build and live in a temple."

An Ending and a Beginning

Shervin was a good father to Zhubin, imparting to him a love of knowledge. He was one of the funniest people I had ever met, with a wonderful sense of humour and a special talent for making everyone laugh at his jokes and unique stories. He was also a very intelligent, well-read and cultured individual.

However, the struggles I had faced had changed me and tested our marriage: our sudden flight from Iran; worries about family left behind; financial problems; adapting to a new country; and concern for Zhubin's peculiar sleep pattern. My father's two-year battle with cancer had also had an enormous impact on me. All of this and more caused me to suffer a severe depression. I was tired. I did not want to live in Vancouver any more. Everything seemed sad and bleak to me. I soldiered on, but six years later my marriage fell apart when Zhubin had just turned 14.

Despite the end of our marriage, I will always be grateful for Shervin's compassion both towards me and my mother, whom he continued to visit often following the divorce. And in the wake of Zhubin's death, Shervin and I were fortunate to find some solace and comfort in one another: speaking often, crying and sharing memories together.

"All kind touches are holy."

Two years after my divorce I met my second husband Zyg, who also had one child – a son named Adam, ten years younger than Zhubin. Each was an only child, perhaps explaining their immediate affinity for each other. Their love for one another, which developed over the years, and the fun times they shared kept their bond strong. Zhubin became Adam's idol.

We lived in London for less than a year; then, together with Zhubin, we moved to Montreal, where we were married. Montreal was Zyg's hometown and where Adam lived with his mother. We were all happy about the fresh start in an exciting city.

Shortly after settling in our home, we all agreed that it would not be complete without two dogs – one for each boy. On a crisp Sunday afternoon in late September, together with both excited boys we drove to the outskirts of the city to the breeder we had chosen. Huddled together in a little cage, there they were: three adorable miniature schnauzer puppies. It was difficult to choose which two to take home – and to overcome the boys' desire to take all three!

While we debated the selection, Zhubin pointed to one of them and said: *"For sure, this one; he is so playful."* Picking him up, he unzipped his jacket and cuddled the tiny creature to his chest to keep him warm. It was love at first sight. This dog we would come to name Sam, and he became Zhubin's loyal companion. Meanwhile, Adam decided on the smallest of the three, on the grounds that "we should fatten her up", and named her Pepper. In a car full of joy and laughter we drove back home, the boys perched together in the back seat, each preoccupied with his new-found treasure.

Although our move to Montreal was a happy one, later, when Zhubin's illness reached its crescendo, I would blame myself for ending my marriage and moving to a new city, wondering whether Zhubin would have suffered as much had we stayed in Vancouver.

One afternoon, while preparing dinner, I watched Zhubin as he lay on the kitchen floor playing with Sam like a little boy with his toy, enjoying every moment of this break from the grip of his usual pain. I opened up to him and said: "Zhubin you really deserve to have a good mom, a good home and a happy life." Zhubin stopped his play, looked at me and said: *"Simin, life is not about having good parents or a good home; life is about so much more than what you think. You need to grow up, Simin."* Reflecting often upon this response helped me later on, as I learned to "grow up". Zhubin never talked about my divorce, never asked why, yet I'm sure that like any other child of divorce he suffered inside.

The brothers grew close. Zhubin took Adam wherever he went – to hockey games, rollerblading, or just to the park to play frisbee. Becoming an avid badminton player, Zhubin loved to go to the nearby club where he would take Adam, so he could also learn how to play well.

Adam would stay with us for two weeks each month. Those were fun-filled happy days. We felt so lucky: our new house had everything we wanted and needed, and was even close to several universities that Zhubin hoped to attend. He had been looking forward to carrying on with his studies, having dreamt of Montreal's McGill University even when still in Vancouver.

> Happy birthday Simin! I hope this year will be a pleasant one for all of us; I believe it will be. I am very happy to be living in Montreal and I hope you are too. Things can only go uphill from here. Again happy birthday, love Zhubin.

The card that accompanied the bouquet of yellow flowers that Zhubin, aged 17, brought for me in the deep freeze of our first winter in Montreal.

Searching for the various things our new home needed, Zhubin helped me to choose whenever I asked his opinion. We both cared deeply about our house, and it was a happy time together turning it into a home. Remembering and thinking of those lovely days always brings tears to my eyes, and I thank God for having granted me that taste of the joy of a mother and son, which I will cherish to my last breath.

It was true that our good times were short-lived. I did not know that the hand of destiny was painting a very different picture for us, and that God had other plans for Zhubin and me. About four months after moving to our new home, Zhubin started having painful headaches. Little by little they got worse. And that was the beginning of our nightmare.

"A garden is ever-changing and always in need of this or that because it is alive. So are you."

Onset of Darkness

Almost from birth, Zhubin had been plagued by a condition whose constant symptom had been an inability to get the proper amount or quality of sleep. As an infant he had been unable to sleep like most other babies, instead crying for very long periods of time and snatching sleep in brief interludes at odd hours. He could be quieted only after a long time, either when rocked in my arms or aimlessly driven around in the car by Shervin. When we had sought help from several pediatricians, they had simply diagnosed colic or teething. Somehow we had coped, but this persistent problem never abated and eventually considerably worsened.

Even as a young child, Zhubin had been aware that he had a problem. Often, he would appear in our room an hour or so after being put to bed, still unable to fall asleep. His sleep deprivation later resulted in frequent headaches. On more than a dozen occasions while still living in Vancouver, we had sought medical advice regarding his sleeping difficulties. Often Zhubin was forced to stop what he was doing and lie down until the prescribed painkillers gave him some relief.

By the time he was in grade eight his sleep patterns had become very distorted: he would go to sleep when he came home from school, waking in the late evening to have dinner, then working on his homework until it was time to go to school the next morning. Despite this, he managed to keep up with his studies and activities, as well as having good times with his friends.

Zhubin was almost 17 when we moved to our new home in Montreal. Within six months, his headaches had grown worse, occurring more frequently. Zhubin could no longer control them, no matter what he or I did. When the pain became unbearable, he would writhe on the floor or on his bed, holding his head. I wanted to squeeze it hard to get the pain out but was powerless to stop this agony. The first Montreal specialist doctor we consulted prescribed light therapy and tried other treatments – even electroshock therapy on one occasion. Whatever we did, wherever we turned, we found no help and felt as though we were repeatedly hitting a brick wall. The pain had become a monster, sucking all the energy and joy out of Zhubin's body, affecting every aspect of his life.

Managing somehow to remain positive, Zhubin lived in the hope that his symptoms would subside, and he remained unusually caring, curious and self-disciplined, and was at times very funny. When it was time to enter junior college he chose one that had an Iranian club and a curriculum and activities that interested him. Although the headaches steadily worsened, he was nevertheless determined to do as much as he possibly could. However, his time in junior college would be cut short: after a year of struggling he was no longer able to continue his studies and was obliged to abandon his other pursuits as well.

Although his former teachers kept calling with concern over his status, a return to school remained out of the question. I would explain the problem that he was facing, but they still wanted him back. His calculus teacher told me that Zhubin was his best student and that, even

Aged 15, on holiday in Turkey with the extended family.

if he didn't take all the tests or regularly attend classes, he would still pass the final exam because his marks were that good. However, Zhubin had become too fragile and weak to continue, no matter how hard he tried to remain in school.

As Zhubin's condition deteriorated our desperation drove us to search beyond Montreal for the elusive specialist who could offer a cure, or at least a diagnosis and some relief from these severe symptoms. At last, the Mayo Clinc referred us to the Harvard-affiliated McLean Hospital, situated in a suburb of Boston in the US, an institution renowned for its cutting-edge research in neuroscience.

After two weeks of extensive tests, we were told that the issue lay with Zhubin's circadian rhythm – the roughly 24-hour body cycle generated internally that controls sleep patterns. Zhubin had been born with an abnormal one, and the hormonal changes during puberty had exacerbated the problem, causing this inner clock in his brain to become highly dysfunctional. The doctors informed us that, although a circadian rhythm disorder was not uncommon, to date they had never encountered a cycle as severely distorted as Zhubin's. Recommended treatment was non-surgical: a two-pronged strategy to both search to correct the chemical imbalance that was causing this condition and to realign his cycle by providing behavioural therapy.

Listening to the doctors' initial conclusions, Zhubin remained calm. *"Simin,"* he said, *"what is happening to me is so rare."* Squeezing his thumb and middle finger together to indicate a tiny amount, he said: *"That's how much scientists know about the brain. They are nowhere yet."*

In an effort to address Zhubin's chemical imbalance, doctors prescribed a cocktail of numerous medications. In the course of his research, Zhubin's favourite doctor, a world authority on sleep disorders, had found that a particular kind of lithium, usually used to treat depression, could also help with certain sleep problems. He placed Zhubin on the highest possible dosage in his final year, which meant that weekly monitoring of Zhubin's blood was essential: too high a level of lithium could be fatal.

The doctors also recommended scaldingly hot baths to be taken every evening at 8pm, the rationale being that as the body gradually cooled it would signal to the brain that it was time to sleep. These baths unfortunately did not help and ultimately had to be ceased after Zhubin's skin became dry and cracked from the extreme heat.

During his treatment by McLean, Zhubin remained on his own in Boston on and off – sometimes for weeks, even months. Insisting that he must go through this process by himself, his doctors requested that I return home, but permitted me to visit every few weeks. Although he was undergoing tests, during the little time we had together we did our best to make each visit enjoyable for each other, regardless of his limitations. Before leaving for home, I always filled up his little refrigerator with his favourite goodies, which I had cooked and brought for him. I also left behind encouraging notes reassuring him of my love and reminding him to eat and take care of himself. It was my abiding dream that Zhubin would come back home to Montreal as soon as possible.

Each time, parting from Zhubin was heart-wrenching, as if I were leaving a part of myself behind. When we were apart – Zhubin at McLean and me in Montreal – we would speak every day on the phone at great length, with Zhubin excitedly sharing with me his plans for the things he would do as soon as he got well – a hope we both held onto. As Zhubin knew how hard it was for me to be away from him and understood how worried I was, each time as we said our goodbyes he would say something funny about the dogs, tell me a joke, or come up with an idea for how we could spend my next visit. This was his way of helping me to keep my spirits up and to tell me, *"Take care, Simin."*

The intensity of the treatment precluded Zubin from coming home for his last two birthdays and Christmas Holidays. Wishing to do our best to cheer him up, each time we made the long drive to Boston we brought along both Sam and Pepper to his great surprise and delight. Only God knows what he had to face as he was going through his treatment. It was a frightening time as it became clear that nothing was truly helping him and many other health issues had also emerged.

After he returned home and continued to grow weaker, there were times I had to help him bathe, dress and even support him to walk. I did my best to keep him busy. We would go for short walks – the library and bookshops were his favourite destinations. At night, he would ask me to repeat his beloved anecdotes about my childhood and my family's life in Iran. Favourites included hilarious ones about Baba escaping army training to keep private romantic rendezvous with Mâmân while he was courting her.

As difficult as this physical infirmity was for him, more challenging was the emotional distress – he had been a great student and an active teenager, yet now that he was no longer in school his life was on hold.

Throughout this period of downward spiralling health, Zhubin and I spent a great deal of time together. Being alone in a new city – away from family and friends, dealing with this nightmare day after day, night after night – was a trial for both of us, trapped as we were in a prison defined by his unrelenting and undiagnosable condition. On a few occasions Zhubin said that if given the choice he would much rather have had two different types of cancer than his strange condition, since then at least his doctors would have known what he was facing.

I always, always tried to put on a brave and confident face for Zhubin – concealing how much I was suffering inside, hiding that every night I cried and cried, asking God to help us. Had I been able to do so, I would, without hesitation, have taken on all of his pain myself.

With all his jokes and fooling around, Zhubin pretended that he was all right – only occasionally confessing: *"Simin, I'm not feeling so good."* But we tacitly understood the ugly reality. Our situation and its constraints created an unusually strong bond between us: our relationship was not only that of mother and child, but also of best friends. We held onto and supported each other emotionally, unable to face these difficult times without one another.

Helping Zhubin get ready for bed one evening, I saw that he was struggling to hide his pain from me. "Zhubin, how can you take this?" I asked. "Your pain is killing us both." Looking at me he smiled and replied: *"You have to have it."* Puzzled, I asked, "Have what?" and received the explanation: *"You need to have inner sight to see the beauty in everything, even in this pain. You don't understand it now, but if you are hungry for truth, you will get it. Always go for truth, love and peace. You will learn that one day."* On several occasions I got upset with Zhubin, even shouting at him: how could he speak such nonsense when there was no way out of his situation? Angry and frustrated, I could neither understand what he was talking about nor why he could be so nonchalant. When I could no longer take the craziness of his situation – when I would "lose it" – Zhubin would calmly tell me not to be a foolish mother. We regard our children as just children, yet they are also our teachers – age has no meaning. Zhubin would become *my* teacher. I could never understand where all his love and wisdom came from, how he was able to be so much at peace in the maelstrom of his condition. It was many years before I discovered the answer.

Zhubin's only comforts during the peak of his illness were music, our conversations and our dogs. There were also the wide-ranging telephone calls he had with Shervin and discussions with Zyg about their favourite subjects, as well as the computer and board games played with Zyg and Adam. He also remained in touch with his friends and cousins by phone and email. Whenever granted a break from his pain, no matter how short that time was, he did his best to enjoy life despite his limitations.

Throughout these hard times, Zhubin kept his sense of humour, his enormous kindness, his constant love and patience, and, above all his dignity. He never allowed anyone to see or hear him being anything but strong. In the long-distance phone calls with Shervin or other family members, he would go the extra mile to make sure he spoke with a strong voice, reassuring everyone that he was doing well. As a result, only a few close friends in Montreal had any inkling as to what was really happening to him, or to us and our lives. Although I tried to explain our nightmare to my family, they could not grasp or believe the gravity of the situation.

Zhubin and I slogged on, doing our best to cope with the challenges, living in the hope that better times were ahead. After all, things couldn't get much worse. Little did we know what was waiting for us. Zhubin's sleep disorder would continue to have consequences we could not have anticipated.

"If we choose, our pains can become a source of growth and learning. Life is a journey. We all have come a long way and we all have to go a long way still. We all do. There is no end. This is what eternity means."

Sleep Like the Dead

In the late evenings during the last year of his life, Zhubin regularly fell unconscious on the floor of his bedroom or the kitchen – anywhere in the house, for that matter. We had no idea why this was happening.

It is difficult to describe what happened to Zhubin every night: instead of falling asleep, he collapsed as if in a coma. Indeed, that's exactly how he described it – never "sleep" but a "coma". His coma-like state would come on very suddenly, resembling a fainting spell, his body crumpling to the floor as though he had been administered an invisible injection of a strong sleeping medication. Unlike true sleep, however, his "coma" was neither restful nor restorative. He lay as if dead, yet with a still-warm body. Each night, before I went to bed, I would go to his room to check if he was still breathing. Standing over him I would watch him sleep – or what passed for sleep. Each morning when I went to wake him, there he would be, lying in exactly the same position as the one I had left him in the previous evening. I understand that in a normal sleep mode a person can move up to 200 times per night. Zhubin on the other hand moved not at all, instead lying like a corpse. Because the "coma" rendered his body completely immobile for 14 to 15 hours, he would wake in severe discomfort.

One morning when I went to Zhubin's room to wake him, I found him on the floor next to his portable electric heater. Two of his fingers had been badly burned, yet he had felt nothing. Zhubin explained that he had been holding his hands against the heater to warm them a bit before going to bed, and had then apparently lost consciousness. Thinking of what might have happened to him had the heater been on high jolted me with fear and it dawned on me just how dangerous this pattern of sudden unconsciousness was. It was impossible for me to hide my reaction to this horrible scene.

The helplessness one feels when a loved one suffers has to be one of the most painful of human experiences. Zhubin never once complained about his serious burn, reassuring me: "*Simin, don't worry, it's not a big deal.*" Although, outwardly, he made light of this incident, it, nevertheless, surely disturbed him, as later that day he told me: "*Simin, if I were raped or stabbed while in this coma, I wouldn't feel anything. Just make sure I'm home and safe.*" It was so hard knowing just how much Zhubin had to deal with. From that time on, we were sure to be home on time, and I would then sit a vigil with Zhubin until between 10 and 10.15pm when he would suddenly pass out, sometimes mid-sentence!

Often while Zhubin "slept" I would lie down beside him, holding his hand, speaking to him, hoping he could hear me telling him that we were in this together and not to give up. But doubts crept in, and I asked myself how long he could endure this unspeakable agony and how long I would have to be a witness to it all. I despaired: What had caused my son's condition? Why was no doctor able to solve its enigma? Why wasn't God helping us?

Over the course of Zhubin's treatment, his doctors gradually reduced his dosage of medications. However, when he continued to fall into this "death sleep" his doctors realized to their dismay that the "coma" was a symptom of his disorder, rather than a side-effect of the medication he had been taking. Zhubin described his condition as feeling like *"taking a bottle of very strong sleeping pills with a pot of very strong coffee. One side of my head feels exhausted and wants to sleep; the other side is fighting to stay awake. My head feels like a battleground."* His doctors were stumped, but Zhubin had a theory: *"The brain itself is so smart: it knows that it is unable to produce the chemicals required to cure the sleep disorder so it simply shuts down to at least provide itself some relief."*

It was so poignant when Zhubin asked me not to let anyone other than me see him in his nocturnal state: *"Not even Zyg."* Although I reassured him, I could never keep that promise for I needed Zyg's help whenever we had to move Zhubin's body. But Zhubin was never the wiser.

To seek his thoughts on matters, Zhubin often went to Zyg, who was less a father figure and more that of a wise older brother. Zhubin respected his opinion in general and over time involved him deeply in his ongoing medical treatment. In an effort to brighten Zhubin's difficult days, and whenever his symptoms permitted, Zyg made every effort to organise fun outings to the cinema, bowling alley, apple-picking, or hockey matches.

Zhubin also enjoyed the weekly visits of a friend's daughter named Yassi, who was already attending university and was a little older than Zhubin. Very kind-hearted, she would come by every Tuesday to see him and remained a loyal friend until the end. Zhubin always very much looked forward to her visits and they would head out together to movies, dinners, or the book store. If Zhubin felt too unwell to venture out, they would stay at home, listening to music or watching DVDs. Whenever they went out, usually for around three hours, they were always under strict instruction to return home no later than 9.30pm before Zhubin fell into his coma state.

Zhubin's doctors insisted that it was crucial he get up at 8.15am sharp, trying to establish or imprint a signal onto the brain: it's wake-up time! No matter how difficult a task, it was essential. Not only was it a substantial undertaking just to wake Zhubin, but he would continue in a state of extreme fatigue for quite some time. To get him moving, I would help him to shower and dress, and then we would walk together, him leaning on me for support, to a local coffee shop for a bite of breakfast. If I didn't get Zhubin to start his morning by pushing him to get outside for some fresh air, his state of exhaustion would last for much of the day.

Aged 18, still in full-time attendance at his Montreal college.

I do not wish to dwell further on what we faced by now – it could be a stand-alone book and would open up deep wounds. I confess that the situation and suffering were so dire, that even the thought of helping him to end his life flitted across my mind. I have closed that door.

Well aware that his overall health was fading, Zhubin's strong sense of personal dignity remained intact. It was during the last year of his life that he chose to see almost no one, since he did not want to reveal what he had become – fragile and diminished. But he also told me that he did not want to be tortured by the constant reminder of all that he was missing.

My son was disappearing before my eyes.

"Life is full of challenges and problems until you become like a rock: strong and tough."

Young Wisdom

Despite his youth and serious medical condition, Zhubin was unusually astute and self-disciplined. Approaching things with great thought and painstaking thoroughness, he gained a maturity well beyond his years. This being the case, it was not surprising that he was very involved with all of his treatment, learning a lot about his condition and becoming well aware of the consequences of such an extreme sleep disorder. He grew particularly close to one of his McLean doctors, a world-renowned researcher and authority in the field of circadian rhythm disorder, and enjoyed their conversations together. This doctor acquired a soft spot for Zhubin as he had a son of the same age and expressed his appreciation for both Zhubin's insight and intelligence. Feeling that such information could prove helpful to the treatment of other patients suffering from a similar condition, Zhubin took pains to keep very precise notes on all the symptoms he was experiencing, sharing them with his doctors on a weekly basis.

Zhubin's insight extended beyond his own medical condition. Wise, frank and eloquent, he was given to mature statements about the meaning of life, death and, most of all, living.

He maintained a binder he dubbed "The Master Plan" in which he wrote down his thoughts and insights, sharing them with me in the hope that they would help and guide me. He would become my hero and teacher, my boy grown up before his time.

Some time after his death I went through this binder, filled with his writings and keepsakes, and it was there that I found, neatly pasted onto a page, all the little notes of encouragement I had written to him while he had been in Boston, along with the postcards he had received from Shervin, Adam, and some close friends. My heart skipped a beat, and clutching his big notebook to my chest I was so overcome that I collapsed on his bed and, with tears streaming, wailed aloud: "Oh Zhubin! How did you manage to store so much love in your heart? You even kept all these little notes and cards!" Knowing how much these mementoes had meant to him made me realize how much we had shared, not only as a mother and child, but also as soulmates.

There was so much more to my son than I had ever grasped while he had been alive. I had never recognized the depth of his love for us all, and this knowledge filled me with guilt and regret. Following the pain of loss, guilt was something that I would so often and acutely have to face, learn to live with, and eventually overcome. Much later I would remember what my sister Soussan had said to me after the funeral: "Zhubin was all about love. That is what he came here to teach us."

"You have to – and I mean, have to – look up with your heart, open up with your heart. The focus should be on that."

Shock

In early 2002, Zyg and I visited Zhubin at McLean where he had been undergoing treatment for over two years. We were accompanied by the dogs as well as Adam, who had been missing his big brother a lot. Arriving early Saturday afternoon we quickly made our way to Zhubin's room. He had known we were coming and had been waiting for us. When we entered, we were all shocked: it had been only a few weeks since I had last seen him, but the change in his appearance was devastating. Adam burst into tears, I almost fainted, and Zyg was visibly stunned. Zhubin looked so weak. He could not stand up properly, and could walk only with difficulty. I could not believe my eyes. How could his condition have deteriorated so much, and why had I not been informed?

I was barely able to breathe and, hearing Adam sobbing behind me, I asked Zyg to take him from the room as it was too upsetting a scene for him. Unable to stop my tears, I held Zhubin in my arms, supporting him as I helped him to sit up in the bed. My heart was shattered. How could this happen to my son? As I held him I said: "There is no way I will let you stay here. I'm taking you back home with us today, no matter what your doctors say."

Zhubin tried to calm me, explaining that for the past 82 hours he had been unable to sleep at all and that his condition was the result of extreme fatigue and exertion. He said it felt as if his brain was in a frying pan. He assured me that if he could just get some sleep, he would feel much better. But my mind was made up. In my heart, I knew his place was at home with us in Montreal.

Seeing my son in such a weakened condition was terribly difficult and the memory still deeply pains me to this day. When I found a nurse and insisted that I was taking my boy home with me that very day, I was informed that he could not be discharged without his doctor's permission and, as it was the weekend and his doctor was out of town, Zhubin's release could not be considered before Monday. I made it very clear that this was not an option, but don't know what happened next – the next thing I remember is finding myself on the floor with an oxygen mask on my face and Zyg kneeling by my side. The head nurse relented, contacted Zhubin's doctor and at last we were given permission to take him home. We left Boston immediately.

Due to the abrupt nature of our departure, I was obliged shortly thereafter to fly back to Boston, both to collect the remainder of Zhubin's belongings and to try to solve another problem facing us – the supply of his lithium medication. The form of lithium he was prescribed was not yet available in Canada, which meant that I needed to pick up supplies in the US. After packing Zhubin's things at McLean, I visited his doctors' offices where I explained my need for a prescription of 300 lithium pills – several months' dosage. Relieved to have the prescription in hand, I then hailed a cab and asked the driver to take me to a pharmacy on the way back to the airport. The first pharmacy, however, could supply me with only a small fraction of the prescription. The next one was the same. Meanwhile, the rain had begun to bucket down, slowing traffic to a crawl. As we inched forward and my flight's departure drew nearer, my anxiety grew. In the end, I had to visit four more pharmacies, each time requiring a call to our doctor for his verbal confirmation. By the time I had amassed 250 pills and arrived at the airport, I had long since missed my scheduled flight.

The ordeal was not yet over, however. After catching a later flight home, I still had to pass through Canadian customs. In an agony of indecision, and fearing the precious pills' confiscation, I debated whether to conceal and not declare them. Ultimately, I chose to be honest, showing the pills to the customs officer and doing my best to explain our need for them – but to no avail. He would not let me pass and instead showed me to a room where I sat alone and waited for him to return. A short while later, another officer came to question me. Exhausted and fearful, I couldn't help crying as I showed him my paperwork, begging him to phone our McLean doctor to confirm my story. He took pity on me and told me to wait while he made inquiries. Eventually he let me go, warning me that in future I would need to make a special request on the form he provided. As it turned out, I would have no use for it.

After Zhubin came home to Montreal, I was just so pleased to have him back that I never imagined he would be with us for only a few more months. I am certain that Zhubin felt the same joy at being home again: he had time with Adam, with Zyg and me, and with Sam and Pepper. We all did our best to create a positive and happy environment for Zhubin, helping him to cope. Having him with us during his final days remains a lasting gift. I cannot even begin to conceive of how it would have felt to have lost him while he was away from home.

"There is light when all of us are together. There is a band of love and a promise to hold us all together forever."

Keeping Hope Alive

After we brought Zhubin home from Boston, we believed it was vital for his state of mind to have some kind of daily routine, that his life should approach some semblance of normalcy for a 21-year-old. We felt sure that Zhubin would benefit by being meaningfully occupied as long as he could be, given the constraints of his condition.

It was Zyg who hit on a terrific idea: to contact our very close friends, Binny and Ravi, and ask them if they would consider hiring Zhubin to work in their downtown office – even if only for a few hours a day. These wonderful, understanding friends, in whom we had confided Zhubin's condition and our struggles over the past several years, recognized our desperation and unhesitatingly offered their immediate assistance.

Zhubin knew and respected Binny and Ravi. When I told him that our friends needed some help for a few hours a day, Zhubin asked how they could even consider employing him. What if he couldn't get to work on time? I assured him that it mattered little to them what time he showed up for work. Although the decision had been made well before being officially engaged, Binny thoughtfully gave Zhubin a formal interview, as she would have any other job applicant. Zhubin never suspected that his employment had been prearranged and started his part-time employment, working several hours per day, five days a week.

During his first day on the job, he telephoned me all excited: *"Simin, it's wonderful. I have my own cubicle and my own telephone line. Write it down. You can call me anytime. Do you want to come see my office?"* I was ecstatic to hear him so happy.

As was his nature, Zhubin took his new responsibilities very seriously. A few weeks after he started, Binny called to tell me that Zhubin did not look well at all and that it was painful to see him in that state. Although she had encouraged him to go home, he had refused. I knew how Zhubin was: he would suffer anything to fulfil his duties and stay in the office until he had completed his work. So I asked Binny to let him finish his workday. Despite his struggles, Zhubin returned to the office and continued his work to the very last day of his life. Brought about by the kindness of friends, employment offered Zhubin much-needed purpose to his day.

In March that year, there would be another event to brighten Zhubin's world. Ice hockey is a religion in Canada and there was a lot of excitement in the city that month, as Montreal's Canadiens ice hockey team had made the playoffs and were about to host their opponents, the Carolina Hurricanes. All of Montreal was tense, and most casual talk centred on the playoff series and upcoming games. Interest in other subjects became secondary as young and old alike were keyed up for the first playoff game at the city's main ice hockey arena.

A week earlier, a very close friend who knew of our struggles, as well as Zhubin's love of hockey and passion for the Canadiens, offered us an invaluable gift: three tickets for the sold-out game. I was so happy to accept this kindness – I knew Zhubin would be delighted when we surprised him with the news that we would attend the game rather than watch it on television at home. Indeed, he could not believe it when he saw me holding those precious tickets. We just hoped that he would be well enough to go that evening.

The day before the game we agreed that we would leave early for the arena, as Zhubin did not want to miss a thing. The next morning arrived and we were lucky: he was having a "better" day. He spent a lot of time in the downtown area near the arena, joining the young crowd cheering their beloved Canadiens. He was like a kid in a candy shop. I was thrilled to see him among his own age group, doing what every young Montrealer loved. Being able to participate like this was such a rare and precious thing for Zhubin.

The three of us made our way to the arena, Zhubin proudly wearing his Canadiens' jersey. The arena was sold out – not one of the 21,273 seats left empty. The music, the singing crowd, and the bright lights made the whole arena vibrate with excitement. Like so many others, Zhubin was jumping up and down, shouting and screaming. It was such an ecstatic night, not just for Zhubin, but for Zyg and me too.

"Life is all about simple things and simple pleasures. Everyone needs to be charged over and over with positive energy. Have a good time and laugh. That is beautiful. God is in happy moments and laughter."

To see him so up and full of life made that night unforgettable. The regular game ended with the two teams tied, which meant overtime: the contest would continue for as long as it would take for a team to score the deciding goal. The crowd was going crazy: over 21,000 people shouting at the same time; I thought the roof would collapse.

In the midst of all this excitement, it was Zyg who brought me crashing back to reality, telling me that we couldn't stay for the overtime and should be going home. It was nearly 10pm and he was concerned that Zhubin would soon collapse. Since he was enjoying the game and there was so much noise around us, I insisted that he could not possibly fall into his "coma". But just a few minutes later Zyg asked me to look at Zhubin: his eyelids were getting heavy despite his best efforts to keep them open. We immediately knew that we had to get him home right away. Zhubin really didn't want to leave, but even he knew we had no choice. We helped him up and out of the arena, but by the time we got to the parking lot he was unable to carry on. Zyg and I had to drag him to the car and help him to lie down on the back seat. Before we arrived home – less than ten minutes later – he had already fallen into that nasty, unconscious state. With great difficulty, together we managed to haul him from the car and into his bed.

"Everyone has ups and downs. We plan and plan but we don't put 'unexpected' into the plan."

Just turned 19, looking out over a lake with me while on a family hike with the dogs in the countryside north of Montreal.

The News

After his homecoming, Zhubin remained in contact with his team of McLean Hospital doctors, scheduling for every Wednesday afternoon an extended conference call to discuss his sleep patterns, evolution in symptoms, overall condition and adjustments to his ongoing medication.

A few months after bringing Zhubin home, we prepared ourselves for a return to Boston for a detailed follow-up examination requested by his doctors. I prayed that it would lead to good news. As Zhubin was unwell, it was difficult for him to travel but I pushed him to go.

While I was cooking dinner the evening before our departure, Zhubin came upstairs and asked to speak with me. I was busy and was going to suggest that we talk after I was done, but one look at him told me something was seriously wrong and could not wait. Leaving the food simmering on the stove, I sat down beside him. I looked at him closely: he was so pale, so tired. His extreme sleep disorder had carved its effects on what had been a young and handsome face, robbing it of so much of its youth. I felt run down myself. It was heartbreaking to be so helpless, watching my son endure so much. I could do nothing, yet could not stop trying. Zhubin and I were trapped in a downward spiral. Zhubin began to speak, explaining that he was willing to go through all of the exhausting examinations one more time, but made it clear that he would do so for my sake, rather than his own. We both knew how meticulously he had followed his doctors' advice up to this point, all to no avail. Calmly, Zhubin told me that he wanted the pain to end, once and for all – he could not bear the burden of his illness for much longer. Knowing what he was driving at, I did not pursue the discussion further and turned back to the stove.

The next day we went to Boston, where, over three days, Zhubin was put through a full battery of tests. Back in Montreal a week later, on Wednesday May 8th, the doctor called soon after Zhubin returned from work. The news was devastating: there was no clear diagnosis, no cure, and no idea for a solution to relieve Zhubin's symptoms. The doctors had explored every avenue – they had done everything they could.

I will never forget the look on Zhubin's face when his doctor told him that he would have to learn to live with the condition; adapt to it; make it part of himself. I witnessed his despair, as if all hope had

"I have always said be prepared financially, mentally, spiritually, emotionally for unexpected events. Life has many turns."

escaped his body. Quietly, Zhubin expressed his gratitude for all their efforts but I could sense something in him had turned. Only 21, he had developed permanent, dark, half-moon circles under his eyes and an old man's hesitant shuffle. The child in him – what little was left after all his pain and suffering – that child, filled with wonder and anticipation, disappeared in that moment. "There must be other opinions to seek. There must be other resources for us," I said to him, trying to give him some hope, trying to offer comfort. But Zhubin did not hear me. He was lost in his own thoughts, no longer interested in trying.

We had run out of hope. All that we could do now was to face the facts and try to make peace with them. This was a very dark day, but little did I know that the days were about to become pitch black.

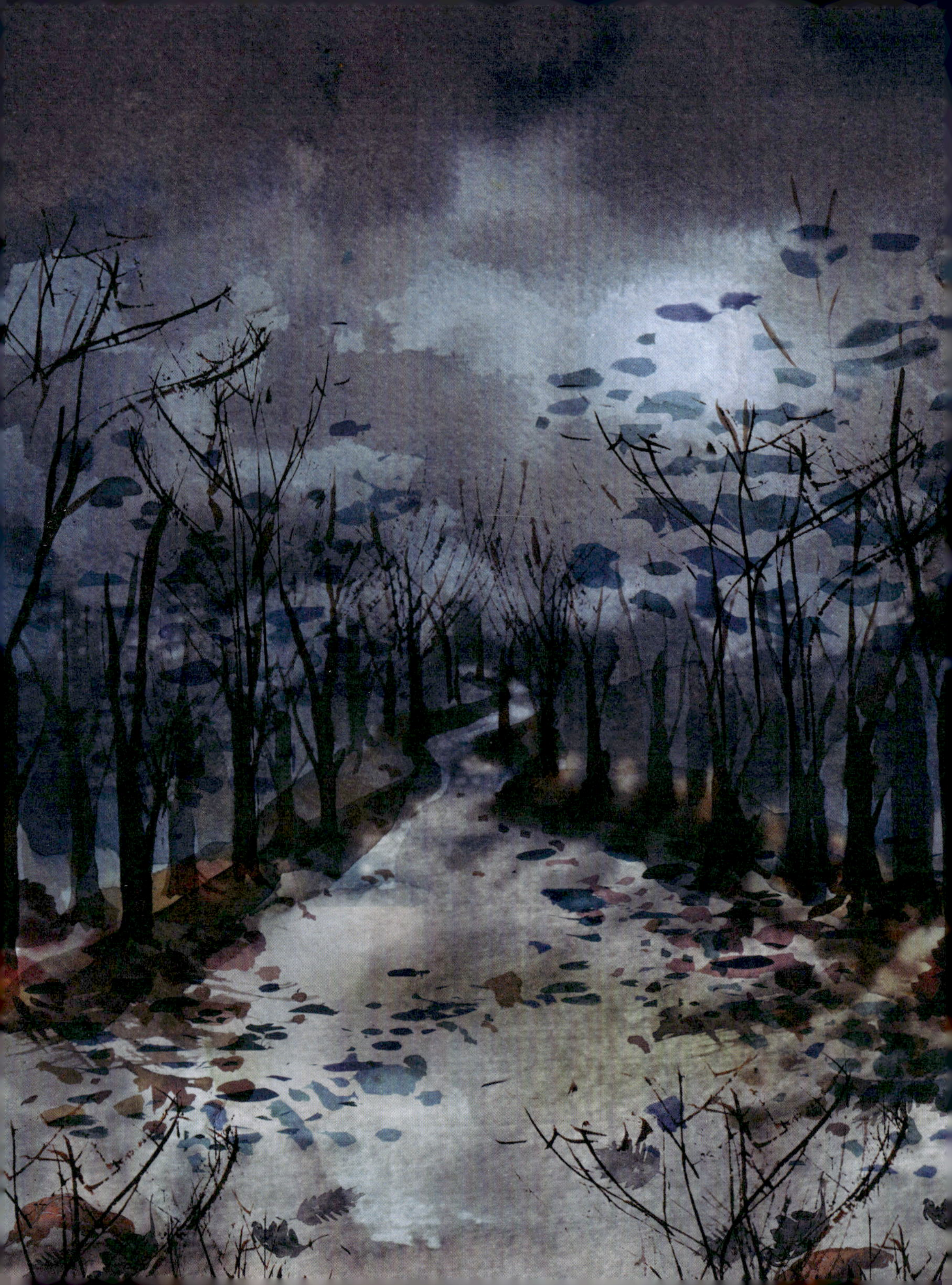

Part 2

Night: Darkness Falls

The Missed Lunch

The day after the doctor's call, on Thursday May 9th, Zhubin left for work at Binny and Ravi's office as usual, saying nothing about the crushing news. It was as if the call had never occurred. When he came home from work he asked: *"Simin, what are we doing tonight?"* "Nothing special, why?" I replied. *"Why don't we all go out for dinner and ask Yassi to come with us?"* he asked.

I loved the idea. It was such a comfort to see Zhubin so relaxed and cheerful – I couldn't believe how lightly he had taken the chilling news. Happy to call his friend Yassi, I hoped that she would be able to join us at such short notice. I rushed upstairs, breathless with excitement by the time I reached Zyg's office, and told him about Zhubin's suggestion and how relieved I was about his upbeat mood. Together with Yassi, we went to a sports-themed restaurant to have dinner while watching hockey on a large screen, enjoying a vibrant evening together.

That evening, after I had helped Zhubin to bed, Zyg asked me: "Did you notice how Zhubin was looking at you? He was staring at you most of the time." I replied: "No, I didn't – maybe it was because I was so happy and he hasn't seen me this happy for a long time – but I did notice him holding my hands very tightly quite a few times."

Zhubin must have known that this would be one of his last evenings with us, and on this bittersweet occasion he had wanted to miss nothing. It was also a chance to see his loyal friend Yassi one more time, perhaps to show her in some way how grateful he was for her companionship and wishing to leave her with a joyful memory.

At around 11am on Friday, May 10th, the last full day of his life, Zhubin telephoned me from work to enthusiastically ask whether I would be free to join him for lunch: *"I have a good idea – I know where to take you. You would like it. It's a nice small place. Do you want to go with me?"* I was so pleased that he was still so positive, despite the devastating verdict received only two days earlier. "Oh, Zhubin, I would love to, you know that, but I already have another lunch appointment and it may be too late to cancel. Let me see what I can do. I'll let you know in a few minutes."

"No, Simin, don't bother. We can do it another time. It's okay," he replied.
"Are you sure?" I persisted.
"Yes, Simin – don't worry."

That missed lunch has haunted me ever since. During that same phone call, Zhubin also mentioned that he had purchased two advance tickets for himself and Yassi to view the Star Wars movie sequel due for release a few weeks later. Unbeknownst to me, he had begun to put his final plan into action and was ensuring that I wouldn't suspect a thing.

Later, after Zhubin's death, I sat in his bedroom sifting through memories and torturing myself over my failure to accept his lunch invitation. The guilt was unbearable. I was the one who had always pushed him to come up with different ideas to get out of the house and keep busy – even if it was only a short walk with our dogs. As most of the time he was not feeling strong enough to be on his feet for long, I had been going out of my way to distract him with activities and outings he enjoyed. So why had I missed this chance to be with him on what would prove to be his last day? I had been able to read Zhubin like an open book. Had I gone to this lunch, I would surely have noticed something odd and perhaps guessed his intentions. Over and over, I told myself that I could have saved my boy. I would have!

I obsessed over the thought that, even though he had made up his mind, he had still wanted us to be together – wanted to be with me as much as possible in what were the last hours of his life. I had lost those precious, irreplaceable moments with him: the joy of seeing him happy, sharing a meal, talking together. I had missed my chance – and that thought grew too much to bear.

In an effort to ease the persistently gnawing feelings of guilt, I would, from time to time, think back to Zhubin's assurance that he would outsmart me – but this recollection provided no relief. Years later, still struggling to come to terms with my loss, my sister Shishi's words about missing this moment came to mind – simply that "It was not meant to be." Now I know this may be very true – things really do happen for a reason. Yet the pain of regret is ever-present. Guilt and regret are just part of the same package. I have paid dearly, over and over, for that missed lunch.

"Don't stay in the past so much. If you were driving and your head was turned around, you would have a fatal accident. Keep your eyes looking toward where you want to go. A lost moment is a lost opportunity."

Zhubin's Going

Zhubin left me on Saturday, May 11th, 2002 – the day before Mother's Day.

The evening before that fateful morning, I had gone to Zhubin's room as usual to help him change and put him to bed. Although we had both been shaken by the doctors' conclusions, I found him to be remarkably calm, relaxed – even joyful. It meant the world to me to see how well he had taken the results, because I was still devastated and in a state of disbelief, telling myself that there had to be – and still could be – a miracle waiting for us somewhere.

Helping Zhubin into bed that night, I reminded him that we needed to pick a place for our Mother's Day lunch with the family, and asked him for some suggestions. All of a sudden, hugging me tightly, he gently asked: *"Mom, Mom, do you really love me?"* I was surprised, not just by his question, but more so by his addressing me as "Mom": he had always called me "Simin". Holding him tightly, I kissed him and said with a smile: "More than anyone and anything in my life."

He was particularly tender and extremely loving, holding me in a long, deep embrace. We hugged often, but for some reason this time it felt different. His grip was unusually firm and he seemed to be brimming with emotion. Leaning back to look into his eyes, I could see they were full of love and gentleness. With another kiss on his cheek, I reassured him that I would wake him at the earlier time he had requested. Having seen him safely into bed, we said goodnight. As I left his room and climbed the stairs I could still feel the grip of his arms around me. I couldn't remember the last time that Zhubin's health had allowed us to celebrate an occasion together – a Mother's Day, a Christmas, or even a birthday – and I looked forward to an enjoyable day together.

At that time, at that moment, I could not have known that this was to be our last hug, our kiss the last kiss, those words his last words to me – that these would be our final moments together. It never occurred to me that he was saying *Goodbye, Mom,* and that he was saying goodbye to me, not just as Simin, but also as his mother.

As I dressed myself early on the following morning, I wondered why Zhubin had asked me to wake him an hour earlier than usual. He had not merely asked but insisted, and indeed made me promise that I would do so. Why? We both knew how crucial it was for him to wake up at exactly the same time every morning, so why had he insisted on it so strongly? I had even tried to remind him that it was difficult enough for me at the usual time, due to the depth of his coma-like state, but he only repeated: *"Please, Simin. Promise me."* Perhaps he wanted just the two of us to spend some time together before our scheduled lunch with Mila, my dear mother-in-law? Maybe he wanted us to share an intimate moment over a coffee at our favourite local breakfast place? Yes, I thought, of course, that's it.

With that thought in mind, I quickly finished getting ready and went downstairs. Sam was already sitting at Zhubin's closed bedroom door waiting for me to let him in. When I entered I was surprised to see the bed empty and already made up, with his neatly folded pyjamas placed on top. Where was Zhubin? I looked for him in his bathroom, but it was empty. Returning to the bedroom I now noticed that the window was ajar, with a stepladder propped outside, leaning against the cement wall of the light shaft that led up to the garden. Then I saw the small "post-it" note stuck to the window pane: *"Simin, do not keep me alive if I am comatose. Promise me that. Zhubin XO."*

"Zyg!" I screamed. "Zhubin is missing! Call the police! Call the police!"

Desperate.

Frantic.

Scared.

A million thoughts raced through my head, each ending with the same question: where was he?

Look at the Big Picture: know it; feel it. That morning, that horrible chilly mid-May morning, I sensed the Big Picture, even if I could not face it. I couldn't say out loud what I feared. Suicide! The very thought of the word filled me with terror, because I knew that Zhubin had not wanted to continue living with his pain.

Zyg was at my side immediately and I had no need to explain. He understood what I was thinking – that if only we could get to Zhubin in time, we could cut him down from a rope that had just become taut. He would still be breathing. We could save him. "We have to find him," I said. "Where would he go?" My thoughts were spinning round and round, always arriving at the same question. Oh, my boy! Where are you?

Then I remembered a recent trip to the Atwater Market on Montreal's Lachine Canal. Zhubin loved it there – the flowing water, the produce stands with brilliantly coloured fruits and vegetables, and the utter sense of peacefulness early in the morning before shoppers began to arrive. On that day, I had caught him standing under the trees by the canal, looking up through the branches as if to gauge their strength and distance from the ground. He had stopped and turned to me grinning: *You think you're so smart, Simin – that you know everything – but one day, I'm going to outsmart you.* The market was where he had gone – I was sure of it!

In a state of extreme panic, we remembered to alert the police and let them know where we were going, before speeding off to search at the canal. Racing from one tree to another, faster and faster, I ran calling Zhubin's name as loud as I could. The police found us on the banks of the canal at around 9am and told Zyg that Zhubin's body had been found. Chasing after me, as I was still running in circles checking trees twice, three times, he finally caught and held me tight.

"Zhubin is gone," he said. "He's gone," he repeated, gripping me tighter and shaking me.

"Gone?" I asked. "Gone where?"

"Zhubin is dead, Simin. The police have found his body. Do you understand what I am trying to tell you?"

"No, no, a thousand times no. It cannot be Zhubin. They are mistaken." My knees buckled and I sank to the grass.

Long before I had even gone downstairs to rouse him, Zhubin's body had already been found, hanging from a tree in Summit Park, a bird and nature sanctuary that was near our home, but in the opposite direction from the canal: Zhubin had completely outsmarted me after all.

For nearly two hours I had persuaded myself that I could find my boy alive, certain that I could save him. At that moment, my hope, and a piece of me, died. I was his mother; we had been so close and yet I had not been able to comprehend either his illness or how this could happen. All I could understand was that he had been suffering, and nothing I had tried had alleviated it.

Like a patchwork quilt with many squares missing, my recollection of what followed this horrifying news can only be gathered in bits and pieces.

My throat felt tight; breathing was hard. I remember an ambulance ride, being restrained on a gurney as I struggled to jump from the moving vehicle. Then in the hospital, strong arms holding me back on a narrow bed in a corridor. No matter how hard I tried, I couldn't get up. Why couldn't these people understand that I must get to my son? He needed me. I begged them: "Please let me go to him. Please. I have to go now."

That afternoon, the police took us to the morgue where we were obliged to identify Zhubin's body. Wrapped in a black plastic body bag, it was partially unzipped to reveal his face: white as marble with a single trickle of blood from a nostril. I gasped in disbelief. My desperate pleas to be permitted to touch and hold my child's body fell on deaf ears and the entire identification process was conducted achingly separated by a plate-glass window – an aspect of this ordeal so cruel that it would be erased from my mind. It was Zyg who reminded me of it many years later. Thank God, I had been spared this memory!

Dazed and broken, we were driven home by someone. Darkness swallowed me. I didn't notice the neighbours standing outside, wanting to help but at a loss as to what to do. I could not eat or sleep – I was a zombie, like the walking dead. Zhubin had wanted to make his death as easy as possible, and he had outmanoeuvred me because he knew I would have tried to hold him back – out of love, out of fear, out of a sense that losing him would mean losing a part of me: my heart.

Trying to sleep, I pictured Summit Park, where he had been found. It was where we had often walked Sam and Pepper, on trails bordered by carpets of white trillium in the spring. Was it an early-morning dog walker who found my son? A jogger? The first pang of guilt: why had I not thought of it? I could have gone there instead of the canal.

But even as I told myself that I could have saved him, I knew that it wasn't true. Following what had been – the police detective informed us

– a carefully prepared plan, Zhubin had slipped quietly out of the house in the early hours of the morning and made his way, first by bus then on foot, to the park where his time of death was estimated to have been between 2.00 and 2.30am. According to the detective's report, he had planned for every eventuality, including the proper length of rope with a pre-tied knot, a flashlight with an extra battery, sturdy shoes for walking up the hill, and, in his jacket pocket, a checklist of items to bring with him. He had also listed his name, as well as our names, address and phone numbers.

I am certain that the timing of his last actions had not been in the least bit arbitrary, instead deliberately chosen to spare us pain: a Saturday morning on a weekend when Adam would not have been staying with us but with his mother as regularly scheduled; his request to be woken earlier than usual, only to ensure that I would be dressed for the police when they came to give us the news; the "post-it" note stuck to the window pane where I could not miss it; his loving farewell the previous evening when he embraced me, telling me he loved me – and calling me *Mom*.

Zhubin was gone. He was only 21.

Burial

On a Tuesday, three days after Zhubin had been found, he was buried.

"We have to get her ready. She looks awful," I heard someone say.

"I think she should wear her black suit. I'll get it."

Someone whispered in my ear: "Simin, get up. We must get ready to go."

"Go where?" I murmured.

"Let's first get ready. Clean you up, fix your hair."

Slowly, I opened my eyes to find my two sisters and Sabine standing over me, gently helping me to get out of the bed. Oh, my God, no, no, not again, I thought. Just let me be alone. Why can't they all go home and leave me alone? Sitting on the bed, I let them dress me up.

The funeral passed by like an old, scratchy, black-and-white film. I was mute, gone, lost. Memories are bleached of colour, just a series of images that seemed out of focus – wrong and disturbing.

Bending over his coffin, I saw Zhubin lying still and ash-white, seemingly in the "coma" that I had witnessed every night for the last year of his life. His eyes were closed. Brushing his cheeks were the long and dark eyelashes that he had wanted to trim, complaining that they made his spectacles dirty. I bent further to kiss him: his forehead was cold as marble. Nuzzling his cheek, I whispered, "Wake up Zhubin! Wake up! Let's go home." There was only silence. "Sam is waiting. Let's go home now." I tried to rouse him, asking him why he had left without me, saying: "Can't I go with you?" There was no response, and then I was gently led away.

A wounded animal wailed as the brown coffin was lowered into the ground. Was that me?

A lightning flash tore its way into my mind: what if he is still in a coma? What if he wakes up? He'll be so scared. He'll be terrified. I was unable to scream aloud the fear that gripped me: "No, no, no, please he needs me. I can't leave him there." I longed to throw myself down into the grave to be with my son, but hands touched me and arms held me back. I remember pushing the hands away, struggling vainly against the restraining arms. Oh my God, these people! These hands! Why do they pull at me so? I wished they would all disappear and be gone.

So tired! So deeply exhausted! I have no memory after that: a void, as though nothing existed any more.

The darkness enveloped me.

"When I leave, my heart will stay in your heart and yours will come with me. You will not be alone."

The First Touch

Following Zhubin's death I was prescribed heavy tranquillizers and so my memories of what happened after the funeral are hazy. I slept most of the time, but only fitfully, drifting in and out of consciousness, in and out of a new reality – one bereft of my son.

I recall lying in bed, waking from confused sleep. From time to time I opened my eyes and saw shadows whispering, but couldn't comprehend why so many people were in my bedroom. A concern that something was very wrong gnawed at me: where is Zhubin? Is he feeling unwell? I must go now to help him wake up! I tried to get out of bed, but each time someone gently held me back. I did not like being restrained and faintly insisted: "I need to see Zhubin." Some soft voice whispered: "He is an angel in heaven now." It was then that I suddenly remembered, and tumbled back into my nightmare...

Most of my family had gathered in Montreal to be with us, including four of Zhubin's cousins with whom he had grown up, and who were more or less the same age. My sister Shishi recounted for me the depth of emotion with which each of them had spoken at Zhubin's funeral, openly sharing their memories of him, their pain and their tears as they tried to comfort one another.

"Don't feel alone; don't feel forsaken; don't feel so misunderstood. There is lots of love, understanding and compassion around you. You have to feel the energy and see the gifts."

I was awash in love and support as the anchor of my family did its best to steady me – but I was beyond consolation. How was it possible? They didn't understand: I had failed my son! All I wanted was to drift away forever, never to return...

I had no idea what was going on in the house or how the family managed to take care of everything. When did they come to Montreal? When did they leave? I am left with but a few vague memories: my sisters and Sabine all curled around me in my bed, feeling safe with them by my side as Shishi told me stories about heaven and its wonders: "This is where Zhubin is now. He is at peace and he is free." How hard I tried to stay awake! I wanted to know where this mysterious place called heaven was, but fatigue kept overcoming me and I could not help dozing off.

Three days after the burial, early in the morning, I was overcome by an urgent need to go and see my son's grave, to touch it, to feel it, to smell it. I couldn't believe that Zhubin was gone. When I asked Zyg: "Please take me to him – I need to go there," he was very reluctant, thinking that such a visit would only worsen my state of mind and emotions. But I promised I would be strong and Zyg yielded. As he helped me dress I studied him. Pale, sad and broken, he still made the effort to prepare me for the visit, reassuring me: "You'll like Zhubin's grave site – it's on a hillside with open spaces all around. There is no gravestone yet, just earth, and it's too early to plant flowers."

During the short drive to the cemetery, each time I closed my eyes all I could see was Zhubin in a black body bag – and yet I could not convince myself that he was gone and buried.

After Zyg left me to approach the last few steps to Zhubin's grave alone, I lay down, pressing my body against the earth as hard I could, trying to get as close as possible to my son. Was he a part of what I was touching? I wanted him to hear my heartbeat, feel my arms around him in a hug, and hear my words telling him: "I am here, Zhubin. I am here. All I want is to be with you. With all these people around me I cannot, but I promise I will be with you soon."

I sobbed desperately, aching to feel his grip, his arms, and his heart against my chest. Lying on top of the muddy earth strewn with rotting flowers, my broken heart felt frozen and as jagged as the sharp edge of an icicle. "Where are you, my son? Who is taking care of you? Is anyone with you, or are you alone? Can you hear me? Do you see me? If you do, then you know I cannot go on living without you. Please help me, I need to know you are safe. I need you to tell me you're safe – please give me a sign."

Distraught, I again stretched myself out over the sodden ground, feeling for my son beneath it – if only to give him the comfort of my embrace. I sobbed: "Dear God, please welcome him; be kind to him – he was innocent."

At last, turning my head, I noticed that the only empty plot in the entire row of gravestones was adjacent to Zhubin's, as if waiting just for me. Returning to Zyg I pointed to the plot: "This is where I want to be buried." When we made our way to the cemetery office, a compassionate staffer consulted her records and informed us that the adjacent plot had been purchased two years earlier. So overwrought that I could barely remain standing, I told her about Zhubin and explained my wish to be buried beside him. "Please call these people and tell them my story," I begged, even offering to pay whatever they asked to give up their plot. The woman assured me that she would speak to her director to see what could be done.

After we returned home, my brother Nader took my hand to help me up the stairs, but I pushed him away and instead walked as though in a trance to the kitchen where I found my sisters and Sabine making tea. For no particular reason, I turned my head to look out through the glass door onto the deck that led to the garden, where the family had left out pots of food that couldn't be accommodated in our fridge.

"Oh my God!" I shouted. Less than three feet away, perched on all fours over a pot he had opened, and calmly continuing to reach for food while intently staring directly into my eyes, was the biggest and most radiant raccoon I had ever seen. I couldn't believe it. Here was this nocturnal creature out in the late morning, the sun shining down on him! Although raccoons are not uncommon in Montreal, this was the first time I had seen one. He reminded me of Charlie, the head of the raccoon family that Zhubin had cared for all those years ago when we had lived in Vancouver.

At my shout, everyone came to the kitchen. There was an air of excitement. Shishi turned to me, took my hand and asked repeatedly: "Simin, did you ask for a sign? Did you ask for a sign?"

"Yes, I did."

"We have been here making tea, but we did not see the raccoon."

She knew of the special bond that had formed between Charlie and my son. "Its appearance was meant for you. Zhubin is safe and sound, and wants you to know he is happy. Do you realize what a big sign this is and how quickly you received it?"

Transfixed by the sight of that beautiful raccoon, I was flooded with memories of how much Zhubin had loved animals, how much he had enjoyed having Charlie in the kitchen, and above all how excited he had been the first time that Charlie had introduced us to his mate and two very young cubs. Soon overcome by these keenly distressing recollections, I turned and went upstairs, climbing into bed with Nader's help.

A few hours later Zyg woke me up. "I have good news," he said. Serendipitously the owners of the plot next to Zhubin's had called the cemetery office that very day to say they preferred a different plot. "So, it is yours if you want it," Zyg said. I was so relieved: "Zhubin, now we can be next to each other soon, very soon, my love."

Looking back now, I realize that these two occurrences were the very first in a string of signs – I consider them miracles – that helped me to open myself up to whatever the Universe held in store for me. Since that day, despite all the food I left out, I have yet to see another racoon outside my house or anywhere else in Montreal, let alone on the deck and in broad daylight!

Zhubin had always been trying to teach me how to live. Preoccupied with trying to take care of and hold onto him, I had not been a good pupil while he had been alive, and had just humoured him instead. Oh, my wise, generous son! Only later would I remember his words, comforting and inspirational: "*Nothing is coincidence. I want you to know and see the Big Picture.*"

"You will be lost at first, but you will find yourself. You will miss me – a small price to pay to be together for eternity."

Agony

I was dead.

How can a mother go through life without her child? How can I?
How will I breathe again? How will I get out of bed?
How will I ever smile again?
How will I find hope?
How can I go on living?
Oh dear God, how? How?

There are no words to adequately describe this horrible nightmare. No words can ever be written to truly express this depth of pain. Words are just symbols. There is no greater pain than that of losing a child.

Cannot believe it.
Cannot understand it.
Cannot explain it.
Cannot accept it.
Cannot give it away.
Cannot share it.
Cannot forget it.
Cannot escape it.
Cannot stop it.
It cripples.
It haunts dreams.
Breathe it and burn to ashes.

It is – all at once, and at every moment – thousands upon thousands of stabs to the heart.

The past was unreal, the present a void, and the future shrouded in darkness. Time stood still. Pain paralyzed me. Slowly I drifted away, dying little by little, welcoming death. Dear dear God, take me to him – let us be together again. I died countless times, over and over. Certain it was only a matter of time before I would be with Zhubin – I just needed to be patient – I marked the minutes of every day, each one passing as if it were a lifetime. Like an addict in withdrawal whose mantra is "One day at a time", mine became "One more day until I join Zhubin, wherever he is." Had he turned to dust in the ground? Was he now merely energy? Might he be an angel in heaven? It didn't matter: I was ready.

"See the beauty of the rose? Your pain for me is a rose."

Was It My Fault?

Was it my fault? Was it? I asked myself over and over again.

Overnight my world became defined by an overwhelming feeling of emptiness, failure and loss. Nothing seemed important any longer. Pain consumed my life. The only thing that felt right was to curl up on Zhubin's bed, waiting for my time to come. I did this day after day – and, as I lay there, a tsunami of guilt washed over me.

Unable to touch anything in Zhubin's room, which had an air of quiet death, I left it as it was:

his pyjamas on the bed;

his slippers beneath it;

his toothbrush and comb in the cup in his bathroom;

his robe on its hanger, still holding the faint smell of his cologne.

Still sitting on his desk was his favourite yellow mug adorned with squares, ladybugs, bumblebees and dragonflies – a reminder of his nickname "Joo-Joo", Persian for "cute little bug".

His CDs and reading materials remained undisturbed: *National Geographic* magazines, Shakespeare, history books, novels and the Star Wars movie tickets – all ready for his return. I was still trying to keep him alive: the little boy walking with his grandfather, his little legs moving twice as fast as Baba's; the wonder on his face as he saw a caterpillar for the first time; feeding Charlie the neighbourhood raccoon; kissing a girl for the first time after his cousins dared him to (he was only nine and generally reserved, but never shied away from a challenge); his school report cards filled with straight As; studying second-year university calculus when he was only 17; the wheeler-dealer who made me sign a handwritten contract agreeing to gift him my ten-year-old sports car if he succeeded in passing his driver's licence examination on his first go (oh, how proud I was of him, and how could I say no when he got it?); and his ability to cut through to the heart of a matter, no matter how blunt he had to be.

Not quite two years old, noticing with delight a fluffy yellow caterpillar in the little backyard of our ground-floor apartment in Vancouver.

How can such sweet memories become so painful? Then the nightmares would come, bearing ugly images that made me shiver to the core: Zhubin writhing on the floor in our kitchen because his head ached so much; the years of drug prescriptions – unceasingly trying to find a combination that would not just bring relief without complications or side-effects, but actually fully restore his health.

Guilt was cutting me to pieces, ripping me apart, with endlessly repeating waves of questions: Did I do everything I could have? Could I have saved him somehow? Why did this happen? Where did I go wrong? Should I have done something different? Had I had lunch with him the day before, would I have known? Why hadn't I suspected or noticed anything on his last night? Why, on this final night, did I let his upbeat mood fool me?

Was it my fault?

I was going mad, hating who I was, asking myself what I could have done differently, what I could have said to make Zhubin want to stay. Finding no answer to these questions did not prevent me from posing them over and over, again and again, on and on, all arriving at one single question: was it my fault?

Often the anguish of guilt proved to be sharper than the pain of loss. Guilt is a feeling that stays with us for a long, long time. Trying to overcome it is an ordeal. I'm certain that every grieving parent must feel the same. It is not easy to talk about, and it is impossible for others to understand it, so we battle it in silence.

The horror of the way Zhubin died haunted me every night. Always exhausted yet never able to rest, I feared what I would see if I closed my eyes. My thoughts circled to his last hours, only to find many more unanswered questions: what had he been feeling when he left home in the dark, walking to the hilltop park alone? Had he been afraid? Did he suffer long? Why hadn't he asked me to help him? I would have.

I waited for Zhubin to return for me – after all, he had promised not to leave me alone. So why was he taking so long? Oh dear God, You gave me this pain and it must be what You wanted for me, but how can I be expected to go on like this? I cannot.

Thoughts drifted to a memory of Zhubin saying to me in a very matter-of-fact tone: *"Remember what you have and not what you have lost."* On closing my eyes, he was there and we were in conversation. Sensing his strength, and before falling back into my recurring nightmare, I would reply: "I'll try. Really, I will."

I wanted to leave – to go far, far away from everything and everyone, and never come back. I needed to vanish, disappear, and be done with it all.

"Mom, sadness is not a cure for your pain. It just traps you. Let it go! Let it go! Live your life. Stay positive. Change your tears for smiles."

Darkness

I was totally lost, feeling like a shadow. The heaviness of the pain crushed my heart. Breathing was difficult and the constant sensation of choking made even walking a struggle. It was a dark dream; it was agony. I was certain I couldn't last much longer. Where did all this pain come from? Did God have any clue what I was going through? How was I supposed to carry on?

I do not recall much of what followed after I was told of Zhubin's death. Through a glass window I had seen a body bag, the zipper opened to the chest – to Zhubin's chest. I had heard a moan. Had that been me? I have but a few wisps of memory from the funeral, the rest remains shrouded by impenetrable darkness.

A few weeks after the funeral, Zyg arranged to take me out of town for a fortnight, but the trip was a blur for both of us and we retained only a few glimpses. Returning to a lifeless home, I found every room hung with an inescapable smell of death, emptiness and sadness. No matter where I turned I saw a painful reminder. Darkness had crept into every corner.

I was sitting looking at a piece of paper. "We need you to sign here," a voice murmured and a finger appeared, pointing to a space on the document. Unable to comprehend what was happening, all I could see were the words at the top: "Death Certificate". I don't recall how long I sat at that heavy table in that large-windowed room, the sheet of paper thrust before me, as I stared at those words. What is this? What does it mean?

"Would you like to be alone for a while? Would you like to have some water?" someone asked me softly. Unable to stop my tears from streaming or my hands from shaking, I couldn't even hold the pen. It must have been Zyg who came to my rescue, rubbing my shoulder and telling me: "Simin we need your signature here." A finger indicated a position on the page.

My memories of those painful days were erased, some forever, others surfacing only years later. How can any parent face these nightmarish tortures? Never before had I known this evil pain. I was constantly shivering.

Unable to believe that Zhubin was no longer with me, I searched for his face – in every crowd, on every sidewalk, in every store and café. My heartbeat would race the moment I saw someone who resembled him, had his hair colour or his gait. In the fading hope of finding him I visited his favourite places – but I was chasing a dream that could never be.

Slowly I began to understand what had happened: indeed, he was gone – really gone, never to return. All I could feel was a cruel and massive pain; a "killer" pain that reached the marrow of my bones, melting me away. I couldn't do anything, nor did I want to. The only thing I did want was to be with Zhubin. Part of my heart had been ripped out and what remained was ravaged.

At last I grasped that my life would never be the same. The heavy weight of anguish was a beast of prey unrelentingly shadowing me. "It will take time to heal," I was told. "You have to be strong." What did they mean? This pain was destroying me, my entire being on fire.

Remembering how much Zhubin had suffered only made it all the worse. My body was numb. My heart was numb, turning to dust. How could it be that I would never again see my son around the house? How could it be that he would never come home? How could it be possible to never again see my child? To never again walk with him? To never again talk to him? Never again tell him stories? Never again take care of him? Never again just be with him? Never see who he would become? Never see him married? Never visit him in his own home with his own family? Never have grandchildren? Never have his love and support in my old age?

I wanted my son back. I needed my only child back – to hold him in my arms and kiss him again and again, over and over, forever. In time, I recognized that looking and waiting for him was hopeless. I had been trying to hold the wind in my hands. He was gone. Gone somewhere, but where? Where had he gone?

"I know you will be in pain but keep your head up and look above.
I will be hugging you and will be all over you.
You won't be far from me.
Have faith."

The First Gift

In Zhubin's room was a box that had filled up with condolences received from family and friends. Even though I knew that each one contained words of love, sympathy and encouragement, I could not and did not want to deal with them. Each time that I opened a card, I could do nothing but cry, with no idea of how to stop my tears. At last, I put the box on Zyg's desk and asked him to take care of them, acutely aware that this was a selfish request: I knew it wouldn't be easy for him either.

Two days later, Zyg called to me: "Simin, come here. You should read this letter. You would like it. It will make you happy." I replied: "I don't want to. Not now." I knew he was referring to one of the letters in *that* box. He asked again, insisting this time, so I quietly sat down near him and he showed me a letter saying: "This is a letter from the senior police detective who went to Summit Park where they found Zhubin's body, and he was the one who found the checklist and other items that Zhubin took with him. Listen to what he wrote."

What I remember from that remarkable letter is as follows: for the past 15 years or so the detective had specialized in cases of suicide, yet he had never encountered one with such a detailed plan of action. Zhubin had planned everything meticulously beforehand: choosing the tree with a rock beside it; selecting a path that was well signposted so that he could locate it in the dark without shining his flashlight and alerting the park security; knotting the rope in advance, with a professional noose. While it was clear to the detective that this had not been an impulsive decision, what had puzzled him was why Zhubin had done it at all. After interviewing Zyg and me to hear our description of Zhubin's journey, and seeing the love and care that had surrounded him, he admitted in his letter to having been deeply disturbed by this case and unable to dismiss it from his mind, suddenly aware of how life can completely change course in a matter of seconds. Shaken by the thought that something like this could happen to his own 17-year-old son, whom he now recognized as far and away the most important person in his life, he shared with us in his letter his decision to devote two weeks' vacation to his first-ever father-son road trip during which he was able to open up to his son and tell him how much he loved him and how important he was. By the end of the trip, he had felt certain that he had succeeded in building a very strong and lasting bond with his son. He ended by expressing his gratitude to Zhubin for showing him the way.

After reading the letter, with misty eyes Zyg smiled and said: "Simin, this is Zhubin's first gift." Still reeling and numb, I couldn't see the letter for what it was – a promise of new shoots rising from desolation. All I could muster before leaving Zyg was: "I'm happy for him and his son."

"Nothing is coincidence; there is a reason for everything. We are so connected to each other in endless ways."

The Passage of Pain

Months passed, seasons changed, and still I awaited Zhubin's return. As I continued to mourn, I tried to follow Zhubin's advice: I put on a brave face; went grocery shopping; made lunch and dinner; cleaned the house; went through the motions of everyday living. Notwithstanding the echo of Zhubin's encouraging words to me, I was bereft of life. The pain and I had become like two lovers deeply in love: intertwined and inseparable.

I had always done my best to look good for him, never letting him see me cry, never wanting him to sense that I was worried about his condition. I had known that I had to be strong for him, and taking care of myself was one way to show him that I had strength and confidence. It had been very important for him to see me "up" and active. One winter's day I had been feeling particularly sad and heavy-hearted, listless, tired of covering up my tears and my feelings, and fed up with pretending. Reading my mood, Zhubin had quietly watched me throughout the morning, waiting for the right time to speak. I sensed his intentions but didn't want to talk. That afternoon, as I sat on his bed folding his clothes, he finally broke his silence: *"Simin, you don't look good today. Are you sad for me? Do you feel sorry that your son is like he is? Do you wish I was healthy and we were happy? Are you feeling sorry for yourself? I have just one thing to tell you. Grow up, Simin. Do you know how lucky we are to have a home, not to have to worry about either food or money to pay for the doctors and all the medication? Do you know how many mothers are out there who cannot even afford to buy medicine for their sick children? Who can't do anything but watch them die in front of their eyes? Why not us? Why not you? Why not me? You do not love me more than any other mother loves her child. I am not more precious than any other kid. Get over your self-pity. It won't help you."* This was my son talking to *me*, his mother – as if *he* were the parent and I the child.

When I went through Zhubin's "Master Plan" binder after he had died, I was stricken when I read: *"Can you dream with your heart? I do it all the time. Good things always happen – be sure to see them."* I tried – oh, how I tried to see it – but how could I? I was black with despair. What was the point of getting better? My son was dead and I felt sucked dry by sorrow.

Weeping when no one would see or hear me, I asked God earnestly:

"Are You there? Are You real? Do You even exist?"

"Do You see me?"

"Are You listening?"

It seemed that God did not hear me, was either deaf or simply ignoring me. I was left alone in the darkness, unable to breathe!

Each time I thought about dying, about ending it all, I would hear Zhubin's voice as if he was in the room with me, expressly asking me to do what he had wanted to do but now couldn't: *"Help all. Open doors."*

In my struggle I was quiet, keeping to myself. When Zyg was not at home, I would make my way downstairs to Zhubin's room to lie on his bed and sob in despair. Zhubin's dog, Sam, would join me, sharing and comforting. For months following Zhubin's death he was listless, missing his best friend so much. During Zhubin's "coma" period, Sam had eagerly followed me down to Zhubin's room without fail every morning, running so fast that I had to let him go ahead of me. As soon as I opened the door he would jump onto Zhubin's chest, licking his face and tickling Zhubin's neck with his muzzle, determined to rouse him from the "coma". How had Sam sensed the need for this invaluable role, which only he could have played with such gusto? Now Sam just lay in Zhubin's room, often without me, waiting for his friend to return. When I tried to tempt him back upstairs with his special treats, hand-feeding him, he rejected my offerings, rushing back downstairs as soon as he could.

One evening I searched all over the house for Sam and eventually found him tucked into the corner of Zhubin's bathroom in the dark. I could not bear to see him suffer like that. "Sam is dying," I told Zyg. "I have to do something." The next day, after Sam had once again raced downstairs to Zhubin's bedroom, I decided to follow our friend Binny's inspired suggestion and take him to the cemetery to visit Zhubin's grave. Together we walked to the grave and sat on the grass. I had a big cry with Sam and said: "Now you know where he is. When we go home, be a good boy."

After that day Sam no longer went into Zhubin's room, comforting me instead. When I found myself alone at home I'd sit on the stairs, sobbing and crying. Then I'd feel a paw and the nudge of a head demanding attention and a return to the present. I would hold Sam's head in my hands, look into his eyes, and tell him: "Sam, I love you for loving Zhubin so much, for never leaving his side. I wouldn't have been able to get Zhubin up without you. You were a loyal friend to him, and now you are a big help who comforts me." Hiding my crying from others, I would hug him, saying: "Sam, it's just me and you now."

Sam was living proof of the special bond that Zhubin talked about that we share with animals.

"We can all learn not just from each other, but even from our dogs: loyalty, honesty, protectiveness, love, curiosity, appreciation, being in the moment, playfulness, and being ever ready for more food. For them, everything is about now."

Aged 19, photographing Sam with Pepper in the background in the kitchen of our Montreal home.

A Circle of Loss

My parents raised their children with watchful eyes. Baba was not a religious man, neither following any rituals himself nor insisting that his children do so. When he occasionally took us to a mosque it was to share with us its visual and artistic beauty. He believed in good deeds and an honest heart, instilling these values in his children.

I am the fifth of seven children: two older brothers (Nader and Ali), two older sisters (Shamsi and Soussan), and two younger siblings (a brother Farhad and a sister nicknamed Shishi). In the course of our childhood, spent in Iran's capital city of Tehran, we changed homes several times. My favourite was in an upscale area with a lush courtyard garden centred on a pool flanked by two mature pomegranate trees, gorgeous when in flower. In time, these flowers would turn into pomegranate fruit, whose skin would slowly crack open under the heat of the sun to reveal brilliantly glistening ruby seeds. I fondly recall sitting with Mâmân on a patio in the courtyard, helping her to make tomato sauce and pickles with fresh herbs. Behind me a glorious wisteria climbed the entire wall up to the second floor, and more than five decades later the scent of those flowers remains with me. Shishi was born there, and I remember this home as a very happy one.

When I was around 11 we moved once again, this time to a new house that Baba had built on a hillside, closer to the mountains. From the start, this home was a disappointment to me. I didn't like its gloomy aspect, and there was no garden or even a backyard. Why had Baba chosen this design – especially with two little ones around? In the end, it proved to be a very sad house indeed: my brother Farhad would die while we were living there.

One bitterly cold and snowy January morning, before Soussan and I left for school, Mâmân took us aside explaining that, as Farhad and Shishi were not feeling well, my sister and I would need to stay with our maternal grandparents for a while. They were doting and gentle, and throughout my life in Tehran we spent most weekends as their guests. Their spacious home within a walled compound had a large multi-tiered garden, which included a turquoise-tiled swimming pool filled year-round with natural spring water. This slice of heaven was a private playground for their 35 grandchildren.

Tehran is an easy place in which to find one's bearings: standing anywhere in the city, one merely has to look up to see the snow-capped Alborz Mountains to the immediate north. My grandparents' home was in a suburb set in the foothills, situated on a steep slope. Although lovely to visit on weekends it was not a very practical place for Soussan and me to stay during the week, being a long way from our respective schools. Commuting to and fro was difficult, especially during that harsh winter, and much as we adored our grandparents, we missed our parents as well as our little brother and sister.

One day after classes, I was surprised and pleased to find my brother Ali waiting for me by the school door. "We're going to pick up Soussan from school," he said, "and then I'll take you home to see Mâmân and Baba." I was so excited about seeing my parents and family again. Although it couldn't have been more than two weeks since we had left home, it had seemed like an eternity. It was snowing heavily

The last photo of my parents together, taken on the deck of the hospital the day before my father lapsed into a coma.

as we trudged the long route to Soussan's school – she was attending junior high by then, while I was still in elementary school. Ali was unusually quiet throughout the whole walk – deep in thought – and I knew enough to let him be.

After meeting Soussan we all made our way home. I trailed behind the two older children, who were deep in conversation. Although I sensed that something was not quite right, I was just happy to be going home. After we arrived, Soussan and I ran upstairs looking for Mâmân and Baba, eager to see the little ones. Before we were able to open the bedroom door, however, I heard someone shout: "No, no! You can't go in there. Farhad and Shirin are very sick. You may get it too." At that moment Baba came out of their bedroom, firmly shutting the door behind him. He greeted us with a faint smile, looking thin, pale, and unkempt. I had never seen him unshaven – he was usually neatly groomed. He hugged us gently. We were so thrilled to see him, but Mâmân was nowhere to be found. I kept on asking for her, and for Farhad and Shishi too. Distracting us with cake and sweets, Baba explained that we could not visit the little ones since they were very ill with a contagious disease that he did not want us to catch. After this all too brief visit, Baba asked Ali to take us back to our grandparents. I remember crying as I had wanted to see my brother and sister so badly and missed Mâmân very much. I am sure Soussan felt equally as sad as me, perhaps even more so – as a young teenager she must have understood what was going on.

A while after that visit – I can't remember how much time had passed – Soussan and I were about to leave for school one morning when my grandmother told us that Mâmân would be waiting for us when we got back. I could not wait for the school day to end, eagerly anticipating seeing Mâmân at last, as well as Farhad and Shishi. I even saved my lunch to share with them – pasta was a special treat for us in those days and my younger siblings' favourite.

As soon as class was finished, I rushed excitedly to Grandma's where I found Mâmân sitting on the edge of the bed by the window, looking out onto the garden. When I threw myself onto the bed to hug her she stopped me. "No, no! Careful of Shirin." Only then did I notice the barely visible little bump under the quilt.

Shishi, not more than three years old at the time, moved her head towards me. Excited to see her, and before even a kiss or a hug, I said: "I brought you some pasta. Would you like to have some?" But Mâmân immediately pushed me away saying: "No, she cannot eat that!"

Unable to smile, Mâmân did not return my embraces. When I asked her where Farhad was she replied that he was not feeling well and had been taken to the hospital, adding: "He is going to come home in a few days." "Where is Baba?" I asked. "With Farhad," she replied.

My grandmother called us away so that Mâmân could be left alone. "She is tired," Grandma said. I did not understand why Mâmân was so sad, hugging her knees and silent – so distant. The truth was that Farhad was never coming home again: he had already died and been buried.

A few days later we all went back home. I kept asking when I could go to the hospital to see Farhad, and every time I'd receive another excuse: "Not now. They're going to send him home soon." Only by accident did I find out what had happened to Farhad, overhearing it mentioned in a conversation. When I asked Mâmân if this were true, the listless response she managed struck me like a thunderbolt: "Yes, Farhad is dead." For the remainder of her life she never uttered another word to me about her loss.

Farhad had succumbed to diphtheria. I learned later that my older brothers had known all along, and I think that Soussan had known too, but for some reason I had been kept in the dark. I guess that was part of our culture – one of secrets and silent suffering. When I finally learned of Farhad's fate, I must have cried a lot, but I don't recall. I've been told that Farhad was a beautiful boy and I had loved him with all my heart, but, ever since that day, when I look at photographs of him his face is that of a stranger. No matter how hard I try, I am unable to remember what he looked like or how we had played together. Is it because of the trauma? Did I block out the pain? I later carried his photo in my wallet for years – even though it continued to hold no meaning for me. Was this strange blank because my parents never spoke of him again? Decades later, when Mâmân was 80 and Farhad's name came up, she requested that we not mention him. I didn't know why my parents chose not to refer to Farhad again and I never asked them why.

Shortly after Farhad's passing, Ali left to study abroad and was soon followed by my other brother. Suddenly our cooking pots were much smaller, the house emptied of all three brothers.

As a young child, I could not comprehend either my parents' faith or their humanity – especially during times of great difficulty. Never asking for anything, content with what they had, they were always ready to help others. As they faced all the challenges that life threw in their path, how could they have been so grateful to God, remaining so hopeful?

For both Baba and Zhubin nature was a divine gift and they saw beauty in everything – even gravel in a country lane. Baba believed in "all is well", no matter how hard life could be. I was unable to understand any of this for many, many years.

Now, at last, I appreciate where all these feelings and godly qualities came from, can comprehend why my parents were so humble, why they wanted to share what they had and why their faith was genuine. They too had been through the dreadful pain of losing a child – two in fact: their adored third son Farhad and their first-born, a daughter named Shamsi, who passed away aged nine months due to illness.

I recall coming home from school one day, not long after Farhad had passed away, and feeling taken aback by how old Baba looked to me. I couldn't figure out what was different about him. Then I was jolted by the realization that his hair had turned completely grey overnight.

> *"Our pain is part of the journey; it allows us to learn what we need to learn and do what we should do."*

The loss of his son, with whom he had felt a very special bond, was more than Baba could endure. In search of relief from this unbearable grief, he grew very spiritual; he chose a path of faith and from then on began to walk with God. Baba's pain became his inner light and that was Farhad's gift to him. By cherishing life and all it had to offer, Baba honoured the love he and his son had held for one another.

After Baba passed away, Shishi found, among my father's few personal belongings rescued from Iran, a pair of Farhad's small shoes, along with a love poem Baba had composed at the time of his son's death. Decades later, in the chaos of uprooting 46 years of their life together – including their home, friends, family and belongings – and, despite the madness of the time, the rush of their departure and my mother's poor health, my father had not forgotten Farhad's shoes and the words he had dedicated to him. By then, Farhad had been gone for 25 years. We never forget our children, cherishing their memories in our thoughts and their love in our hearts.

Mâmân would live for 22 more years after Baba's death. Coming from a very large family, it was lonely for her to live widowed in a foreign land. They had made a few friends in Vancouver, but gradually they too disappeared from her life. Although I saw her daily when we lived in Vancouver and my siblings would travel from near and far to visit her often, the absence of her husband was a harsh reality. Like Baba, Mâmân never talked about either the son or the daughter they had lost.

> *"We have to have hardship so we can continue to grow. I know it is not easy, but be strong."*

For years, I thought my parents' silence was meant to protect us from missing them. But I now know that this was how they had coped with their grief – keeping the pain locked in their hearts, which became a secret sanctuary for the memories of their children.

We all deal with loss in different ways. No one way is better than another; no one way easier than another – merely different.

At the time of Zhubin's passing we were living in Montreal, once again far from my mother. She had loved Zhubin dearly and had held a special place for him in her heart as she had watched him grow up. Two months or so after Zhubin died, I visited Mâmân. She had become frail – not strong enough, I felt, to withstand the news of Zhubin's death. The visit was excruciating as I could not share my grief with her and receive the comfort of my mother's love. Instead, I had to put on a cheerful face and pretend – but inside I was screaming with the memories of Zhubin's Vancouver childhood now surrounding me.

During each of my many subsequent visits, Mâmân would ask after Zhubin, wondering why he had not come along and asking when he would come to see her. Each time this question arose, I had to come up with a white lie.

As she got older, Mâmân's memory began to fade and she became so weak that she eventually needed care around the clock. I was fortunate to be able to visit her often, each time grateful to God for granting me these few moments alone. I sensed our time together would not last much longer and wanted to be with her as much as I could. During these visits I loved to give Mâmân her bath, washing her old and fragile body with great care and affection. The memory of one such particular time is carved into my heart. While washing her fragile hands and fingers my thoughts travelled back: I pictured Mâmân at a younger age, recalling how innocent and selfless she had been; how she had watched over all of us in her own tender way; how much she had sacrificed for her children; and the way she had hidden her secret tears when longing for her lost children. In that moment, out of love and admiration for her, my tears poured down and, while caressing her gnarled fingers, I told her in my heart: "My beautiful Mâmân, I share your pain. I know it and I love you even more for your broken heart." I felt closer to her than ever before, certain that our hearts were connected: just then she reached out to hold my face in her hands and wordlessly return that same love – a memory that my spirit will carry wherever it goes. That night, I cried for her, and for all mothers.

My parents never revealed their grief and sadness over their losses, keeping them hidden in their hearts. True faith was their anchor.

"Everything in life is circular and it is a circle that binds us all together. We truly never leave each other. This is because we all become part of one another."

Brothers

Adam and Zhubin only had four years together. Despite Zhubin's limitations, these were years packed full of laughter, adventures and memories. Sadly, the good times were often overshadowed by periods when Zhubin's symptoms grew severe. However, even when Zhubin's headaches were intolerable and he had no choice but to shut himself away, Adam would not abandon him and simply sat on the floor outside Zhubin's bedroom until his "big brother" felt better. Sometimes, Zhubin would tease him, addressing him as *Flea*.

"Know that with young souls you should keep them safe and be ever watchful. Be positive and encourage the positive within them, without lectures. Love is the way."

Once, to cheer up Zhubin, Adam purchased with his own money a gift from his school bazaar: a pack of hockey cards to which he attached a handwritten note: "To the best brother in the whole world." After Zhubin's death, I found that pack in Zhubin's "Master Plan" binder, along with its accompanying note.

When my brother Ali and the rest of the family came to Montreal for Zhubin's funeral, he and Zyg had to consider how to break the news to Adam and determined it best to talk to him with his mother at their home. To this day, I have not had the heart to ask Zyg how they did that or how Adam reacted. At only 11 years of age, I have no idea how he was able to handle such devastating news.

I learned that Adam placed one of Zhubin's badminton birdies in the coffin, a symbol of the game they had both enjoyed, but that he kept Zhubin's racquet as a precious memento.

It was difficult watching Adam coping with this loss at such a young age. He missed Zhubin so much. "He is my real brother," he used to say. I had nothing to give Adam at that time: my every thought was about Zhubin, and everything around me evoked his memory. From time to time we would talk about him, hug each other and have

With Sam on the day we brought the dogs home. Adam cuddles Pepper.

a good cry. Adam was extremely sensitive to my sorrow. At the end of the crying, he always talked about Zhubin's jokes, reminding me of the funny things he used to say and do. This was Adam's way of bringing a smile to my face and cheering me up, reaching out to help and comfort me as best he could.

I know that the love our sons had for one another will be with Adam forever and the memories of the good times they shared will be cherished always. Today Adam is a skilled badminton player and part-time coach, perhaps his way to honour and remember Zhubin.

"Keep all your memories as that is what makes a difference in our lives. So be in the moment and make sure that you treasure it all. Enjoy your time with family and love them in every moment – when we are together we are all blessed. Spending time with loved ones is a great gift."

My Confidante

Every evening, when Zhubin was still with us, I had taken the dogs for a long walk. He would accompany us whenever he was up to it. Our neighbourhood is very quiet, with graceful old trees and elegant streetlights emitting a foggy yellow glow that makes one feel as if one were in Wonderland – all the more so in the summer when the fireflies show off their flickering beams. It would prompt Zhubin to whisper in wonder: "*Simin, look: it's magic – just like in a fairy tale.*" Sometimes Zhubin preferred to rollerblade, taking Sam's leash and skating so fast that Sam was left collapsed on the ground panting after the chase. All four of us had loved these evening walks, and it had made me especially happy to see Zhubin enjoy them. It was just one more thing that I would miss.

A few weeks after Zhubin's passing I went on a trip. Returning afterwards to a home without Zhubin was a nightmare. Never would he walk with us again. My loneliness grew sharper, leaving me with an acute feeling of emptiness – dead inside.

Crawling my way out of the prison walls of my mind, I resumed my late-night walks with Sam and Pepper: it was my time to be alone with my grief, just the three of us, without pretending, always tracing the same route Zhubin and I used to take. As I knew that Zyg had not only to cope with his own emotions but also be strong for Adam, I did not wish to add to his burdens. I had no one to talk to and yet I needed to talk, I needed to cry and I needed to grieve. I even dreamt of seeing Zhubin appearing around a corner or hearing his voice calling out to Sam.

One night as I was walking and talking to myself, I glanced up through the leafy trees to the sky and was treated to the sight of the full moon. At that moment, it was as if she was looking down only at me and wondering why I was crying, so I told her: "If you want to know, I will tell you my story. It is a sad one. You look so beautiful up there. I don't want to make you sad." The moon did not answer, but when I lifted my gaze up to her again, her face glowed on, lighting my way, tacitly inviting me to go on – so I confided:

"I am jealous of the grasses growing on Zhubin's grave.

I am jealous of the rain that waters those grasses and keeps them fresh.

I am jealous of the sun that warms them and helps them to grow.

I am jealous of you, on dark nights brightening his tomb with your silvery sheen.

You are with him now, at this moment."

That night I welcomed the moon to my heart as a friend, opening up without fear to tell her my story bit by bit. The moon became my confidante: silent, true, wise, loyal and gentle. No matter how much I cried, no matter what I said or how much I had to tell her, the magnificent moon always listened, never judged, never told me to be strong, never told me it was or wasn't my fault. Always there, she waited to comfort and listen. Her majestic serenity was what I needed to calm me.

I remembered a peaceful evening that I had spent as a little girl with Baba by a lake in the countryside. The moon had been large and her reflection on the still water had looked radiant. Pointing to the shimmering lake, my father asked me: "Do you see the moonlight on the water? See its silvery colour? That is the meaning of your name, Simin – silverish." I loved the way Baba had explained to me my name. Not only has that memory vividly stayed with me all these years, but from that moment on I felt a special bond with the moon. Maybe it was meant all along for the moon to come to my aid now?

On my solitary walks I said to my new friend:
"You beautiful moon,
my son is as beautiful as you are,
as shimmering as you are
and as unreachable as you are."

As though playing hide-and-seek, she sometimes concealed herself behind patches of cloud or sprays of leaves, saying:

"Now you see me, now you don't, but you know I am here.
Sometimes I appear with different faces, but you know it is still me.
Sometimes you won't see me at all, no matter how hard you look.
That may sadden you, but you know I will be back.
You just have to be patient."

When she was absent I thought perhaps she was somewhere else in the heavens helping another broken heart. Knowing that my friend would never leave me for long, I searched the dark sky, watching for her return. And then, after some time, I espied her, though she did not reveal all her beauty at once: little by little, ever so slowly, she emerged, until a few nights later there she was showing off her true grace – a full moon. How glad this made me!

One late evening, the sky was filled with dark clouds and the moon was nowhere to be seen. Forced to wait for her for another night, I felt especially lonely and downcast. I needed my friend. As I continued on my way, all of a sudden – as if reappearing just for me – the moon emerged from behind the clouds, huge and luminous. That night I went to bed with the silvery moon in my thoughts, sure that she was urging me never to give up quickly and teaching me not to believe only in what I saw. She was telling me: "Yes, your son is as beautiful, as luminous and as unreachable as I am, but, like me – ever present, even when unseen – he is also always with you."

Then I asked myself: What if there is something out there? What if Zhubin is somewhere in the Universe, can see me and hear me? I concluded that I had to have faith – and to let God work on me. My suffering had created faith in me. Then I heard Zhubin's soft voice reminding me: "*Let faith fill your heart. Believe in the unknown,*" and I felt and understood the essence of what Zhubin had written in one of his last notes to me:

"*Look at the sun and the moon,*
And see me.
Look at animals and yellow flowers,
And see me.
Our bond is forever."

That magical moon gave me love, gave me courage, taught me that nothing is lost, nothing gone forever. She became my healer. I still talk to her, still open my heart to her, but it is with the joy and certainty that Zhubin is with me.

"We will be together when the time is right."

I realized that I had already been given many signs to help me carry the burden of pain that had been weighing me down. The connection I felt with the moon was one of Zhubin's ways of showing me and telling me: "*I am always with you.*"

"Always learn from nature. There are many hidden beautiful lessons in nature. It is the biggest teacher. Always love nature and pay attention to all its details."

My Winding Road

Life without Zhubin was impossible to imagine. Gradually the stark truth dawned on me: I would have to live the rest of my days without my son. At last I admitted to myself that he was not coming back – that his body, riddled with its horrible illness, was now in the ground.

I was unable to stop agonizing over the way Zhubin had died – all alone, without me to hold him in my arms until the end. It was impossible not to dwell on the extent of his suffering. The sight of him in that black body bag had shattered my heart into a thousand pieces! Try as I might to put these heart-shards together, their razor-sharp edges sliced my fingers. Through these broken pieces I saw the tears of my soul.

Could there have been any reason for God to permit such cruelty to be visited on an innocent child – one who had been all about love? I couldn't believe that He could first infuse a mother's heart with love and then inflict this much pain and suffering. How much I prayed to God during the extremes of Zhubin's illness, begging Him to "Take Zhubin if You want, but end his nightmare", and promising that I would never ask why. Now, the pain was mine, only mine: a black hole sucking the life from me, so crippling that I was unable to get out of bed, wishing only to be left alone with my grief. I told God that guilt and emptiness were tearing me apart, piece by piece, and that I could not go on any longer. "You know it. So why are You keeping me here? I have no more questions to ask. Don't You have any answers for me?"

I was waiting for something, or someone, or maybe even nothing at all. My mind had grown weak and fragile, like my body. Everything in my life was so difficult; every day a century. Yet there was a longing in my heart to keep my promise to Zhubin – I needed to feel alive and to rid myself of this torment. But how?

It was time for me to do what I needed to do to survive this tragedy, and I sensed that this meant seeking by myself, and for myself, the true meaning of life. The void my life had become was vast and the road towards my new destination was daunting – as long as eternity, a brutal and lonely track. Unable to fight this battle alone, I told God that He had given me the greatest gift of all – my son; that He had also taken him away – taken from me my love, my teacher, my friend, my life; that I accepted the pain but did not want to grieve for the rest of my life. I pleaded with God to help me keep my promise to Zhubin. When there was no one and nothing to help me, when the flame of Zhubin's death grew out of control and I could no longer deal with it, I turned to God alone in the darkness:

"Show me the way, I will follow.
Teach me, I will learn.
Tell me, I will listen.
Ask me, I will do."

I prayed for God to give me courage, to help me with His blessings, His miracles and His love. I prayed that He would not abandon me.

"Do not always ask for answers. Find questions. Find God. Let everything go, but work on your faith."

Only God can heal a broken heart – but even for Him it takes time, as He must put back together thousands of pieces. What I needed was to trust in a Higher Power to work on and protect me.

Slowly, with baby steps, I learned that my faith did not necessarily mean belonging to any particular house of worship – I could seek solace in any one of them. Relief and counsel were not necessarily to be found only in prescribed religious rites or visiting a psychologist's office once or twice a week to unburden myself. Instead, I found help in my everyday life: in the wind; in the flowers of my garden; in books about loss and mourning; in a simple yoga stretch; in advice given in an afternoon television talk show. The secret to my becoming whole again was through spirituality, faith and patience – by opening myself up to the Universe. It was here that I found a means to fight the battle against darkness and sorrow.

I did not appreciate then that the Master plans everything ahead of time for all His children – even for me. While I was lost in the void, where everything was pitch black, I had no idea what miracles awaited me. And yet, I found solace at this time in Zhubin's words.

"I know you will suffer, but you should learn what this is all about. It is a new phase for you and you have to guide yourself on your own. Step by step, you will learn and know, I promise. But move on with faith and peace."

Where Do They Go?

More than anything I worried about Zhubin, certain that he needed help. Who would take care of him? Where had he gone? He was nowhere to be found. There was no trace of him. How could he be here one minute and then vanish the next? Where should I look for him? How could I find him? Although I had seen his body and knew it was buried, I wanted to know where the rest of him was. I had never thought about the soul and the spirit. What were they and where were they? From the depth of my grief I made a vow: "I will search for you for a thousand years, and will wait a thousand more."

It was only after I came back to myself a little after those first few months of numbness that I started to ask how Zhubin had been able to do what he did. How was it that he had not fallen into his recurring coma that night? How had he been able to be so alert and aware as he carried out his plan to end his life: writing out a checklist; ensuring that our names and telephone numbers were in his jacket pocket; leaving the note for me stuck on the window where it could easily be seen?

I recalled one afternoon, during Zhubin's coma period, when I was about to take the dogs for a walk and asked him to come along. He had not been feeling well but came anyway. As we were walking I told him: "I am so concerned: if something were to happen to me, who is going to take care of you?" In a very casual tone, he replied: "*Simin, you worry too much about me. Don't. I will go long before you will. Anyway, either there is nothing so I won't suffer anymore, or there is something and I will have a second chance. Don't worry.*" Really angry with him whenever he spoke this way, I demanded that he stop spouting such nonsense. But this time he continued: "*Simin, you need to learn about the Spirit.*" When I replied, "What are you talking about?" he explained: "*When you become curious, it means that you are hungry for the Truth. This way you open your heart to the Universe and only then are you ready to learn the truth. The Universe teaches you in so many different ways. Trust in that.*"

Faced with this recollection, I pledged: "I will trust, and I will learn, I promise."

How could Zhubin have talked this way, concerning himself with such profound matters? Is there really such a thing as a soul? If there is, is it possible that while he was in his unconscious state his soul had actually travelled to the unworldly place that he spoke of with such joy and excitement in his voice?

One morning, when Sam and I were struggling to rouse him, and before he was even able to open his eyes, Zhubin whispered: "*Simin, you have no idea how much I know. I cannot even begin to tell you. You know I don't brag; you know I do not like to show off.*" Later the same day, when I asked him to explain what he had meant, he answered: "*Simin, it is too hard; you cannot understand. But I can tell you: the entire Universe is based on two things: love and mathematics.*" Zhubin often shared with me his thoughts, his beliefs about the "Big Picture", but as his health and well-being were my only focus and concern at that time, I hadn't really been listening or bothering to understand.

Much time passed as I pondered all this. I felt in my heart that there must be something somewhere to help me understand.

> *"A loss is not a loss – it is a change. Through change comes growth, and there is always reason to celebrate growth."*

Thinking of my parents' and Zhubin's faith and love, I decided that, from this point on in my life's journey, I must travel the same path that they did. I wanted to find out, feel and grasp how they had been able to do it. I wanted to experience what Zhubin was talking about. Where did all his faith and wisdom come from while his life was being pulled out of him? What was the origin of his peace and gentleness? Why did he never ask why? Why did he never cry or rage at his illness? He never asked for it, and did his best to fight it, enjoying every little respite that came his way. How could he have taken it so bravely and even joked about it? What was the source of all this strength? And I thought again, and this time with more hope, that there must be a way.

I began to think that maybe my life was not ending after all, but was about to begin. This was a blissful moment. At last, I could take a deep breath. At that time, I did not know that God had heard my prayers and I did not yet realize that by turning to the Universe my spiritual journey was about to begin – a journey towards the light.

With whatever was left within my heart, I embraced the Divine.

"When you lose all your sadness and pain, it is then that you will see the Light. It is then when magic happens."

The Tombstone

Many months had passed and I still hadn't chosen a tombstone for Zhubin's grave. I just hadn't had the heart to deal with it. But how was it possible to do so? What parent can ever imagine the need to consider the choice of tombstone for their child? From time to time, I strolled around the cemetery looking for inspiration, searching for a tombstone that would speak to my heart, one that related somehow to Zhubin. It was an agonizing task, made even harder by the limited choices permitted by the cemetery's regulations.

I needed an idea for a monument, one with warmth and feeling. Meanwhile, it was painful to see Zhubin's plot: still just an untidy mound of earth. I felt as if I was letting him down by not attending to this quickly.

To get away from the loneliness of Montreal, I travelled to England to spend some time with my brother Ali and his family. One morning, my niece Ina put into my hand a pile of photos, saying: "I do not know who has sent these to me or why, but it isn't a bad idea for you to take a look at them. Maybe you'll find something you like." The photos were all of tombstones. Even though I could not see clearly through my tears, one of them really caught my eye: a bas-relief carving of a ewe standing with her lamb beside her. I could not shake the image of Zhubin and I standing together, forever. My choice had been made for me.

To this day, each time I go to the cemetery, I wrap my arms around the tombstone, placing kisses on both the ewe and her lamb, and whisper: "Zhubin, you are both my mother and my child; you both teach me like a mother and love me as my son."

I truly love this tombstone – it is just what my heart had wished for. I am certain that it was meant to be: a gift from above sent through my caring niece. I was so touched by her kindness and awareness of my need, even while she herself was in the midst of a two-year recovery from a near-fatal car crash that had required her to undergo a dozen or so major surgeries. It takes a big heart to remember others when one faces severe challenges of one's own. In the most unexpected and unimaginable ways, the Universe always chooses the right one as His hands.

Part 2 – Night: Darkness Falls   101

"Know also that people are blessed by choosing to be an instrument."

The inscription reads: "Gentle caring son / He loved Animals and Flowers / But most of all he loved God."

Feeling the Bond

Days turned to weeks, months sped by, and still I remained crippled and broken, unable to live with only memories and a few photos. Well over a year after Zhubin's death, day-in and day-out I continued to spend time in his room, which I had left untouched: his bed, empty; his chair, empty; his room, empty – empty like my heart. Lying down on his bed, I would tell him:

"I have to look for you.
I must find you.
I cannot live without you:
Like a fish that needs the water;
Like a desert thirsty for rain;
Like a tree needs the earth;
I am the fish – you are the water;
I am the desert – you are the rain;
I am the tree – you are the earth;
I need to breathe – you are the air."

Living in dreams that spiralled one into another, I thirsted to find him. This is the torture we grieving parents face: searching for our children, waiting for them to return. Not one of us can ever forget either the raw pain we have been given or the darkest times we have been through.

Zhubin's room became a private refuge – a safe haven where I could cry or talk to him the way I wished to, with no concerns about explaining what I was doing. The room came to be my sanctuary, where I could be "with him" in the only way left open to me. Like an addict I needed the fix of my morning visit to his room, without which it felt as if I could not survive the remainder of the day.

Throughout the first year following Zhubin's death, I had been in a thick fog, in shock and unable to understand what was going on in my life. But by the second year the fog had started to lift and I slowly got a better sense of the disaster that had befallen me. Although I knew by then that Zhubin was gone, never to return, the need to "look" for him remained with me. I was searching for something, but I had no idea what – I was so desperate.

Sitting one day in Zhubin's room, staring at his photo, I was struck by a horrifying thought that had not occurred to me earlier: he no longer existed in the way I had known him or the way he had looked, the way he had been – surely his body had turned to dust by now? When I asked myself, "What is it that I am missing so much?" an inner feeling answered that I was missing someone who was no longer here, did not exist and could not be found anywhere. At that moment my heart plummeted to a new depth of sadness – a heart-stopping realization that caused me to cry and cry.

I saw that what I had lost was the ability to "feel my son": the pain, the guilt and the regret had emptied my heart. What is brutally ripped away and goes missing when a mother's child dies is the pure God-given gift she was granted the moment she felt her baby next to her heart: the most noble, irreplaceable, treasured love without equal – a golden cord connecting the souls of mother and child. The loss of a child severs this golden cord. To survive, a mother's need to find a way to stitch it back together is as vital as the air she breathes.

Drowning ever deeper and deeper in pain, I despaired of finding any way to reconnect with my child.

How?

Zhubin had assured me: "*We are never alone. Trust God.*" And so I did. Humility and faith were the only strengths I had left at that time. I repeatedly went through the notes and letters he had left for me in a big red binder titled "The Master Plan." Each time it felt as if he were speaking to me – just like in the old days. One day, while sitting on Zhubin's bed reading through these notes, I had a wonderful idea: why not rewrite all his words in the form of new letters addressed to me, adding stories to them to make them seem more real? Oh! I loved this thought – a hope born of frustration.

"Life is a journey and a process – not a one-time event."

It was as if a door had opened – an escape hatch from the agony, even if at first offering only momentary relief. A bright light had suddenly shone into my heart, like the first star in what had been a pitch-black night sky.

With lifted spirits I started the work and wrote many, many letters written as if from Zhubin. In each, I copied word for word one or more of his notes to me, decorating the pages with stickers of the different "joo-joos" and animals he had loved since childhood and occasionally adding his photo. In my mind, it was as if he had travelled to a faraway land, where he continued to live his life, married with children, and from where he kept in touch through these letters.

> *"Do not go to the past and do not concentrate on loss, but on the gain and the future, otherwise you will walk backward."*

It took my heart some time not just to accept, but also to believe in, this unfamiliar means of connecting with Zhubin. At last I was in touch with him again – and with each letter understanding more of what he had been telling me. This letter-writing exercise wrought a miracle: Zhubin was coming back to me; I could feel him again; I could talk to and hear him again. What magic!

As time passed, many things I had not known before would be revealed to me through the notes Zhubin had given me. Not only was my son still with me but he was actually helping me to grow and learn about the wisdom of the Universe. More importantly, I came to understand my son at a much deeper level than ever before. Slowly, my heart had found a way to piece itself back together. Zhubin now lives through his words to me.

The Universe is filled with love. I know the letter-writing idea had been put in my heart. We all need to find a way to feel our children. It is so healing. Healing is freedom. Healing is power.

Blessings From a Broken Heart

"Do you hear me, Simin? Do you understand what I am saying?"

On a cold afternoon, just before we left for what turned out to be the final round of testing in Boston, Zhubin asked to speak to me and we had sat together by the warmth of the fireplace. It was there that he opened up and confided to me his final decision: if his doctors concluded that there was no way out of his illness, he would end his life.

We had tried everything to help Zhubin get better, but to no avail. We were at the end of the road, and, although my heart denied it, of course we both knew it. He was determined, yet full of concern, both for me and the other loved ones he would leave behind. He tried to explain his decision to me gently, needing me to understand.

I remember the slight trembling of his fingers; the pain in his innocent eyes fixed on mine and filled with love and tenderness. His voice was unwavering, with no trace of fear or sadness. *"I am going to tell you something that will be hard for you, but I need you to hear me out. My health is getting worse and my body is giving up. I won't last for even another two years. If my doctors give me the slightest hope, and even if the healing time would take ten years, I would go for it, you know it. But, if they say there is no cure, I will not*

This pair of soaring eagles represented to me how parents' souls will one day take flight to reunite with their children.

wait even one more day. Do you hear what I am trying to say, Simin? If you want me to stay with you when I cannot get relief from this pain, then you must be a very selfish mother. How could you expect me to live like this, because you won't let go?" He repeated: *"Do you understand what I am saying, Simin?"* I understood what he was telling me and why – and I knew that he wanted me to say: "Yes, I understand." But I did not; I could not; I did not want to understand; I could not listen – a mother can never give up, always has hope and fights on.

And yet, how could I not give him what he was asking for? How could I not give him peace of mind, if only for a moment? How could I deny the depth of the pain that had driven him to this decision? I looked into his tired eyes: he was talking to me through them. Feeling with every cell in my body the enormity of his pain, I knew I could do nothing. Looking like a wounded bird, with pleading eyes fixed on mine, he waited for my answer. I knew he had made up his mind and I was now powerless to change it. With pouring tears and a broken heart, I nodded.

"But what will happen to you, Simin? What will you do?" Zhubin asked. With difficulty, I lifted my eyes to look at him, seeing him only dimly through my tears. "I will die too," I whispered. He reached for my hands: *"No! No! No Simin! You cannot say that. You have no reason to. You are healthy, you are still young and you have your family. There is no excuse for you to say that. You can do what I cannot do. Help all. I know broken hearts. Help them – it is your blessing. Promise, Simin! Promise!"*

I did not know it then, but I know now that my blessing and promise to Zhubin were my gift to him.

I have learned that it was not for me to ask why. It was not for me to decide who had to live or who had to die. Some live longer, others shorter. Some children go before their parents. Some parents lose one child, others lose more than one. I could not be the judge of that. It was not up to me to save my son: since nothing could have saved him, he had to be allowed to go – his journey and his time with us had come to their end. He knew it, I am certain of it.

"Every life, every chapter of life has a story. Make it worthwhile. Our lifetime here is less than a dot in eternity."

At home in Montreal at age 20 – his last photo.
Aware of his failing health, he no longer wanted
to be photographed.

Remembering the Promise

For a long time the grief had left me nothing but bitter despair. I had felt that no life endured within me, that I had nothing to grasp onto – my only remaining possession, a heart dedicated to mourning the loss. I had seemed cast away, the pages of my life's book filled with agonizing scars of guilt and regret; that I had been given more than I could bear. I had tried to expel the pain, although success had seemed not just remote but impossible. And yet something deep inside of me had told me to hold on.

I began to find some relief in Zhubin's words and in my connections to nature. I had glimpses of a new beginning that might await me, but still had healing to do: a heart that is dead needs to be rekindled. There is a great space in the soul that needs to be filled with love and trust. But how? Each time I thought about dying, I remembered how Zhubin had asked me to take on the work that he yearned to do but couldn't due to his illness:

"Be a source of light where there is darkness."

Zhubin had known that I must live. Now I would come to know it as well. I had promised him that I would open doors. I had to keep this promise, but how? I needed help – I couldn't do it by myself.

"'Could' must be replaced by 'can'."

"Don't ever discount relationships. They are so intertwined. There is a bonding, like roots to soil."

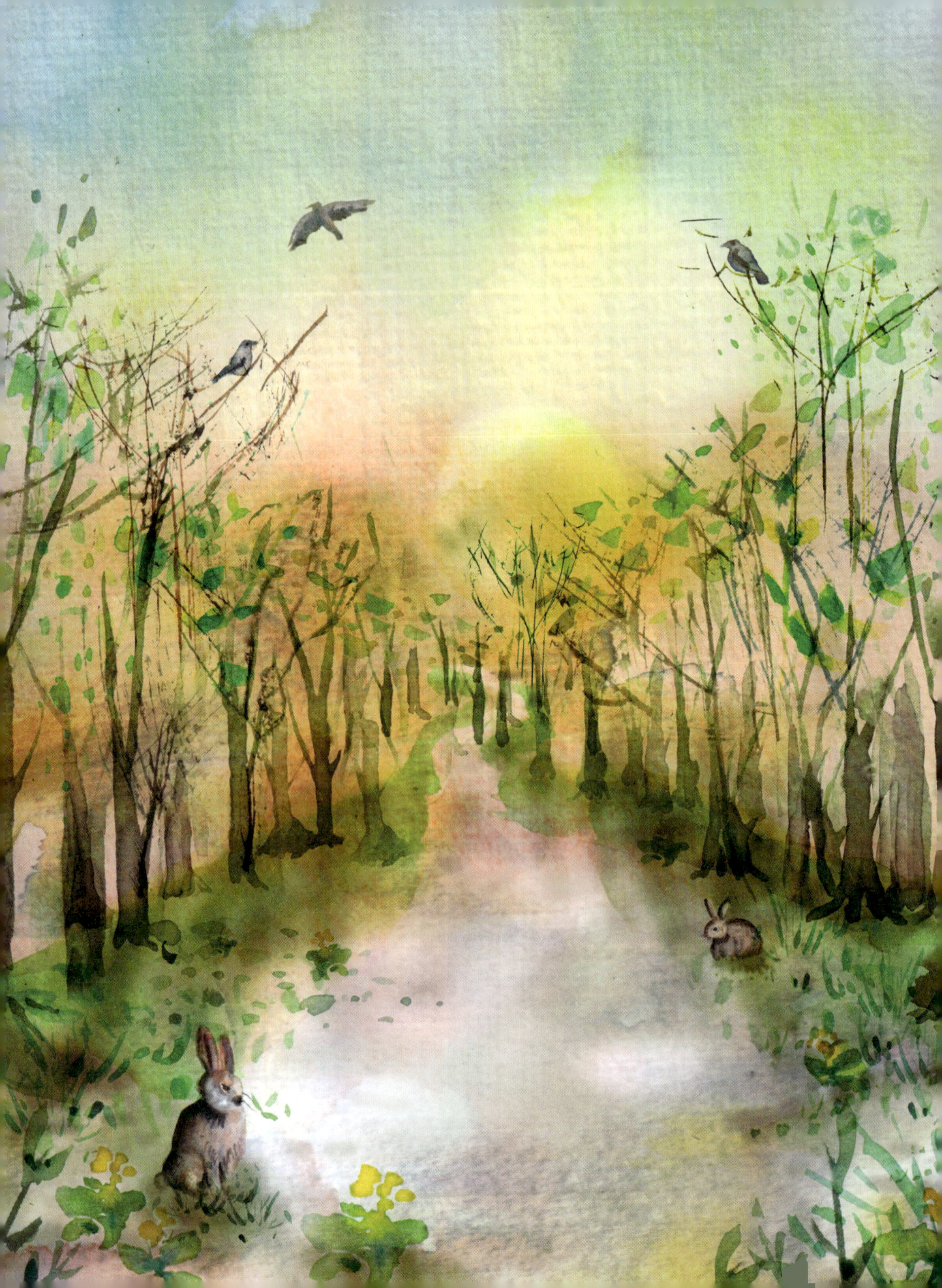

Part 3
Dawn: The First Shoots

Mya

While Zhubin was alive I had spent my days taking care of him. In the aftermath of his death I did not know what to do. I had no purpose. These were my darkest days and my grieving had to be stilled. I felt an enormous first tug: like a fish needs water I needed to be with children. This maternal instinct was even stronger than when Zhubin had been alive and desperately sought an outlet, but where, and how? I asked the Universe for help.

A mere five months after my son's death, God put me next to some of His purest and most special children. It was one of those black mornings when I just couldn't get out of bed, did not want to face another day. As I lay there thinking of my Zhubin a new thought pushed its way into my head: on my daily comings and goings I passed a daycare centre close by and had noticed young children in wheelchairs entering and leaving the building. More than an impulse, I felt a longing to be with them. What got me out of bed that day was a strong desire to find out what I could do to help these children.

I set up an appointment with the director of this daycare centre. As I would find out later, it was rather unique in that it opened its doors to a 50–50 mix of children with and without special needs. I told her my story, of my compelling need to be with children, and asked if I could volunteer, willing to do anything: wash dishes, clean bathrooms, mop floors, *anything*. A compassionate young woman, the director listened patiently. Although my story and my plea touched her, it was with tears in her eyes that she informed me that as I had no training or experience in working with severely handicapped children she couldn't accept my offer to volunteer – adding that the centre's insurance policy would not permit it.

Devastated, I was tearfully shuffling my way out of the building when I heard my name called and turned to see the director running after me. Taking me by the hand, she said, "I don't know why, but for some reason I cannot say no to you", and then led me into each of the centre's five classes. Each room had two caregivers and she introduced me to everyone in turn, saying: "This is Simin. Please welcome her. As of tomorrow, she will be here to help out in any way she can." As I was about to leave her face suddenly brightened and she said: "Actually, I have something for you to do. Maybe you can help with Mya. She is a little girl who needs to be fed. She can only eat puréed foods. It takes a very, very long time to feed her and the caregivers don't have enough time to devote to that task. If she doesn't gain some weight, she will have to be tube-fed." Mya had severe cerebral palsy and was a quadriplegic. The day after her birth she had suffered a massive seizure and had to remain in intensive care for 17 days. I was stunned when I first met Mya: a gorgeous girl not yet two years old, curly lashes framing beautiful dark eyes, skin like caramel, her frizzy hair neatly arranged. It was love at first sight. We came into each other's life at the right time. I now had a reason to wake up every day, a place to go to, and a job to do. I felt God's presence that day. He had made this happen.

Each day after feeding her I placed Mya on a plastic floor mat and lay beside her. Her laughter brought me joy, sensing that she was communicating that we could love these simple, yet precious, moments

Mya celebrating her 15th birthday at school.

together. Teachers and their lessons come at different ages and different times in our lives. From the way our paths had crossed, I knew that the Universe must arrange things way ahead of time, and that Mya's presence in my life was a gift. If Mya were a part of what God had planned for me, then I had a reason to live and to love after all. As time passed, I realized that it was in helping others that I would be healed, and that things would only get better.

"The seed of life in your heart will grow fast. Your love and feelings allow the seed to grow – keep it up.
Give yourself a mental, emotional and spiritual task every day.
Keep giving yourself a purpose."

What Kind of Bird is a Dove?

A few years after Zhubin died, I visited my brother Ali in London. We had always been very close and I knew his nephew's passing had taken a heavy toll on him. Early one glorious morning we were out in the countryside walking his dogs, steeped in conversation yet enjoying the peace and quiet of nature that enveloped us. Ali told me how happy he was to see me getting stronger, and how pleased he was that I had found a way forward.

"I probably shouldn't tell you this," he said, "but I didn't think you'd survive Zhubin's death and was so worried. On the plane coming over to Montreal for Zhubin's funeral, I was thinking of what I could do to save you. It was then that I came up with the idea of starting a foundation in his memory." As we reminisced, I kissed Ali's cheek and, looking into his misty eyes, said: "It was from above that God chose you as His hands." That was how it had come to pass. Less than a year after Zhubin's death, using seed money from both Ali and ourselves,

Zyg established the Zhubin Foundation. The foundation supports charitable organizations that provide services to families with children of multiple and special needs in the Montreal area. Zhubin had made me promise to *"Be aware of broken ones, help them all"*, and the foundation is all about love, sharing, and lending a helping hand. As one of the most important miracles that has occurred since Zhubin passed away, I treasure the foundation. It has allowed me to both keep my promise and helped me to heal.

From the very beginning, the foundation engaged my husband: it is his baby as much as it is mine. His devotion and ongoing generosity to it have touched me deeply. I am also grateful to our many friends whose support and belief in the work that we do on behalf of the foundation has sustained us year after year.

Children and the foundation have played and continue to play a very large role in my life. I still see some of those very first children with whom I worked at the daycare centre – all teenagers or young adults now – and continue to have a strong connection to each of them. What they gave me during those difficult times is beyond words. The children who crossed my path at the lowest point in my life have lifted me up to the highest, their innocent spirits moving me to carry on with purpose. I can never explain how much of a miracle they were to me. As a dear friend once said, it was like finding "golden threads in the ashes of a great fire". God took one child from me but gave me many back.

Before its launch, Zyg and I determined that we first had to identify what the foundation's focus or mission should be – in short, what "spoke to our hearts". This took quite some time, particularly since we were still dazed from the shock of Zhubin's passing. We were surrounded by

The logo of the foundation.

many true friends, however, who were both knowledgeable and willing to guide us in our search. One day I received a phone call, an offer of help from a dear friend named Rachel who had considerable experience with a much larger charitable foundation: "Simin, we need to choose a logo for the foundation. If you come to the office tomorrow, I will help you choose one."

While reading one of my favourite books that evening, I started a new chapter – one describing a white bird, a dove – although I mispronounced the word, as in "He *dove* into a swimming pool." I asked Zyg: "What kind of bird is a dove?" After correcting my pronunciation, he explained: "It's a small white bird that usually symbolizes peace and purity."

At my appointment with her the following day, Rachel said: "I've set up the computer for you. There are millions of sample logos to choose from. I've picked a few just to show you how it works." Staring at the

With Daisy, Panagiota Boussios and Nadia Weekes dress up for a Valentine's Day celebration at the C.A.R.E. Centre (supported by the foundation).

four examples on the computer screen, one immediately caught my attention: I couldn't believe it – it was a dove! In my heart, that was it, and there was no need whatsoever to look any further. Pointing at the dove I said, "This one." Surprised, Rachel looked at me: "Don't you want to at least see some of the other possibilities?" But I was quick in my conviction: "No, no, I'm sure. This is the one." Rachel instantly understood and smiled, saying: "Then it must be a sign for you." I related to her how I had learned only the previous evening about what the dove symbolized, and she loved the story. It would be Rachel's husband Jim who designed the foundation's logo. As for me, it was the story behind its selection that was so reassuring. I knew that it was meant to be.

"Don't spend too much time with yourself. Lose yourself in others instead."

Healing Through Helping

Volunteer work would prove to have a very powerful effect on me in many different ways, providing me with many eye-opening experiences and making me aware of how many people and families suffer with unimaginably difficult challenges of all kinds.

Not only would it prove to be a way to learn about life, but helping others would also became a very unexpected way of healing myself.

My first experience was with the centre for handicapped pre-school children, where I volunteered for five years. I later moved on to an adult long-term care facility and then spent over five years helping out at a seniors' assisted-care residence. My many years of experience feeding handicapped children proved invaluable when working with the elderly. The nursing staff awarded me the title of "Champion Feeder": I had the time and the patience to make certain that the residents assigned to me, each of whom became a friend, ate every bit of their allotted food. I attended the seniors' residence seven days a week, sometimes twice a day, returning for the evening feeding. It was a responsibility that I relished.

The most touching and humbling experiences I had were those in which I was witness to the passage of patients from life to death. Sitting bedside, I held a hand, praying with or for the dying patient. Here I learned that at the end of our time all of us have the need to turn to a Higher Power.

Even those who had no faith of any kind during their lives wished to connect to something in their final moments. It was thanks to these experiences that I learned about the soul, and how to connect with someone who was no longer able to communicate. As always, love was the universal language.

Zhubin had said me: *"You have to go among unusual people and unusual places. Do it. Make the right changes in the right places and in the right way. Passion in your work is a must."* It took me seven years to fully comprehend what he meant. At the seniors' residence, I met an elderly gentleman – very fragile and quiet, never with a visitor. Feeling sad for him, always silent and all alone in his chair, I made a habit of sitting with him in his room. One afternoon I noticed that his lunch tray had been left untouched. When I asked if he wanted me to feed him, with a blink he indicated Yes. As I moved the soup spoon towards him, he opened his mouth wide in anticipation. At that very moment, it dawned on me what Zhubin had meant by the most unusual places. Indeed, these places and centres were ones I had never visited before, yet now they had become an important part of my life. During the next spoonful, while looking me in the eyes, the gentleman stunned me by uttering the first words I had ever heard from him: "I think that you'll make it." Certain that my ears had played a trick on me, I advanced yet another spoonful just as a nurse dispensing medication entered the room. The old man held my gaze and spoke once again: "I know that you'll make it." The nurse and I couldn't believe that "The Silent One" had spoken. I repeated his words to the nurse, asking if she had heard the same thing. The nurse, who knew of my loss, replied, smiling: "Yes. It must be a message for you." I had just received confirmation that I had indeed grasped Zhubin's message to me, and the path I had chosen was true. My heart began to mend itself, and I felt myself coming back to life, bit by bit.

"When a tree loses a big branch, either it rots or so many little shoots start to grow in its place. In the same way, when a parent loses a child, many opportunities to help and provide service will manifest themselves. You should start the healing process of your life in a deep way: by helping others to heal."

A willow tree near Zhubin's grave had been drastically pared due to disease – reminding me of how I felt. The trunk stood barren until the third year when shoots reappeared.

Letting in the Light

I heard an inner voice whispering to me:
>I am knocking on your door. Are you there?
>Open the door. Let Me in.
>I am here for you.
>Listen, listen carefully.
>I am the divine love within.
>Open the door and welcome Me.

I did listen, opening the door and welcoming in the light. I did trust. On my winding road I was longingly waiting for God to come to my life, but He is polite and came to my heart only after a truly sincere invitation. When He did come, it was with all His might to help the one calling Him. He knows the pain. As He does His work, our faith and feelings of peace get stronger, the learning and growing get deeper, the heart and mind expand, and hope and joy become possible again.

In turning to God, I touched upon something that had always been present yet buried so deep that it was unknown to me. My faith was conceived in the desire to believe. Faith was my starting point – a feeling in my heart allowing me to believe in the unknown, helping me when my mind and reason could go no further.

"Faith has to be the centre of everything that we are and do: faith in things that we do not know; faith in the unknown."

Faith became both my refuge and a source of powerful healing energy through which strength comes, illuminating a new path and bringing me many gifts. Faith is a sacred feeling, difficult to describe: a cool breeze on a burning body; a light on a dark road; a whisper of hope that, little by little, becomes the voice of wisdom and peace that helps us find what we believe we have lost; a light whose first spark stirred life in me. Realizing that it was up to me alone to take the first steps, no matter how difficult, I prayed that I wouldn't fall, wouldn't fail. I hungered to see, smell, touch and taste the goodness of life – all the wonders that Zhubin had so often spoken of. I became curious.

I learned that faith comes first, and only then can clarity, understanding and insight follow. Through my new-found faith, I arrived at an unforeseen place: the spiritual world, whose light and knowledge spread to soothe my burns and heal my wounds, dispelling the darkness in which I had been.

Learning from everyday life experiences, both past and present, came slowly. My new insight had to ripen, as if it were a fruit. Each lesson had to come at the right time, and only once I had properly understood its message would I be ready for the next one. I was offered opportunities to atone for my wrongdoings and, if I failed, was given chances – again and again, and in different ways – to learn the same teaching, until I passed the test. As Zhubin said: "*No shortcuts. Think about it.*"

"*Live your life in a curious as well as in a trusting way.*"

With my heart teaching and guiding me, I realized that the joy of the learning was in opening myself up to its lessons. It took me years to grasp this. There was no quick or easy way.

No matter how many times I fell, or felt broken or thought I was dying, I always reminded myself that tomorrow was another day and that I wasn't alone. Often I was fed up and tired, crying in secret, but through spirituality I began to believe that I could win the battle against sorrow. The Universe and Zhubin's words provided many signs of confirmation that I was on the right track: books came into my hands at just the perfect moment when I was ripe to receive their message; the "right" sentence in another's conversation was overheard by chance; a car bumper sticker expressed a thought that helped me; inspiring phone calls were received just when I needed them; a chance interview appeared on television with someone who bore a message or taught me a lesson. Each of these small events helped me along the way; every little thing counted, allowing me to move forward and search. It was not the passage of time alone that could help me – no, it took much more than that; it was a willingness to embark on my journey of discovery.

My faith was an invitation to God to help me to see the light through the cracks of my broken heart. As the 13th-century Persian poet Rumi said so aptly: "The wound is the place where the Light enters you." Of course, I would still tumble back into the darkness, but in time my heart became a healing chapel.

"God is holding you. You can find yourself in His light. Know that. Always! Always!"

Cemetery

Zyg chose Zhubin's final resting place, sensing that I would appreciate its lush open view with only a few neighbouring plots. I visit often. I love this cemetery – its serenity, majestic old trees, magnificent statues and tombstones from long ago, loved ones buried beneath. I love the fresh grass, the wide blue sky with patches of white clouds, the sound of the wind gently rustling through the leaves, and the smell of the earth where I kiss Zhubin's grave. Most of all, I love the quiet, interrupted only by birdsong. My time in the cemetery is always tranquil and inspiring.

The cemetery is not just an ending but a beginning as well. My journey started here. My miracles started here. I first felt God's love in this very place and it was here that I was shown His magical gifts and assured that all is good, all is well. It was in this peaceful setting that the seed of my faith, planted many years ago by my father and then watered by Zhubin, took root and grew to become my core and my anchor. It was here that I began to understand that pain is a fire, one that burns yet is capable of forging faith. While here in contemplation, I felt that I could never be broken inside and would not let the torment that Zhubin and I went through come to nothing. I sensed that I was about to open a door to the unknown and felt the need to start the "work". The shadow and heaviness of pain shone a light, revealing a passageway out of my grief. I had to go through it, no matter how murky or arduous the road. I felt certain that this was my way – a winding path to my inner Universe where I could make my home with my son, myself, God and therefore with all in existence.

It was here that I came to thank God for my life and for Zhubin, and came to believe that He hears us across this glorious Universe. You see, the Master always hears us, but we must be awake to hear *Him*.

> **"If people knew that life experiences are meant to be, then their grief would change its shape and get replaced by reflection."**

I felt a strong bond to this bronze statue very near to Zhubin's grave: a graceful mother sits at her child's grave, streaks of rain tracking her face, as she keeps her long vigil.

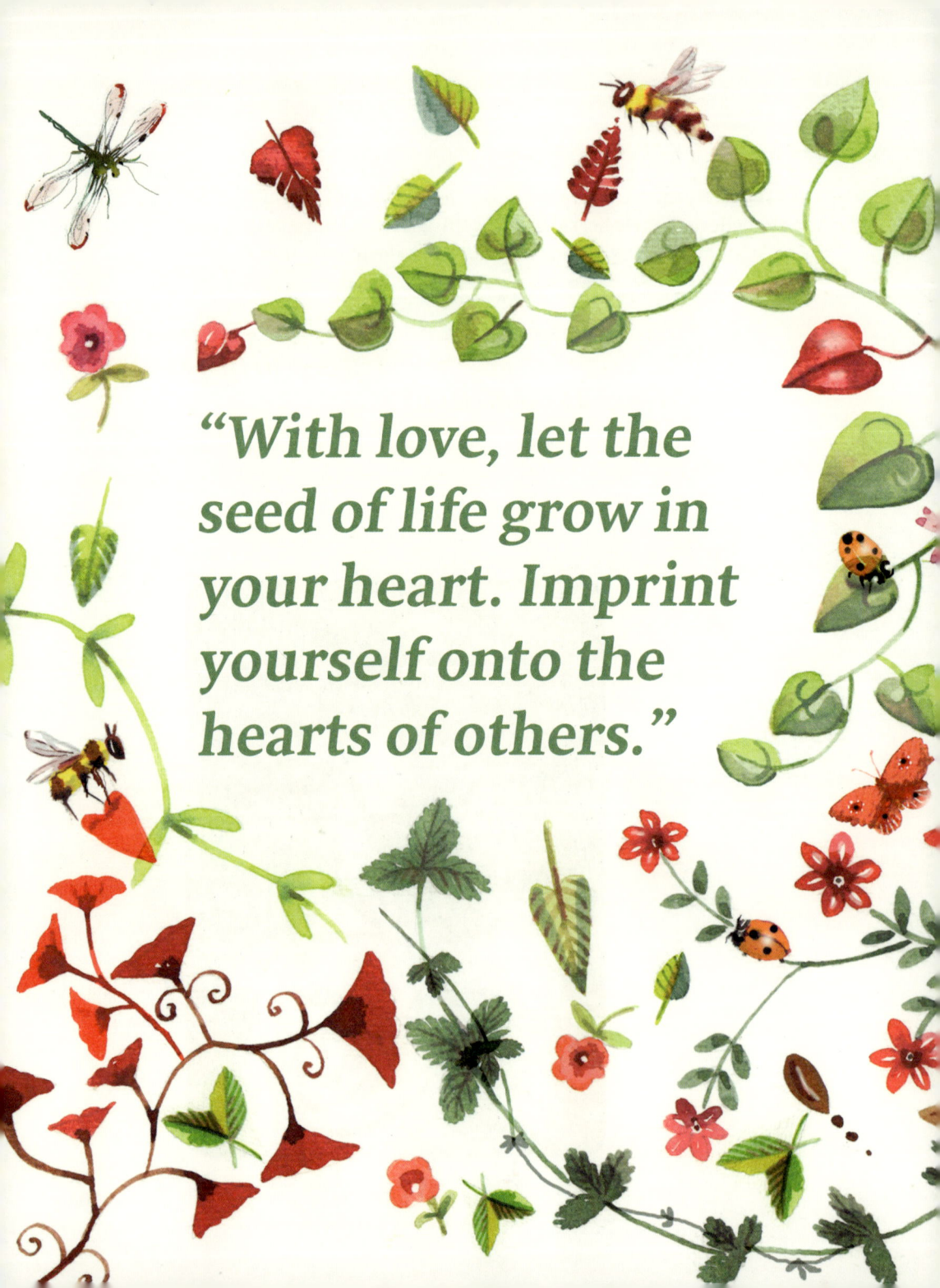

"With love, let the seed of life grow in your heart. Imprint yourself onto the hearts of others."

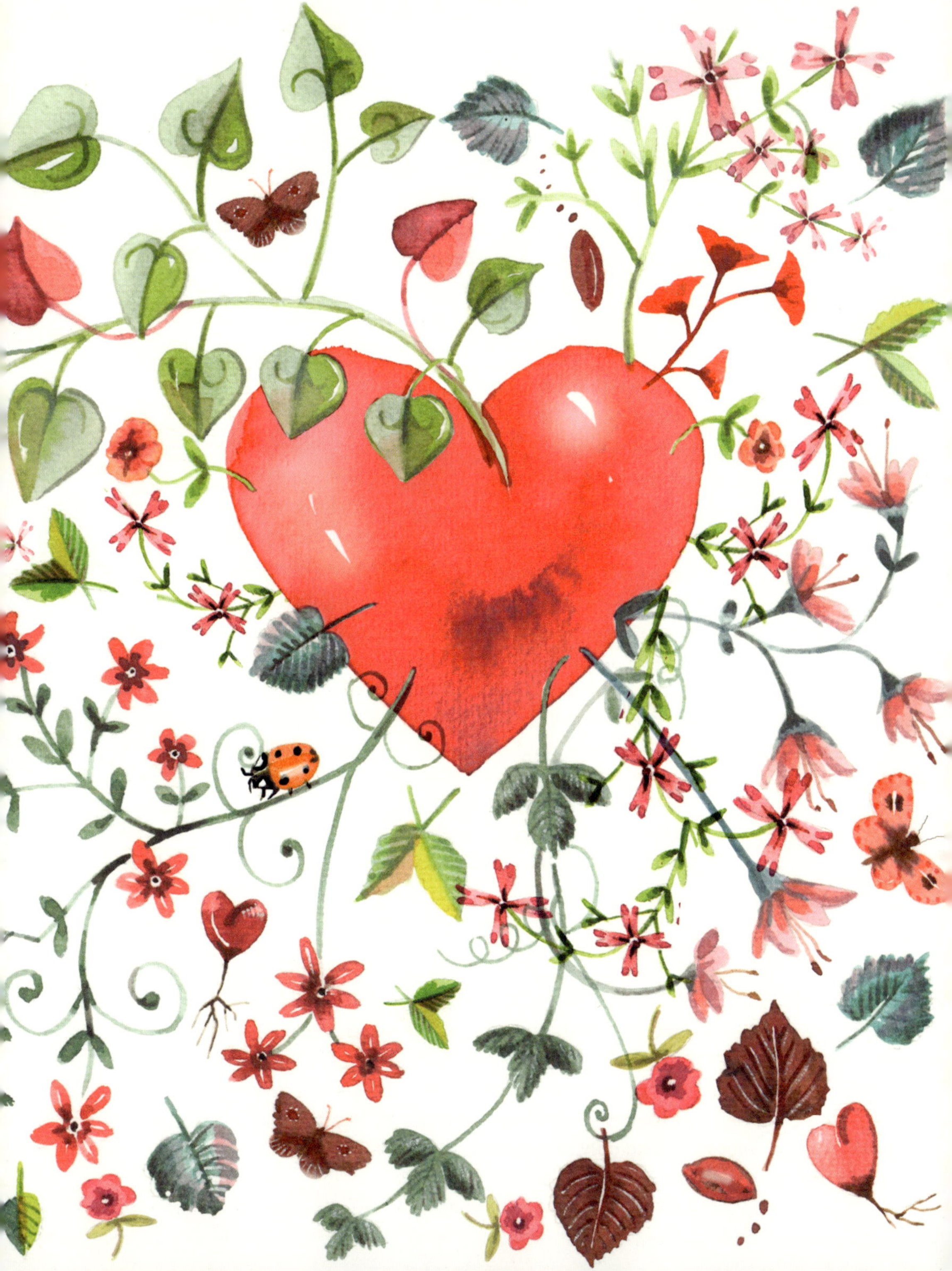

Self-mastery

Pain turned out to be but a tool: once eventually mastered, it helped me to gain control of my life and view it in a new way. It woke something deep within me – a longing to search, to see and to understand.

We all know, or at least suspect, that each of us has a particular path to follow, a particular destiny. We all yearn to know our life's purpose – what each of us is supposed to do while we are here. Some may think they have to do big things. In searching for my purpose, I came to the realization that what is most important of all to me is that I am here to learn; that I do not need to do big things to change the world; and that by changing myself I could do more. It boils down to self-mastery. To achieve this, one must have a deep desire and a strong willingness to go forward, requiring discipline and constant self-awareness.

Zhubin had talked to me about how he believed life should be lived, often referring to self-mastery and explaining how important it was to be master of my own mind and to control my feelings. He had tried to make me understand that I must rid myself of the negative thoughts and feelings hurting me so much, turning them instead into tools for good. I never ceased to be surprised by his views about life in general and how to deal positively with its challenges, as well as his optimism, his serenity, and his acceptance of it all. Often I remarked, "Zhubin, you are in dreamland!" yet he never grew tired or frustrated when I had difficulty understanding him or struggled with certain issues and would reply, smiling: *"It may sound hard to do, but you will learn it one day."*

I regularly return to these conversations about the wonder of life, rereading his words even though I know them all by heart. Each time I do so, I draw a new insight, refreshing my heart and soul. Zhubin's notes have been both my motivation and a guide to be my best self for myself. It's an ongoing process, through which I have learned to channel towards love all disturbing thoughts that unavoidably come with the grief of loss. But it also permitted me to see that there was another kind of faith – a faith in myself: to believe I can do it; that I can move on; that I can heal. Self-mastery and peace go hand in hand. Self-mastery comes first and only then peace.

To me, self-mastery is:
learning how to teach myself;

believing and trusting myself and all that I do;
learning more by being aware of my surroundings;
looking at everything as a priceless experience;
being patient;
knowing how far we can go, how much we can do, how strong we can become;
and being at peace with the Universe.
Self-mastery is lying on the grass where Zhubin is laid to rest, looking up at the sky, and smiling at the Universe: "Thank You, I love You."
Believing in all this is self-mastery.

"Self-mastery is about being in the moment and enjoying little simple things – going with the flow of life, not against it."

The Glove

My late mother-in-law Mila had been very fond of Zhubin, holding a lot of respect for him. Despite their age difference they had found much in common, speaking to each other at length whenever the opportunity presented itself, and, with a shared love of movies, occasionally going to the cinema together.

Mila experienced a lot of difficulty in coming to terms with his passing: she was angry, unable to make any sense of his illness and the fact that nobody had been able to help him. Feeling devastated when he died, she refused – almost to the end of her life – to accept his passing. Mila shared with me that when the rain had poured unceasingly on the day of Zhubin's burial, she had been convinced that the heavens themselves were crying at his passing. She worried about how the trauma of Zhubin's death would impact on all of us.

For four years following Zhubin's death, I not only dealt with my own grief, but also tried to help Mila come to terms with hers. When she wondered how I coped with it all, I explained that I had come to believe that I could still connect with Zhubin through signs bestowed upon me, feeling certain he heard and was guiding me. I spoke about how, while I no longer experienced Zhubin as a physical presence, I now did so in a different way. Each time I described these feelings, however, Mila would be taken aback and upset: "Simin, surely you don't believe in this nonsense – have you gone mad?"

On one early, bitingly cold morning in January 2007, I picked up Mila at her apartment in order to drive her to the Montreal General Hospital for what was supposed to be a routine examination. Climbing into my car, she was a little short of breath, so when I dropped her off I suggested she mention it to her doctor before telephoning me to fetch her when she was finished. When by 11am Mila had still not called me I began to wonder what might have happened. At last, at 1pm she telephoned to let me know that her doctor had held her back to run some additional tests on her lungs and that she would call me again as soon as these were done. When she next telephoned later that afternoon Mila was distraught and sobbing: the tests had indicated that she had advanced lung cancer, and her doctor was immediately admitting her for further examination by specialists over the following days. Zyg and I rushed to the hospital and found Mila in a hallway, lying uncomfortably on a gurney. Understandably, she was very upset as she tried to explain what she had been told.

I could not believe this disturbing news. Mila had looked so well; we had thought it entirely possible that we would be blessed to have her with us for another ten years or more. As there were no empty beds available, we were advised that Mila might have to wait for several days before a room and bed could be arranged. Zyg and I stayed with her as long as we could that evening. As Canada has no private hospitals, it was not within our power to move her somewhere more comfortable. It was difficult leaving her in that state, but I held her hand promising that I would return early the following day. Pointing skyward, I said: "Mila, ask for help. What is there to lose?"

As I was getting ready the next morning to go and see her, I received a call from the hospital to let me know that Mila had been transferred to a room on the eighth floor. I was so relieved to hear that welcome news! Entering her room later that morning, I couldn't believe it: not only did she now have a proper bed, but she was in her own small private room with a view of the snow-covered mountain. To my surprise, Mila's first words were: "Simin, you told me to seek help – and I asked Zhubin to help me." Apparently, during the night a young doctor had passed by and seen her crying. After looking at her chart, he had realized the seriousness of her condition and had the kindness to immediately arrange for the room. I was happy to hear her interpretation of how she had obtained the hospital room. It gave me hope that Mila would find some inner comfort and strength with which to face the challenges ahead.

While awaiting the biopsy results and specialist's diagnosis during the first several days, Mila was extremely nervous and very frightened, though not in any discomfort. Remarkably, she required no painkiller or other medication throughout this final hospital stay. Zyg and I were shaken, but we did our best to calm her.

One day while helping her eat, I told Mila about the things I had come to know and learn, hoping to give her some peace of mind and a better understanding of why I believed in the Universe the way I did. Although she listened intently, she did not respond, leaving me with the impression that I was getting nowhere. When I had to return home for a short time, Mila watched as I put on my coat and gloves. I was almost out of the room, when I turned back to her and said: "Look, Mila." I took off my glove and tossed it onto the bed. "The glove is like the body: when there is no more need for it, you can take it off. The hand is like the soul; it stays with you. When our body's work is done and there is no more need for it, it is simply removed and dies; but the soul lives on forever. You are just getting ready to go Home, the real place you came from. Your parents are there. Zhubin is there, too. I would change my place with you right now, if I could." Mila looked first at the glove on the bed, then at my bare hand, then glanced again from the empty glove to my hand. At that instant, she appeared to have been transported somewhere else, and I was certain that she had just had her biggest "Aha!" moment. Without saying another word I left, hoping that she would meditate on it.

When I returned to the hospital later that same afternoon I found Mila sitting comfortably in the large chair in her room, seemingly asleep, oblivious to my entrance. As I slipped quietly onto the bed waiting for her to wake, she all of a sudden began to talk as though conversing with someone else in the room. Pointing to the sky through the window, she asked: "Where do they go?" After a brief pause she asked again: "Where do I go? Which way? That way?" I was immediately convinced that someone, maybe her guardian angel, had made contact with her from the spirit world. Having read about such deathbed phenomena, I was sure of it in my heart. On quite a few occasions later, both during my volunteer work at a geriatric centre and, even more poignantly, on Mâmân's deathbed, I would witness the same contact.

A brief moment later Mila opened her eyes, looked at me very alert, and said: "Oh Simin, did you see that light? Did you see the colour? It was not blue. It was not green. It was just beautiful." I replied: "No Mila, that was meant only for you to see." She continued, still very coherent: "I don't know what it was. I was not dreaming and it was real. But I have no idea where it came from." Mila looked absolutely serene. That afternoon when Zyg came for a visit, even though her breathing had become laborious by then, Mila went to some length trying to relate what she had seen.

The following day, Mila's specialist informed Zyg that her condition was inoperable and terminal: the expectation was that she would not be with us for more than two weeks. It was so hard to believe. It was left to Zyg to break the news to Mila, but when he did so he was the one who broke down in tears. Mila already knew her fate and was entirely reconciled to it. It was Mila who found the strength to console her son. What a remarkable journey she had travelled in the five days since I had dropped her off at the hospital!

That evening I planned to leave the two of them alone, so that mother and son could have some time together. Before I left, Mila asked me for her handbag. She had always been a discreet and rather private person, yet now she took out her wallet and proceeded to pull out every credit card, phone card, video card and the like. She informed me of the balances owed on each of the cards and instructed me to look after it. It was as matter-of-fact as if she were giving me a grocery list. Smiling serenely, she handed me the $150 cash that remained in her wallet, saying: "Simin, too bad we can't spend this on lunch together."

Mila passed away less than a week later, in complete peace and surrounded by her loved ones. I am sure that Mila had help from above.

It is never too late to believe. I was blessed to have been with Mila at her special moment. Not only was this experience a confirmation from the Universe indicating that I was on the right path, but, in time, I realized that it had also given me a sign that I might be of some help to others. This was Mila's last and greatest gift to me.

"Listen with your heart. Nobody can understand, imagine, or hear it for you."

Spiritual Mysteries

Between the seen and the unseen, the known and the unknown, there is a space, an expanse. There, in that mysterious place, is where faith is to be found. If we were to believe that what we can't see doesn't exist, then we would never grow spiritually and would remain closed to the Universe. How can we expect to have sunlight when we are in a room with drawn curtains? The sun is "out there" – all we need to do is open the curtains and let the room fill with its warmth and brilliant light. We must allow ourselves to be open to the invisible yet dazzling light of the Spirit.

The Universe helps us in endless ways. I was waiting for something to connect me with my Zhubin, unaware that he had remained with me, albeit in a different way. With faith, I became conscious of an indescribable power. Slowly but surely, I started to get the feeling and the message. Bit by bit, things began to unfold and I could sense that perfect love – a divine love – reviving, creating stepping stones to my new life's gateway.

On one occasion, when Zhubin was trying to talk to me about the intelligence of the Universe, I failed to take him seriously, amusing myself by pestering him with questions. I'm now sure he knew that it was scepticism that drove me to make fun of him – how silly I must have seemed to him! In the end, looking at me as if I were a child and doing his best not to laugh, he said: *"Let me put it this way for you. Don't try so hard to understand. The human mind can never understand the work of the Universe. It is not capable of doing it. Comparing our mind to the mind of the Universe is like comparing the IQ of a dead fly to the intelligence of the human brain."* I had to laugh then – and it still makes me laugh today. Small wonder he often teased me by addressing me as "Genius"!

Some years later, still struggling to grasp the concept of human versus universal intelligence, I sought guidance from Nader. He offered an analogy of the relationship between the baby toe and the brain: a baby toe is a very small appendage of our body, yet even this part has its purpose. It was only some time later before I could understand my brother's analogy. Indeed, this funny baby toe has its own purpose: it feels the coolness of a sandy beach, the pressure of a tight shoe, and helps us to keep balanced when walking or standing.

"You can work and learn about life's spirit. Do not worry about not understanding and being confused. You have to be confused before you can have understanding."

Yes, that odd little toe may seem insignificant when compared to other parts of the body, unable to understand that it is the brain that controls it and takes responsibility for the role it plays in helping the rest of the body. Just because it does not understand it, can the baby toe deny the existence and the work of the brain? It is the same with us. With our tiny little brains how can we understand the Master and His plans for us? It is impossible!

One afternoon, while on a beach watching sandpipers playfully scampering about dodging waves, I reflected on how happy they appeared, seemingly without a care in the world as they searched for any morsels that the sea might have left exposed at their feet. They darted about to pick up food, retreating quickly to avoid being caught by the next wave. Did these tiny creatures realize that the ocean was their provider? Did they have any idea what was going on in this vast expanse of water? Could they grasp that their very existence depended on that ocean? How could they? So it must be the same for us: how could we ever understand the vastness of the Creator?

We are all deeply connected, not just to one another, but also to something much, much greater than ourselves, something beyond our understanding. Our name for that does not matter – God, Jehovah, Allah, Buddha – it is the source that is important. Like a magnificent Persian carpet, connected from the very first knot to the very last, we are all part of a greater plan. It makes no difference where the knots are, or what colours they may be. The hand of the Master weaves the threads together, putting them in the right place and in the correct order to create an astonishing masterpiece.

I have come to believe that we are spirits and so we never die. We come to this life at a preordained time – at a particular second, minute, day, week, month and year. Similarly we depart it at a preordained time and manner, but in doing so we leave behind only the physical body, whereas our spirit returns home. That is how one day we will all be with our beloved children, whom we mourn so much today. And when that time comes, it will be pure joy!

"There is a sheer intelligence in this amazing Universe and it is super-duper advanced. But our brains are not made to understand it."

Learning to Live Again

How often must grieving parents suffer the well-intentioned assurances that in time they'll feel better? Although I soon sensed that the passage of time alone could not cure my grief, I could apply it to a search for a means of survival. There would be many lessons to absorb before I could find a way to live again.

What turned out to be my key lesson was that suffering was but a teaching tool – to be taken advantage of in my pursuit of insight and growth. Anguish taught me both how to endure and the importance of enduring.

"Sometimes it is hard to see the blessings in the difficult times."

Accepting pain, living through it, and experiencing every bit of it has helped me to replace the dreadful emptiness of loss and guilt with a feeling of being alive again. I came to understand that, to persevere through hardship and emotion, grieving parents have no choice but to find on their own a means suited to them.

A curse whose spell shackled my feet – guilt – was the most difficult challenge I faced after losing Zhubin. I hadn't been able to save my son. I was unchained only when it struck me that my journey was one through the heart and soul, and that as long as I clung to shame and guilt I would not be free to travel further. If I could not be truthful with myself, then I could not be truthful in a real way with others, unable to give what I did not have. I faced a long and difficult task: to learn to forgive myself, thereby ending my guilt. I learned that forgiveness is a fundamental law of the Universe. Bringing its own gift of liberty from shame and guilt, forgiveness proved to be a doorway to spirituality and a healing light. Most importantly, it taught me compassion and humility.

"Have the right knowledge to move forward and create."

Longing to do and to give became a necessity that both sustained me and brought me satisfaction, nourishing both my heart and soul. In this way, the love I could no longer give to Zhubin, I now give to others. The love I can no longer receive from Zhubin, others now give to me. It is through caring for others that I continue to feel him. Through their eyes I am able to see his love. The birth of this new feeling has brought me peace – a bridge that allowed me to cross over from despair to where freedom awaited me. This healing force of helping is not momentary but tangible and permanent, never to be lost or disturbed.

I learned that there is no magic cure for grief and that I had to fight to live again. To know how to fight, I first had to know what I would be fighting for:

to overcome the emptiness within;
to be humble;
to be eager and willing to start the work;
to accept my challenges;
to have the courage I would need;
to continue on my journey with dignity and hope:
and to have joy, no matter what.

At last I realized that I was capable of standing on my own two feet. I knew the path ahead would still be steep, but understood that I could not give up and had to do something with my life. I could learn from my mistakes and, like a child after falling, could pick myself up and teach myself to walk again.

"Not many people get second chances. You have a clean page to work with: write on it wisely."

I came to understand that life could be wonderful, irrespective of what it might bring. I could decide who I wanted to be, how I wanted to live and what I wanted to take with me into the hereafter. Armed with faith, I could strive to live fully, fearlessly, and with joy.

> *"The best way to show ourselves is by being great at what we do and how we do it."*

The Happy Learner

I have learned that every minute counts and that there are no ordinary moments. The simplest things in life can be the most complex. Even the smallest things are huge. Nothing is insignificant; everything is magnificent in its own right. Life is about learning through a spiritual journey.

Along my journey of adventures and lessons I came to learn that:
- no true love is greater than another;
- no true pain is greater than another;
- no true lesson is greater than another;
- no true learning is greater than another;
- no true life experience is greater than another;
- no journey is greater than another; and
- no one person is more precious than another.

Essential to my survival was learning about the true meaning of love:
- it sees the divine in everyone and everything and therefore does not choose one over the other;
- it is kind and remembers all kindnesses;
- it cannot be selfish or possessive;
- it is incapable of hurting anyone or anything;
- it is always thankful;
- it taught me that the most difficult people can be the greatest teachers of tolerance;
- it knows the importance of everyone and everything, respecting all;

it teaches me not to judge, reminding me of my own past wrongdoings;
it always offers a helping hand to those in need.

I learned that:
it is never too late to admit to my mistakes and make them right;
it is never too late to bring peace to my heart;
it is never too late to say, "I'm sorry";
it is never too late to hug and kiss;
it is never too late to say, "I love you"; and
love will never fail us.

Love is the greatest gift, one that I could not allow pain to take away. In giving love I can heal myself; as Zhubin said: *"This is self-love."* Knowing kindness is free to give makes me happy. We have arms with which to embrace, lips with which to smile.

In the same way that our society has laws and order, the Universe has its own spiritual laws and order with love as their very basis – like a giant sheltering tree adorned with many colourful blossoms. For strength, I learned to rely on no one save for the precious force of the Source, present and available always. The bounty of the Universe is limitless.

I learned that, in the same way that I need God, He needs each of us too. When we love each other, we love God.

> *"God is a cool partner to have.*
> *God is an awesome partner."*

The Divine is in all of us, binding us. Like the sun, it has countless rays – each one of us is an inseparable ray from the single source of the Divine Light. God put us next to one another for a reason. Why? To be together, to help, inspire, love and care for each other. We are all connected, not just to one another, but also to every snowflake, every drop of rain, every leaf. The lesson of spirituality is that we are all one – and that God is indeed love.

Like God, our love for our children, and their love for us, is timeless. Our children bring us something much greater than their physical presence: they bring us the spirit of life. In the eyes of the Divine, we are all His beloved children – no matter what we look like, where we are born, or what we believe. Each of us is created and born with the same love. I believe that we all derive from one place and in due time will return there, where we truly belong and where our children and our loved ones are or will be – the place Zhubin called *"home"*.

Nourished by love, my soul expands – the greater it is, the bigger my soul – and the bigger my soul, the wiser it is. It is the richness of love and peace in my heart that brings joy. Living for love and with love is happiness – now I am a Happy Learner.

> **"What a wonderful day and what a wonderful life! Celebrate your life, my life and everything – pure thoughts and feelings, and nothing but love in your heart."**

Finding Blossoms in the Darkness

As I stumbled along the twists and turns of my road, I would wonder: "Where am I now?" But each time, I would hear the same answer: "You're not there yet!" I was not over the pain, its sharp claws still torturing me with cruel games.

I have met many mothers struggling to survive on this same battlefield and have realized that, in every corner of the world, each life's journey is about love, pain, trials, disappointment, challenges and hope. We all love, suffer loss, mourn and grieve in different ways. But pain is the same.

Drowning in grief for the first few anniversaries of Zhubin's death, I had been unable to stay at home and escaped by visiting my sister

Shishi in Seattle. As each anniversary approached, I could not help but dwell on the thought that he had left me on the day we had planned to celebrate Mother's Day. Then, one day, I had an epiphany while working in Shishi's garden on the fifth anniversary: God had given me a gift by taking my son on the day before Mother's Day; his passing on that particular day was not a coincidence – my Mother's Day gift was certainly one of pain, but, more importantly, one that would force me to grow and *"see the Big Picture"*.

Clawing my way out of the dark and journeying through the unspeakable agony – from the seed of my parents' secret grief at the loss of their son to my own bereavement – I discovered that pain itself has a purpose. In time, this discovery has helped to open me to the Universe and find an unbreakable faith in God, in signs, and in Zhubin's words. I had to cut myself open, not only to let the pain in, but also to give it a way out. I could not, and did not, understand this for many years after Zhubin passed away. I died again and again, every day. But now I know why.

Pain comes to us, whether we like it or not – in different ways, and at different times along our journey. I now understand that suffering is another law of the Universe, with its own concealed gifts and teachings, whose purpose is to purify us. It takes courage to embrace it, time to understand it. The decision has been mine to see it as an opportunity in my search for a measure of wisdom and insight.

Bearing this burden requires discipline, hard work and constant awareness to carry on – but each of us is surely capable of obtaining what we seek, albeit slowly and quietly. Insight comes through pain – I am convinced that in time, though with difficulty, we can each learn its true meaning. It is pain that teaches us how to connect with the invisible realm, which for me is the Divine Spirit.

Pain is a bitter medicine. A mother whose child faces a terrifying disease will administer with determination and hope the medicine prescribed, despite its miserable side-effects. My pain was an inoculation delivered with a long needle directly to my heart, making me yelp in hurt, yet ultimately saving my soul. Pain is both the infliction of and remedy for the heart's wounds and all the unwanted ugliness carried within it. Surprisingly, we can turn pain into something positive, using it as a tool to purify this most precious place.

How can one explain the power of love one finds in the agony of losing a child? Mysteriously amazing, this unbearable pain has brought me closer to my soul and taught me how, and in which direction, to grow. Yes, it is a fire within that can melt me, but, at the same time, it is bliss and joy. Tears flow when I spend quiet times with this feeling in me.

I had seen a lot in life, but then realized how little I had understood. It was pain that made me look for something more. I needed to make a fresh start. Pain trained me to see the good in everything, the loveliness of all I had never known, never seen, never felt and never understood. My memories I now love in a very different and special way. Even those that are darkest are near to my heart, as there are lessons to be learned in every single one of them. Pain brought back the lost child in me, returned my long-forgotten innocence.

Do I still feel the pain? Of course. The bitterness of absence never leaves. I would be untruthful if I were to say that this "missing" part no longer hurts. If I were to vow that there will be no more tears, I would be deluding myself. From time to time, the agony comes back like a wild beast, growling, making my body shiver, and tearing at me with its sharp teeth.

I no longer fight it – I have no more need for that. It can rush in suddenly like a tsunami, submerging me entirely, and I drift for a few moments until I am able to shake off its spell. It is good for me to re-experience this pain from time to time, both as a reminder of my earlier black days and as a reason to be thankful for the present. I no longer own the pain – and pain no longer owns me.

"Pain can take us to a different realm. It can also break us. Feel your pain and this will become the road back to God."

Do I miss Zhubin? Always – every day. I miss our late-night talks. I miss his holding my hand, teasing me when he addressed me as "Genius". I miss his hugs and his making fun of our crazy days and our dogs. I miss his calling me by my name. Yes, I still miss him deeply. However, it is no longer a "killer" pain. It is not emptiness, loneliness or regret, and it is not like dying over and over again. Zhubin's absence on Mother's Days, birthdays, weddings, family gatherings, Christmas and all other celebrations is no longer unbearable. Certainly, I miss him, but I hold on to the "Big Picture" and feel overjoyed thinking of the future, perhaps distant, when we will be together again. Hope and joy make the lost and intervening years much easier to bear.

> *"All the good feelings in the heart come from the Light. Open the door of your heart. Show your faith and let God work on it. Life does not last forever, but love does."*

Even now, as I put these words next to each other, the subtle beauty of it moves me. The heartache of Zhubin's going has been replaced with so many wonders. The foundation is but one of the many gifts showered on me as a result of my son's death. Accepting and then letting go of this pain has shown me a way of life, and a way to live. It is all about love. Finally, the window of my soul has been opened to this amazing Universe.

I can now taste the nectar of divine love spread all around us. Although I will never have any further earthly experiences with Zhubin, his spirit remains with and feeds me every day. I believe I will continue to have many great blessings and joys, but in a different way. Zhubin taught me how to live and how to look at life through the very core of my being. I hope to leave a footprint in the field of life for any parent who has faced the crippling pain of losing a child. By sharing Zhubin's life and his words, I feel that I am spreading Zhubin's wings of love, which brought me comfort and hope.

I am growing into the person I wish to be. I may have come a long way – and yet I know that there remains a long way to go. I hope my soul will continue to bear more fruits of wisdom in my search for a life of purpose.

Truly embracing my challenges opens me to the Universe, which in turn allows me to get all the help I need to go on. Little by little, with patience and faith, the unknown becomes known and I realize that this crippling pain is in fact part of the "Big Picture" and a true gift from God. Unbelievable becomes believable. Unreal becomes real. Both Zhubin's arrival in my life and his passing were, and continue to be, a gift. Both are equally precious and blessed. I now view my journey with love and would not change any part of it.

Passage through pain unveils dreams and hopes. To find hidden beauty in pain is like finding blossoms in the darkness.

"Don't worry that good times have come to the end. Just be grateful that we had a chance to be together. Don't be sad that a life is over. Be happy that you had the privilege to deal with it."

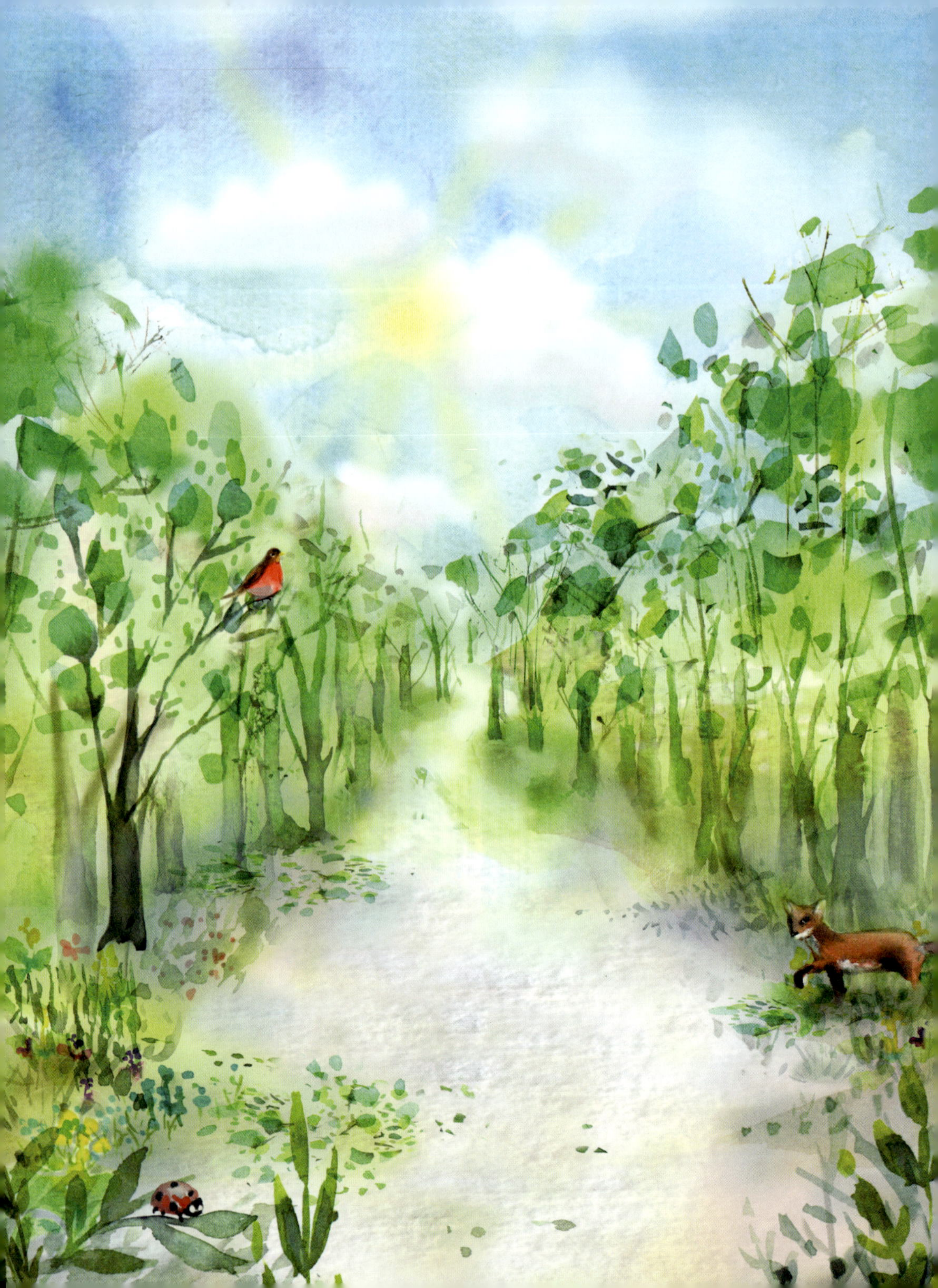

Part 4

Rays of Light: Messages and Signs

"There are many different ways to be helped. Open your eyes to broad horizons – you can learn 'how'. There is no secret way – it is for everyone. One needs to be open. It is like going to a river to collect water: some use just their hands, some a cup, some a bucket, and others jump into the river and merge with the ocean."

Ladybugs From Joo-Joo

Within two weeks of Zhubin's burial all of my family had departed Montreal. I wanted it that way: no more talking, no more comforting hugs, no more anything. Zyg organized to take me away for two weeks, but, wanting to just remain at home with Zhubin's memory, I felt reluctant to go. On each of the three mornings prior to our departure I made my way alone to the cemetery, to be with Zhubin as much as I could.

I have no idea how I managed to make my way to the cemetery and find Zhubin's grave in that vast place. The plot hadn't changed since the first time Zyg had taken me there. Sitting on the cold, wet earth beside the muddy grave and reeling from the odour of rotting flowers, I couldn't make sense of anything. How could Zhubin be under all this earth? Could this be true? Could it be real? He must be somewhere near: hadn't he promised never to leave me alone – and hadn't we always kept our promises to each other? If I just waited here, surely he would come? I spoke silently to him: Zhubin, I am here, but where are you? You told me we would always be together, so how come I don't see you? When are you coming back? How much longer do I have to wait?

Lost, cold, numb, staring into space, I sat and waited. After a while, as I was wiping my tears, I blurted out: "Zhubin, if you're alive somewhere, if you see me or if you can hear me, can you show me a ladybug?" Joo-Joo, cute little bug, had been Zhubin's nickname. Had I entirely lost my mind? What a crazy thing to ask for – a ladybug! Who would ask for such a silly thing? Moreover, don't ladybugs live among fresh flowers and not in these smelly, rotten ones? In early May the earth in Montreal has not yet softened from the harsh grip of winter and it's still too icy to plant flowers, so the cemetery was barren. I chastized myself, convinced I had gone mad to be pleading to someone who was no longer alive – someone who was dead. Let go, Simin, I told myself, let go! Zhubin is dead – he will never come back! Look where you are; look where you are sitting!

Something in my heart compelled me to ask again, and so I did. Then, crawling out of the heap of rotting flowers strewn beside me, a red ladybug appeared. Could the creature I saw before me have any connection to the sign I had just asked for? Sheer coincidence! Who would believe in such a thing? Certainly not me! But back I went the next day, and again asked the same question. Once more, a ladybug crept out, this time orange in colour. I didn't know what to make of this, but I couldn't wait for the following day. When I returned to the cemetery on the third day and asked yet again, another ladybug emerged, this one yellow and orange, sporting three black dots on its back.

Zhubin, are you really here somewhere? I don't see you, but do you see me? Do you really hear me? I had no idea what was going on, but as I watched the ladybug I wondered whether my son was somehow connecting with me. "Please forgive me Zhubin, but if this is really from you, if you do see me or hear me, can you make the ladybug come and touch me?" Sitting still, I held my breath, keeping my eyes on the ladybug. Suddenly she took flight, but before I could cry out "Oh no! No! Don't go away!" that beautiful *joo-joo* landed on my hand and then crawled up onto my arm and sat there for a moment before taking off again.

Then and there, the ladybug became for me a "sign" from my own Joo-Joo, and I realized that I had, in fact, already been bombarded with ladybug imagery, which adorned several condolence cards and gifts.

Since those first encounters in the cemetery I received the ladybug sign in the most surprising places, at the most unexpected of times, and carrying various messages: some of hope, some to cheer me up, and others just for fun. I've received this sign countless times and still do. Ladybugs appear in the middle of winter in my home, on the car windshield while driving on the highway, on my dog Sam, on my books, or on the cherry tree in Shishi's Seattle garden. I see them while walking with friends, and even in my dentist's office. They've arrived in different colours and with different numbers of dots – uncannily, most often 21! Never before had I realized that ladybugs exist in so many different colours and with so many markings.

For a long time, I could not make sense of why this had started at the cemetery and why I had even asked for a ladybug in the first place. Eventually, I came to understand that some words and ideas are not of our own making, but are given to us. We are not even aware of our thoughts during moments of acute emotional pain and fear. I had asked on the spur of the moment. The impulse to ask for a sign to connect with a loved one is a gift to us – help from the Universe.

At first I neither realized nor believed that Zhubin was communicating with me in this way – it took quite a while before I learned to

Part 4 – Rays of Light: Messages and Signs   149

"connect the dots" and understand the Big Picture, as Zhubin used to call it. Only then did I see what he had meant when he said: *"I won't be gone. I'll always be near you; our bond is forever."* In the end I realized that it did not matter whether I was receiving these signs and messages from the Universe, Zhubin, or both of them – they were a confirmation that not only did my child still exist, but he would also be there to guide me on my path.

"It is very important for you to learn about first collecting the dots and then connecting them. See how connections work?"

Ladybugs were a reassuring sign of Zhubin's presence while I wrote the book – one landed on a card I'd received and another surprised me by crawling out of a bunch of parsley that I was washing.

Garden of the Heart

My family organized several trips for me after Zhubin's death, but, with the exception of a few flashes here and there, I have very little memory of them. A visit to my sister Shishi in Seattle took place some two months after Zhubin's passing. I was emotionally and physically spent – the pain so very fresh, acute and unbearable. One afternoon Shishi led me into her back garden, which was muddy from the rain and quite a mess with overgrown grass. It didn't look like a garden at all.

After directing me to a chair, she pointed to the corner and said: "Look at this cherry tree. This is Zhubin's cherry tree." Glancing in that direction, I saw a sapling in a sad state – half dead, with a few cherries limply hanging on its branches.

The cherry tree: a sickly sapling in its first year; then, only a year later, in full blossom.

With both excitement and sadness in her voice, Shishi then told me its story. Zhubin had been buried on her birthday of May 13th. On the flight back to Seattle, following the funeral, she had hit on the idea of planting a cherry tree in her garden in memory of Zhubin. Arriving home on May 20th, she had discovered this poor sapling at her front door, left by a friend as a birthday present, and immediately sensed that this was a sign from Zhubin: how often does one get a cherry tree as a birthday gift? At that moment, she had felt Zhubin strongly, was certain he was happy and safe in good hands, and gained a feeling of peace and relief.

Having sat in the shade with no water for a week, the sapling had been in a bad way, but Shishi had nevertheless planted it right away. As she sat me down in a chair in her desolate garden, she hoped that I would feel Zhubin's presence in or through that cherry tree in the same way that she had two months earlier. Gazing at it I was reminded of Zhubin at the end of his life: fighting to survive – or perhaps, just giving in. What would be this sapling's fate? How could I look at this dying tree and feel my child? How could I even believe in such an idea or feel my boy this way? But Shishi insisted that I sit there quietly, so, reluctantly, I obeyed. As I contemplated the tree, I pitied it, musing: You are like me, barely alive. I don't know how much longer either one of us will last, so do whatever is good for you. If you want to die, die – it is okay with me. I won't be hurt. I will understand.

I don't know how long I sat there wordlessly "talking" to the sapling, eventually relating the story of my broken heart, how much pain I was in, and how much I just wanted to be with Zhubin. Tears rolled down my cheeks and grief choked me. And now I was supposed to "feel" Zhubin's presence by looking at this tree? What kind of nonsense was this! I felt nothing save for the shards of my shattered heart.

I don't know why, but at that moment I felt compelled to address God: "Please give me another sign. Let me know whether Zhubin is all right. Tell me if he is somewhere safe, if someone is taking care of him. Please help me, I cannot go on." I would count the cherries, I decided, and if there were 21 – because Zhubin was 21 when he died – it would be a sign that Zhubin was safe and with Him. I asked for this particular sign, despite my extreme scepticism. I made my way over to that pathetic tree (ignorant of what an important role it would come to play in my life) and started counting its cherries: one, two, three – all the way up to 19. Tallying them twice more, I reached 20 each time. Defeated, I returned to my seat.

When Shishi came to me a little later and asked whether I had felt anything, I replied: "No, nothing." I told her that I had asked God to allow me to find on that tree 21 cherries, as a sign that Zhubin was all right. But He didn't want that for me – there were only 20 cherries. Why hadn't He shown me 21? Why? Why wasn't He helping me? Taking my hand, Shishi led me back to the tree. "Let's count again," she said. We counted from the top, and this time she spotted a little cherry I had missed: caught between two leaves, its back was pink but the front was green, which was why I hadn't spotted it earlier. What joy that 21st cherry brought to my heart: an affirmation for me of Zhubin's existence in another realm! I felt God had responded to me: "I heard you. Be comforted. Know your child is safe with me in my arms." Shishi and I hugged one another, jumping up and down screaming with joy. My entire body trembled with excitement. I could not believe it. For us this was an unmistakable sign – the first real and definite step in my healing. To keep Zhubin alive, I now felt the glimmer of a determination to change, to search out miracles in the everyday. I had already received three important signs – the appearance of the raccoon, the cemetery plot's sudden availability, and the ladybugs at Zhubin's grave. This fourth sign melted the rest of my scepticism. Although it would not be an easy road, these moments persuaded me that I would not be travelling it alone.

Zhubin had entreated me to celebrate life and our journeys. With this sign I believed God was giving me a place where I could mark Zhubin's anniversaries and birthdays, a place to be with Zhubin at crucial times. Most importantly, God had taught me a lesson in His own way: to not lose faith or abandon hope in times of utter darkness, as He always hears and never deserts us. From that moment, both my heart and the Seattle garden started to transform. I dug up every inch of the ground, pulled every weed, cleaned the soil with my bare hands, watered it with my tears and nourished it with the love locked in my heart. What had been a dead garden and a dead heart, a forgotten place and a forgotten heart, fused to become my sanctuary. The garden and I started to work on our roots, growing together and slowly maturing, never imagining how strong and resilient they were.

"The garden in your heart is our shrine. Make it cozy and very spiritual."

The garden is now my meeting place with Zhubin – where our worlds become one. When I work there I talk to him and to the flowers, giving them love while they return the favour. The more I give, the more I get. It now seems no coincidence at all that, in one of his discussions with me, Zhubin had used the metaphor of a cherry tree to make his point. And so that Seattle cherry sapling came to be symbolic for me of a greater meaning for our existence here, the living proof and explanation of Zhubin's words: *"This is our journey. This was meant to be. The mission is the Master Plan."* Shishi knew how much I loved and cared for her garden. Certainly it was hers, but she wholeheartedly let me do with it as I wished. Throwing myself into long hours of work tending to the plot, I communed with Zhubin. With each visit, the garden slowly but surely took shape, becoming healthier, fuller and more colourful. I had a vision of the garden complementing "Zhubin's" cherry sapling as it matured into a beautiful tree.

As I started to make even more substantial changes, I realized that the garden would require someone to maintain it when I was not visiting Seattle. Shishi had arranged for help here and there, but nothing permanent had come of it. One day, however, she introduced me to a young man named Francisco, a recent immigrant from Mexico. The moment I saw him I was reminded of Zhubin: he seemed young and innocent. It was clear that he was desperate for a job and I was certain that he was just the person we were looking for. Francisco did not know a thing about gardening – he didn't even own a shovel! – but he was eager to learn and willing to work hard. I told him about Zhubin and the story of the cherry tree, and so he understood why this garden meant so much to me. The care he has since lavished on it has given me peace of mind about the garden when I'm away from it and the garden has even won awards. Over the years Shishi became like a business counsellor for Francisco, teaching him sound commercial practices. In no time, he learned it all and today he owns a small business with his own truck, all the equipment he needs, and a few full-time employees. Each time I visit Seattle, usually in May or September, Francisco sets aside time for us to work together in the garden. We have all come to love, trust and respect him very much, and whenever I'm there on Mother's Day he makes sure to put a smile on my face with a big hug and a bunch of flowers. Francisco was "chosen" for this garden: he from Mexico and me from Iran, meeting in the USA, each at a crossroads in our respective lives. Miracles come in different ways, with different purposes and meanings.

Today "Zhubin's" cherry tree is tall and strong, each year bearing a bounty of fruit that is shared with neighbours – as well as with the crows and raccoons that also call this garden home! Whenever I am there, I try to remember and focus on what Zhubin said to me: *"Remember what you have and not what you have lost."* I have since learned that in medieval art the cherry is understood to symbolize the sweetness of performing good deeds. It is sweet, indeed! And I hope that my soul will be as fruitful as my cherry tree.

The cherry tree – 16 years later and magnificent!

"Look at a fruit tree, for example a cherry tree. If not for the soil, the tree would not grow. If it were not for the tree, there would be an empty dead space. Together the two produce flowers, fruit and shelter. Do you know how many birds rest on the branches? How many different birds and animals eat the fruit? How many insects love and enjoy and need the branches? There is also the beauty of the tree for the pleasure of our eyes. There is a lot more but you don't understand. Everything has a thousand connections, and connections are what make you."

My Lucky Number

The cherry tree standing in the corner of Shishi's garden was only the beginning of my special connection with the number 21. It now seems that no matter which way I turn, it appears: the time still remaining on a parking meter when I'm inserting coins for payment; on my ticket in a queue at our popular local pastry shop; the amount of change that I find left behind, whether on the floor of an elevator or on a sidewalk; a table number assigned to us at a restaurant; and when I turn to see the time displayed on the microwave or the television – almost invariably it's 21 minutes past the hour.

     Each of these encounters with my lucky number, no matter how trivial in day-to-day importance, serves as a reminder of the path that has been shown to me – and I am so grateful for each such appearance.

"Count your many blessings to help you through your journey."

One day I spotted one dime and a second one lying close beside it. Certain I'd find a penny to total 21, I looked and, sure enough, this battered coin lay partially buried in the gravel next to the other two.

A Chance Encounter

A year or so following Zhubin's death, dark grief had shrouded me, hanging heavily. At one time I had been feeling particularly shattered: it was one of those unbearable days where, no matter how much I cried, no relief could be found. Retreating early to bed that evening, I had hidden in the dark and quiet.

The next morning I awoke very early, having promised to pick up my mother-in-law, Mila, and drive her to her appointment at a nearby hospital. I got myself ready and glanced outside: a sunlit June morning, birds twittering. Since I had more than half an hour on my hands before I was due to collect Mila, and feeling an impulse to refresh my heart and mind, I thought of taking a stroll in a hillside park part-way to her apartment. After but a few minutes' walk, and for no reason, I changed my mind, returned to my car and drove to another nearby park instead. As soon as I entered the second park I heard the loud trilling of a robin singing as if only for me, trying his best to cheer me up. Loving his song and message, I stopped under a magnificent oak tree to search for him, craning my head skywards – and there he was, a red-breasted male perched on a branch at the very top, seemingly delighting in the freshness of the early hours. I stood quietly to share this moment with the robin; in my heart I was speaking to him: "Are you singing your love for your Creator? I am sure He loves it. I love it too, little one! You make me very happy, thank you." Still entranced by the robin, I became aware of someone else behind my shoulder, also peering up at the tree. When this person walked away, I thought fleetingly that he must either be a fellow bird lover or just curious as to what had caught my attention.

After saying goodbye to my little singing friend I continued with my walk, soon reaching a pond where I sat down on a waterside bench. Watching the ducks swimming, I remembered a time when I had visited Zhubin in Boston and we had gone together to a park to feed the ducks. I was warmed by the memory of his smiles as he gently touched the ducks' glossy backs while they took the seeds from his hands. Lost in my own little world, I heard a voice asking me: "Do you love nature?" I looked up to see the owner of the voice and right away was certain that this was the same person who had shared in my moment with the robin. Looking at him, I replied: "Yes, very much." But he simply repeated his question: "Do you love nature?" At a loss for words, I continued to look up at him, holding his gaze. He was first to break the silence, asking me the oddest question: "Why do you cry so much?" I jumped to my feet, losing all emotional control, tears pouring out and rolling down my cheeks. Tongue-tied, I just stood crying, looking into his eyes while he stared into mine. After a pause he asked of me: "Do you know who you are to God? You are His child, He loves you."

I was unable to utter a word, even had I known how to reply. I was just eyes and ears. I saw a man of medium age, height and build; thinning hair and a stubbly beard; clothes somewhat threadbare; a small, old knapsack slung over his shoulder. His voice was calm yet firm. He reached for his knapsack and pulled out a book. After opening it seemingly at random, he started to read aloud a few lines. After finishing, he shut the book and said, looking at me: "This is who you are to God."

While I had been unable to pay close attention to what he had read, I could understand the gist of it – that God has love for each of us. The man then thrust the book into my hand. I turned my attention from him to the book: it was brand new, looked unread, and bore the title *Conversations with God*. I could not imagine the reasons for his words, or why he had given me the book. But I remained transfixed by his initial question: "Why do you cry so much?" From his appearance, it was easy to see that the book was a materially substantial gift for him to make. I was disappointed that my stream of tears had made it so difficult for me to speak. I wanted to offer him some money, but my lips were sealed with the certainty that I shouldn't – that I was truly not "allowed" to put a price tag on his kindness.

Leaving me with the book in my hand, and without saying a further word, he started to walk away. At last I found my voice, managing to ask: "Who are you?" Without turning to face me he replied over his shoulder: "Never mind who I am. I am here for you now. You will not see me again." I remained frozen, watching him until he disappeared from sight. How could he have known that only the previous evening I had called out to God? Was he an angel, I wondered. It took me some time to pull myself together, get back in the car and pick up Mila. Several times that summer I returned to the same park at the same time in the early morning, hoping to meet this mysterious man again, but I never caught another glimpse of him.

I could neither stop thinking about him nor could I put down the book he had given me – one that would come to help me enormously. Although it was the first volume in a best-selling series, I had never heard of it before. Who could ever believe this intense encounter? It was months before I digested it enough to feel that I could share it with Zyg.

I understood that God had told me:

"I am like the wind.

You don't see the wind, but you feel it.

You don't know where it's coming from, or where it's going.

Sometimes it's so quiet that it seems not to exist.

Sometimes it's just a gentle breeze, refreshing and soothing.

Even when its violent gusts are stormy, in time it passes and is becalmed.

It is the same with Me: you don't see Me, but you can feel Me.

I have been talking and showing you how I am piecing together your heart's shattered pieces, shard by shard.

Don't lose faith.

Don't lose hope.

Believe.

Trust in the unknown.

Know I am here."

"Think that you are going to an amazing destination... Instead of packing objects, you are packing qualities: faith, love, patience. By learning these you are packing for your trip – a trip to heaven."

Jarred

On the afternoon of the day following the discovery of the 21 cherries I was resting in bed. Downstairs I could hear the laughter of my nieces – playful, joyful, and making all too much noise. "Simin, come down to meet Jarred," Shishi called out. I didn't want to get up, preferring to remain alone, but when I didn't answer my sister shouted up to me again. Easing myself out of the bed, I shuffled over to the top of the staircase and bent down to sneak a peek into the living room: Shishi was animatedly relating to a young man the major sign we had just received; her pre-teen daughters meanwhile played with his hair, curling it into little ponytails. All this pulling and shouting didn't seem to bother him one bit – indeed, it looked as though he was enjoying it as much as his "tormentors" were. Listening to Shishi's story with an ever-growing smile, he was apparently very pleased by her account.

Growing curious, I continued to furtively study him and sensed in him a great deal of inner peace. When I made my way downstairs I was introduced as "Simin, Zhubin's Mom" and he was introduced as "Jarred, Jenny's partner and the one who planted the cherry tree". Jenny is another niece, this one Soussan's daughter. Jarred had been welcomed into my extended family a few years before Zhubin's death, but I had not previously met him as Zhubin's illness had greatly limited my ability to travel and I had seen little of my family. Instantly taking to him, I was happy to hear that it had been this young man, not much older than Zhubin, who had planted the sapling.

Although we would meet only a few more times, I grew very fond of Jarred. He had a humble and generous heart, and was a particularly gentle and kind person. Despite needing to work to pay his way through university, week in and week out he still found time to volunteer, teaching underprivileged children. A devoted son, older brother and friend, Jarred's inner beauty was apparent to everyone that came into close contact with him. I saw a lot of Zhubin in him and developed a maternal feeling for him, which was very soothing.

Tragically, Jarred's time with us proved short-lived: only two years after Zhubin's passing, he was killed instantly in a head-on car collision in upstate New York, where he had been living with Jenny. Once again, I was crushed by grief, and this second sudden loss tore open my far-from-healed wound over Zhubin. The loss of Jarred was a grievous blow to his mother and three younger siblings, as well as to my family and his friends. All our love and hope was replaced by the pain of dealing with his death.

Only a week or so before he died, Jarred had brought home a gift for Jenny from the local animal shelter: a gorgeous black cat with big, shiny, green eyes. They christened it Joo-Joo, intentionally choosing Zhubin's nickname. Joo-Joo proved to be not only very smart and playful, but, following Jarred's death, he would also play a crucial role for Jenny as a comforting reminder of both Jarred's big heart and her cousin Zhubin.

A number of years later, as the anniversary of Jarred's death approached, I felt particularly sad. To ease my anguish, I "spoke" to him, telling him how much I missed both him and Zhubin, and asking them to embrace each other for me.

The watermelon that brought greetings from Jarred.

Jenny's amazing gift.

> *"Know that we all are bound together forever, and that our bond is very powerful."*

Preparing dinner later that afternoon, I remembered the large watermelon I had purchased the day before and left in the car. After retrieving and placing it in the sink to wash, I was about to slice it up when I caught sight of the sticker on the outside rind: "Jarred's Best". "Oh my God!" I screamed. Jarred was talking: he had heard me, was sending me love, and was saying that embraces had been exchanged.

As yet another anniversary of Zhubin's passing grew near, it was so hard to believe that he had been gone for ten years and Jarred for eight. Finding it too difficult to be without my siblings at this time, I travelled to Seattle with Zyg to spend Christmas with my sisters and their families. When we were all gathered in Shishi's home on Christmas Eve, Jenny presented me with a little box as a gift. I can still remember her expectant eyes, awaiting my reaction as I unwrapped it. I didn't disappoint her, stunned when I saw what was inside: a medallion with a painting of a figure of a black cat, not only a dead ringer for her pet Joo-Joo but also adorned with ladybugs' wings and perched on a little mushroom set in a garden.

> *"I want you to know that I am in your heart and you are wrapped in my special bubble."*

Jenny told me that she had wanted to give me something especially meaningful. She had been searching online for long hours, on countless websites, and then, at 2am, just when she'd been about to give up, she had found this necklace and been amazed at how perfect it was – and astonished that some artisan had been inspired to combine the two creatures that carried so much meaning for her Aunt Simin. It had been Jenny's heart's desire – and the Universe had made it happen. When a desire is pure and selfless, it will come to pass. What artist would compose a scene of a black cat wearing ladybug wings?

Jarred shares a moment with Joo-Joo.

"I want you to see and understand the eternal aspect of our connection. That is when understanding and growth comes about – this way you will understand the Big Picture and the Master Plan."

A Gift Deferred

A simple gift, whose story began long before Zhubin died, is perhaps my most amazing "sign". Just before Zhubin began his last year of high school, he and I had been making the move from Vancouver to take up residence with Zyg. I had gone ahead to get the house ready, while Zhubin remained to spend some additional time with his father and friends.

Before he departed to join me, Zhubin had purchased a gift for his paternal aunt, Soodi. After wrapping it, he left it with Shervin for safe-keeping until he could send it to Soodi in San Diego. As it happened, the wrapped present was placed in Zhubin's trunk in Vancouver and forgotten.

Eight years later, and three years after Zhubin's death, Shervin and Soodi undertook a trip to Montreal to visit Zhubin's grave for the first time. Before leaving Vancouver Shervin opened Zhubin's trunk, intending to bring me a few childhood mementoes. It was only then that he chanced upon Zhubin's gift, which had never been delivered to Soodi.

Shervin had already suffered through two heart attacks following Zhubin's passing, and I was concerned as to how he would bear the strain of the trip to Montreal and his first visit to his son's grave. In the two years that had passed since Zhubin's death, Shervin and I had found a measure of solace by periodically sharing our grief over the phone or when we met during my visits to Vancouver. In time, as I progressed, and with the hope that Shervin would also find them uplifting, I revealed to him more and more of the signs and messages I had received. Although many others in my family and circle of friends were aware of these events, Shervin remained sceptical.

Soon after they had separately arrived in Montreal, Shervin presented Soodi with Zhubin's forgotten gift. I am told that when she unwrapped it she burst into tears, unable to believe what she saw.

We were scheduled to meet the following day at the cemetery. I had always been very fond of Soodi and also knew how much she had cared for Zhubin. Knowing how painful it would be for the two of them to be at the graveside, I was determined to make the occasion as special as possible, so had prepared a little picnic. I was delighted when they arrived wearing smiles and carrying colourful balloons. As soon as Soodi saw me, she approached, clutching something tightly to her chest. Her first words to me were: "Simin, you have to see this. It is so hard to believe." Unfurling the hand clasped to her chest, she revealed a small cushion adorned with three ladybugs, each bearing seven black dots – for a total of 21 of course!

In the immediately ensuing torrent of hugs and tears, the first words that in turn I could muster were: "*This* is the sign for you, Shervin! Joo-Joo, our little bug, is telling you 'I am fine, Daddy'." With tears in his eyes yet a smile on his face, Shervin managed to say: "Imagine my surprise when she opened it!"

When I saw what a positive impact this sign had had on Shervin, I was relieved and certain that Zhubin had at last found a way to provide his father with some support. So our picnic kicked off with elated hearts – and my excitement with this latest sign encouraged me to share with Shervin even more of my other signs. It was a bittersweet moment. But as we were talking and fighting off the effects of the chilly air by drinking hot coffee from the thermos I had brought, we were treated to yet another sign for good measure: a ladybug flew over Zhubin's gravestone, perched on it for quite a while (I still have the photos), and then flew over to me and sat on my hand. To us, this was an unmistakable confirmation that kept our hearts warm on that difficult and cold day. This latest "sign" changed my world forever: I believed, and my faith had become unshakeable and solid as a rock.

Returning home that afternoon, I went directly to Zhubin's room where I sat down on his bed, feeling compelled to tell God how much I loved and trusted Him. It was then that I felt Zhubin telling me: "*Mom, rid yourself of my stuff. You and I are above these things now – let go!*" The next day I at last found the courage to contact a local centre for homeless

A gift that waited eight years to be delivered to his Aunt Soodie, the cushion photographed that day in the cemetery. As Zhubin was fond of saying: "*What are the odds?*"

youth and ask them to send a pick-up truck. An older gentleman accompanied by two young men came by two days later to collect Zhubin's belongings. The day before the collection I had neatly packed and readied everything, an emotionally hellish task. Each item elicited a memory – one heartbreaking, another happy and pleasant. As I stood watching my son's belongings leave forever, I was crying inside but also happy in the knowledge that they were destined for homeless youth – a cause that I knew had been near to Zhubin's heart. After the truck had been loaded, the older gentleman said: "Whoever these things belonged to would be very pleased to know where they are going and who will use them." He hadn't asked any questions, but I was certain that he sensed that not only were these things my son's, but also that the owner of these possessions was no longer with us.

"My desire is for you to become strong, like a rock. See rocks and imagine what kind of rock you want to be so that will guide you to what kind of person you will become."

The Red Fox

Two months or so after Shervin and Soodi's visit, instead of enjoying the warmth of that sunny summer day I was bent over in pain, missing Zhubin very badly. Will it ever stop? I wondered. Telling Zyg that I was going to the cemetery to water the flowers, I needed, in truth, to go and let out my anguish.

Driving slowly, I made my way to the cemetery and parked close to Zhubin's grave in my usual spot along a narrow lane. As I was about to step out of the car I was stunned to see, only a few feet away, a resplendent young fox. Turning his head to regard me calmly, we held each other's gaze for several seconds before he continued on his way down the lane. I was drawn to follow him, ever so slowly inching after him in my car. Very much aware of my presence, he glanced repeatedly over his shoulder as if inviting me to continue. Without a trace of fear, he allowed me to remain close enough so that I could see his shining hazel eyes. We continued in tandem to the border of the cemetery, where the ground becomes hilly and empty of graves. Here the fox turned once more to stare at me for several seconds – and I was sure that his message was: "Don't come. Don't follow me further. This is not for you." With a great leap, he disappeared over the hill, leaving me in tears of sadness for the fleeting moment of the connection we had shared.

Rushing home excited, I called: "Zyg! Zyg! I saw the most beautiful red fox, a young male fox with a thick tail. A big sign from Zhubin!" With a straight face, he replied: "How do you know it was a fox? Have you ever seen a real one? Could it have been a cat? And how do you know it was a male?" I assured him that I'd seen foxes on TV and that males have thick bushy tails and are much more attractive than vixens. "I know what a fox looks like," I told him with dignity. But being the sceptic that he was, he persisted: "No, Simin, it was a big cat. We don't have foxes here in the city." I left the room and said to myself: "How silly – a cat! He doesn't believe me..."

Three months later we received in the mail the annual calendar published by the cemetery, and on its cover it featured a photograph of a fox standing beside a gravestone, with the following caption below: "A fox – rare wildlife in the Notre-Dame-des-Neiges Cemetery." I immediately ran upstairs to Zyg's office, brandishing the cover, and triumphantly demanding: "Is *this* a cat or a fox?" Despite considerable time spent at the cemetery, for the remainder of the year I did not see another fox and reluctantly stopped my search. The following summer, as I drove through the back gates of the cemetery and approached Zhubin's grave, my heart skipped a beat: the same fox was standing dead ahead, in the exact same spot I'd seen him the year before, but now he was fully grown and sporting a shiny, reddish coat with a much bigger and bushier tail. He had filled out and grown majestic. As before, we stared at each other eye-to-eye, holding each other's gaze for even longer than the previous year. This time I immediately parked the car to get out and follow him on foot, sensing that he recognized me and felt safe. Once again, he walked ahead of me, turning around every so often as if to make sure that I was following. Passing a couple planting flowers and cleaning their loved one's plot, I wanted to shout, "Look! Look at the fox!" but kept quiet lest I scare him. Nobody paid us any attention. Indeed, I was happy that we had remained unobserved and could enjoy this private moment together, as if he and I were in our own little world. I followed him down the same path to the edge of the cemetery where he repeated his actions of a year earlier, turning to face me as if to say: "That's it, come no further." After giving me that same farewell glance, he leapt over the crest of the hill, disappearing into the underbrush.

Although I cried this time as well, these were tears of joy: through the medium of the fox, Zhubin had sent me yet another sign! I was certain that he wanted me to know that, like the fox, he had come into his own now, filling out over the past year and gathering in strength.

"Look at animals and flowers, and see me."

The same fox that I first saw in the cemetery as a kit, now fully grown. This was taken by the cemetery's photographer and appeared on their calendar the same year I saw the fox. Notre-Dame-des-Neiges Cemetery (Montreal).

A Hand-stitched Message

After completing a first draft of this book, I wanted Zyg to read it over and provide me with his initial feedback. It had been a long winter and I felt very tired, despite the relief of at last finishing the manuscript. Zyg perfectly read my mind and mood when he offered to get away from work the following week, suggesting we go to Mexico and spend it in the sun reviewing the draft together. Where better to undertake this task than in a place where nature is so generous, inviting and tranquil?

It was extremely important to me to get Zyg's opinion as to whether the draft was on the path to "doing my job", true to my goals and promises. Determined not to jeopardize either Zhubin's or my dignity, I sought help: "Dear God, if this book is meant to be and You approve of it, please show me a sign. I need Your confirmation." Asking for confirmation from the Divine is one of my most deep-rooted means of connecting with the Universe. It is now impossible for me to make any important plans without first asking for a sign to confirm that I am on the true path and doing the right thing. Signs and messages are the Divine's means of guiding us.

Just a few days later, well before dawn, we left for the airport. I had kept things simple and hadn't packed much – only a few summer dresses and a bathing suit. But when we checked into our room, hoping to immediately go out and enjoy the afternoon sun and heat, I found to my dismay that I hadn't packed my bathing suit after all. I owned three and could have sworn that I had packed at least one – after all, how is it possible to forget one's bathing suit when leaving for a beach vacation? My family and friends know me as a very organized person, so this was most unusual.

The resort we were in was far from the nearest town, so Zyg suggested that I go to the hotel lobby to see if there was a resort shop. Tired from our long trip and the short night's sleep, Zyg expressed no interest in joining me, but when I got to the hotel lobby and glanced over my shoulder I was surprised to see him following.

I was in luck: the resort did have an elegant and quite well-stocked store. Zyg remained outside in the sun while I was shown the selection of bathing suits. After a while, when I had completed a review of the entire store and sat down to try an array of sandals that had caught my attention, Zyg surprised me again by coming in and casually looking around. Shopping in general, and browsing in clothing stores in particular, usually makes him tense and is something that he rarely volunteers for. Seeing that he was relaxed, I had returned my attention to the sandals when he called out excitedly from the far side of the store: "Simin, come look. This is just for you! You must have asked for a sign." When I went over and looked I was stunned: Zyg stood holding a small, red clutch purse, bearing a hand-stitched message – one written in English, whereas all the other purses on the shelf were adorned with Spanish phrases. What did the embroidery say?

"Be free.

Trust your heart.

Trust your story."

On the reverse side of the purse were three stitched hearts surrounded with shiny gold sparks, the middle, larger heart adorned with angel wings and raised above the other two.

"Trust me.

Trust yourself.

Trust your heart.

Be free."

These are the words that Zhubin had said and written to me many times. Staring at the words "Trust your story", I hugged Zyg and burst into tears of gratitude. Even now, as I remember that moment, I break into goosebumps. The saleswoman naturally had no idea what was going on, or why I was both crying and laughing, but she soon joined us, crying and laughing and pointing skywards with her hand, repeating: "God! God!" She too must have been certain of the presence of a divine love and touch.

For this to have occurred, I had to uncharacteristically forget to pack something – a bathing suit, crucial for a beach vacation – making it necessary for me to venture out to a store, and then Zyg not only had to follow me but atypically enter the store and look around, then find something that had escaped my notice. Ringing in my head, clear as a bell, I could hear one of Zhubin's favourite sayings: *What are the odds? Just connect the dots.*

Zhubin's words to me uncannily stitched onto the clutch purse;
the shop assistant standing with me holding the purse.

A sacred object: this is what that purse was to me. Not only a striking confirmation for the book, its "wings and heart" design represented to me Zhubin aloft between Zyg and myself, guiding us on the right path. Of course, I purchased the purse. To this day, whenever I look at it, my spirits soar.

> *"God is in your life.*
> *I am in your heart.*
> *Soar with me.*
> *Be free, Mom, I am your energy."*

Daisy

When our miniature schnauzer siblings named Sam and Pepper died more than eight years after Zhubin had left us, Zyg and I didn't consider getting another pet. Four years later, however, I began to feel a longing and a readiness for another dog to fill some of the quiet and emptiness of our home. To make it easier to care for, I wanted one even smaller than a miniature schnauzer. Zyg immediately agreed with the idea.

A neighbour had two miniature Yorkshire terriers with whom I played whenever I saw them out for a walk. Why not get a Yorkie? As it seemed a perfect fit for me, I asked the neighbour to give me the details of his breeder. On reflection, however, I decided that instead of approaching a breeder I would first visit the local animal shelter and try my luck at rescuing a small dog – even if it wasn't a Yorkie.

I called my dear friend and neighbour Jill to share my plan. She loved the idea: "I'd like to come with you, but this week I'm busy. Can we go next week?" I didn't mind the delay, as I really wanted her to accompany me. Only half an hour later she rang me back to say that her afternoon appointment had been cancelled. If I wanted to, we could go right away. With great anticipation, off we went.

On arriving at the shelter we explained that I was looking for a small dog. I was given an extensive application form with many questions for me and Zyg about our reasons for wishing to adopt a pet. After Jill helped me to complete the form, we were shown into a large kennel. On our way, in a room reserved for cats, we met a rooster roaming free, whose crowing made us laugh. The dog kennel was clean and airy, with cages around the periphery of a large room. It was heartbreaking to see all the little faces behind bars, looking at us so hopefully and wondering whether we would be the ones to bring them home. I was in tears, recalling my visits with young Zhubin to an animal shelter in Vancouver to walk Lucy the blind poodle. I wished I could take them all. As we circled the room, all we saw were enormous dogs of various kinds and ages – each far too big and strong for me to handle. Returning to the attendant, I explained the problem. "There is a little dog in the last cage on the right, near the door," she replied. We went back to look again and, sure enough, this time we saw a fluffy little thing curled up on a blanket in the far corner of the cage. Jill opened the cage and picked it up. "Oh Jill, she's a small one," I noted, and then: "Oh my God, it's a Yorkie!" We were both so thrilled. The little creature was shivering, fragile and lost, and so tiny. I fell in love with her right away. The attendant explained to us that the dog had been brought to them only two days earlier and that her name was Daisy. What a perfect name!

I made it plain that I wanted to take Daisy, but the animal shelter's strict policy required that all adults living in the home first present themselves to make sure it was a good fit. In other words, Zyg had to come to the kennel to meet Daisy before I could bring her home. "But my husband is at work visiting a client and there is no way he can come here now," I pleaded. "I assure you they will be fine together; there won't be any problem. I promise." Although my entreaties fell on deaf ears, I was granted half an hour to comply before Daisy would be turned over to another lady who had expressed an interest in adopting her. I started to get nervous. While I was negotiating with the attendant, Jill had been inspired to take a photo of Daisy in her cage and email it to Zyg. As it happened, his client meeting had finished early and he had just turned on his smartphone. When he telephoned Jill to ask for an explanation of the mysterious image, she let me explain. It was meant to be that his client's offices were nearby, and I was in disbelief when he marched into the animal shelter offices less than 15 minutes later. The instant Zyg saw Daisy, she stole his heart. That afternoon we left the shelter with very, very happy hearts and our Yorkie snuggling in my arms.

Daisy enjoying the garden.

Daisy turned out to be very well trained, loving and gentle not just with us, but with all dogs she meets. The animal shelter had not revealed to us why she had been given away. Whatever the reason, we were the lucky beneficiaries as Daisy has proven to be yet another gift from the Universe: how was it possible for a creature this small to brighten our lives with so much joy? After deciding on a Yorkie, why did I change my mind and try my luck at the shelter instead of the breeder? What were the odds of Jill's meeting being cancelled at the last moment? How was it that Zyg had a meeting so close to the animal shelter that day? And how was it that this four-legged ray of sunshine had been given away only two days earlier? Daisy is another precious miracle.

"Sit with your soul.
Smile at life and move on.
Wonder, and wonders you will see."

What Do Signs Mean to Me?

Signs and messages came to me quite suddenly and unexpectedly. In the beginning, I didn't quite know what to make of them: should I believe or not? Trusting in the unknown was not easy. If I believed in these signs, what was their meaning? Little by little, I began to feel something other than just pain:
- a delicately pale ray of light aimed at me;
- a whisper in my ear, "Don't lose hope";
- a fresh breath of air to bring me back to life.

As I learned more, the signs evolved: at first they simply gave me hope, later becoming richer in meaning. Each carried a unique message, delivered with the right instrument at the right time. They persuaded me that beyond this life is a vast Higher Energy and offered an explanation for my journey through life without my child, which had been thrust on me. I believe that signs are God's way to allow us to connect with Him, bringing us closer to Him and the unknown.

"The soul has been given its own ears to hear things the mind does not understand."
– Rumi

Carrying a promise of eternal love and bonding, each of my signs encouraged me to work harder and learn more. Slowly I absorbed the richness of the Universe and came to believe that its love is ever present. By telling me that God's love is unconditional, no matter how poorly I thought of myself, the signs allowed me to overcome my guilt and regrets. I cannot help but marvel at these gifts, each one reinforcing my faith.

I have shared with you just a few of the signs that have blessed and guided me. I think of them as "my little miracles". I am unable to share many other moments; they are as impossible for me to describe as they would be impossible for you to believe.

"Miracles do 'happen'. They really do. Believe and believe more."

On many occasions, friends with whom I shared certain signs have asked: "Why you?" And my answer is: "Why not me?" I have never asked "Why?" God knows, and I have learned to listen gratefully to His voice. I have also been asked how one looks for signs and messages. Are they not merely coincidences? I believe they are not coincidence, that God does not believe in coincidence, and that the Universe does not understand coincidence. Once both my heart and my mind were open, I got a glimpse of the unseen world. It had always been there.

"As far as it goes, the energy of the Universe does not stop. We are all a part of life and a part of this Universe forever."

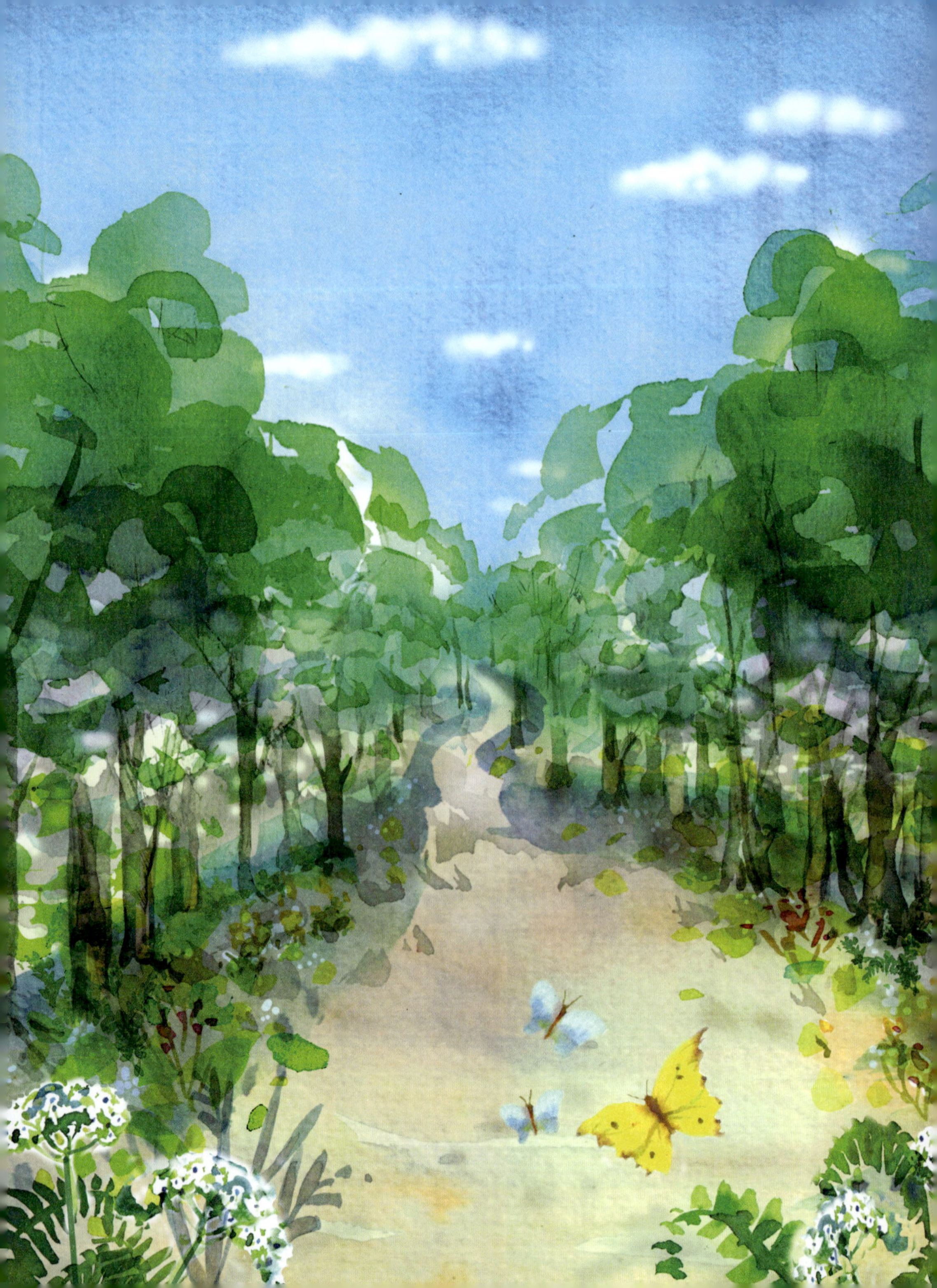

Part 5

Sunshine: A Peaceful Heart

The Biggest Show Ever

I have come to understand that life is full of "events" and all of these things make life what it is.

> Little surprises – big surprises
> Little challenges – big challenges
> Little bumps – big bumps
> Little hills – big mountains
> Little pains – big pains
> Big pains – huge pains
> Huge pains – unbearable pains
> Small miracles – big miracles
> Small learning – big learning
> Small faith – big faith
> Small growth – big achievement
> Little money – great fortunes
> Small people – big people
> Funny things – sad things
> Small houses – big houses
> Disturbing things – peaceful things
> Fast things – slow things
> Acquaintances – true friends
> No trust – little trust – absolute trust
> Little love – big love – unconditional love
> Small family – big family
> Mother's love – lovers' love – all kinds of love
> Small experiences – big experiences
> Silly things – wise things
> Day-to-day headaches – day-to-day joys
> Small happiness – big happiness
> Little hope – big hope
> Bad things – good things
> Wrong things – right things

Life is but a hodgepodge, a mishmash of experiences and possibilities. Each of us has a role and each is unique; each has its own purpose, and not one is more important than another. Possibly we'll never feel ready to play our roles in our individual stories, but we are obliged to play them as best we can. Each life story has its happy and its sad, its good and its bad. A grieving parent's story is one of tragedy, but also one highlighted by unexpected and magical moments to help them through. One just needs to be open.

"Let everything happen, and love whatever happens. There is a blessing and a lesson in all of it."

Back in My Garden

Leaning back on the bench in my garden, with Daisy tucked in beside me, memories of the past dance through my mind, tracing back all the footsteps I have taken in my life without Zhubin. Now I ask myself: are things better after all these years? Taking a deep breath, I listen… Yes – definitely, Yes.

With these last few words escaping through my pen, the story comes to an end. This is the moment to tell Zhubin that I have tried my best to keep the promise I made to him: *"Be my voice and spread my words."*

Looking back at my life, my greatest achievement has been how I faced and learned to live with the loss of my son. I know the Universe has given me a grand chance to recognize the Big Picture and to discover my journey's purpose. So in a way I do appreciate the challenge the Universe sent me.

"A journey without purpose is empty."

Etched in gold on my heart is Zhubin's guidance: *"Mom, know and remember what you want to be and where you want to be. Visualize that. Let that feeling guide you to the end. Let your heart work for you. The truth is in your heart: go in it, and don't come out."* This is what I continue to work on. Each day as I wake, I rejoice in the new day offering its own teaching – whether a brand-new lesson or an earlier one not yet mastered.

"Remember there is no end to learning. We go from phase to phase. Higher and higher. Deeper and deeper. And that is what eternity means."

When my time comes to leave this life, I do not want to regret that I should have done more, shared more, or learned more. Knowing now that life is a breath of love, I cannot let the fleeting, precious time I have left slip by without doing the best for myself and others. There remains much to learn, much to do, and all in so little time. In doing my best I am doing what I can: yes, that may be insignificant in the eyes of others, but in the eyes of the Universe it matters a great deal. Knowing I did my all will make my departure peaceful. In the end, what matters is how the Universe sees me.

Now I understand that nothing in life is commonplace or dull – not even peeling a potato! I look forward to the rest of my journey and its new experiences. Sure, hard times may come again, but this time I am prepared, armed with this God-given drive to move on, my angels here and above, a caring family and true friends, and, most of all, the love and support of this magical Universe.

"Life is a wonderful and amazing journey – just enjoy it! Our journey started from the moment that we are born and ends at the last breath we take. In this short time we have here, there are endless possibilities, ways to love, give and learn. One has to go along the road with faith and courage."

I accept all of life's offerings to the end of my days, certain that there is no place or time in which God is not present. Faith has taught me to live without fear, to trust without doubt, and to ask with hope. For now, I do not need to know all the answers.

I will always have Zhubin in my past. I have him still, but in a different way. Surely, in due time, we will be together again – even closer than before.

My life now is simple yet rich. My world now is small, yet my heart is big. I can never be the same. Learning about the real essence of love became my spiritual remedy. This unconditional love is like a gentle, devoted mother who gives birth to all. To me, love is the highest, most exquisite and noble of God's creations. Love and faith was the way for my parents, then for Zhubin, and now is the way for me. At last I have come to the end of my winding road full of peaks and ravines, holding a handful of blossoms that I found along the way through darkness towards light.

"To see beauty in everything needs skill and practice."

My constant companion while I wrote in the garden.

Part 6
Wings of Words

Who Was Zhubin?

Zhubin is an ancient Persian name, meaning "a man who touches the sky".

Who was Zhubin? Really, who was this child that God put in my arms? How could he not only know, feel and understand all the things he said, but truly live them as well? How could someone gain as much depth of insight in such a short lifetime and under such tortured circumstances? What was the source of his strength? How was it possible? As I set out on my own path to seek and learn, I repeated these questions over and over to myself. Slowly, ever so slowly, I began to understand why he had been the person he was.

In time, Zhubin had discovered an escape hatch from the trap of his agony: in giving himself to God, he accepted all the hardship and the limitations with which his life had presented him. Extreme suffering and unwavering faith, his unconditional love for everyone and everything took him to another level of understanding. Somehow, he had touched something – or something had touched him. His abiding faith in God had allowed Zhubin to make a connection with Him. Zhubin's tolerance and measure of wisdom were God's gifts to him in return, a reward for his love and appreciation.

Zhubin was a simple and quiet boy, yet somehow he gained a rather deep understanding, which in turn brought him much peace. He became master of his emotions and thoughts. He owned his destiny and respected his life with dignity. His pain became his secret refuge – in a way, a source of blessing. I am certain of that. It was depth of faith that allowed Zhubin to bear his pain for as long as he did. Yes, there was sadness, but there was also joy. He appreciated life, enjoying everything about it, yet living in a very humble, quiet and gentle way.

Sharing many things with me, Zhubin taught me as much as he felt I could understand. "*Beauty comes out of pain. Blessings also come out of pain*" are words Zhubin often repeated to help me in difficult times. Zhubin taught me about faith, making me believe and trust in God. He taught me to live my life with all it has to offer. He taught me patience, courage and how to move on – how to look in the mirror, smile and say "Thank you, Life, you are *bellissima*!" Because of him, I look at every situation through eyes of love and know that, deep inside, all is well – all is right. By example, he taught me how to let go of my wounds and scars, my pain of guilt and regret, and how to be selfless. He showed me how to love myself and stand on my own two feet.

Above all, Zhubin taught me how to walk with the light.

Spending time alone in my quiet place, I still feel the pain of separation, but there is now a joy that comes hand in hand with pain, making it not just tolerable, but even rewarding.

Zhubin demonstrated how one can have a life filled with meaning, despite overwhelming challenges. He not only lived his life to the fullest extent possible, but also helped others. He came to believe that the Universe is not at all about cruelty, but about love. Zhubin's story is not about how he died, it is about how he lived.

Why did he come into my life, choosing me as his mother? I had nothing to offer him. I had no gift for him. What did I do to deserve this child? I have no answers to these questions. His coming to my life saved my soul when I did not even appreciate that I had one. I am forever thankful for him – and to him for his gifts. I believe Zhubin was touched by God. One thing I know for sure is that Zhubin came here for a purpose. He had a difficult life in which to accomplish much. He chose to reach towards a higher understanding of existence, knowing that his path had many hidden blessings. Like a shooting star, he was with me for but a moment, showing his light before disappearing.

So Zhubin's life came to mirror his name.

"To become a master, one has to have a life story. Trauma, loss, misunderstanding, grief, loneliness, are all a part of life. Accept it all – do not ask why. Face it all with courage and, most of all, with acceptance and unselfishness – it is the only way."

The Master Plan

Zhubin shared with me the notes that he compiled in his *"Master Plan"* red binder, which dealt with the issues we were going through. All his thoughts, observations and advice reflected our times together – both the good and the bad.

From an early age, Zhubin saw himself as my teacher. His understanding went well beyond his years of life, grasping what lay beyond our daily challenges, and he was clear about what we had to do to learn about and improve our time on earth.

Zhubin's words are straightforward because he believed in simplicity. But each of his teachings held a gem for me to discover. I found a healing quality in them. Touching hidden pockets of my consciousness, they are about the truth, the kind that comes from the heart and goes to the heart – and what goes to the heart is from God.

After posting some of Zhubin's words on the Zhubin Foundation's website, others were able to read them and many visitors provided feedback, remarking on the deep impression that his words had made. I have often been asked this question: how can someone so young have demonstrated such surprisingly mature depth and wisdom? I always answer that the time one spends on earth is not the measure of the soul's maturity.

In the following pages I have shared Zhubin's words about love, learning, growth, gratitude, God and the myriad other subjects that he discussed with me. In considering how best to present them to the reader, I was torn between leaving them "as is" in the chronology that he wrote them or instead grouping them by theme. After months of soul-searching, I concluded that imposing the prism of theming onto his original words would unavoidably change their spirit and eliminate any sense of how Zhubin's thinking and beliefs evolved. I have already written about Zhubin's childhood, and now I leave to the reader the best way in which to connect with, and what to extract from, his words – in the hope that they may gain their own sense of who Zhubin grew to become. Apart from adding titles drawn from the entries themselves, I have left his notes unvarnished, leaving the occasional repetitions with which he used to further explain and emphasize. Like me, each reader has their own "doors" into their individual true understanding, and so this repetition is merely an exercise at knocking on different doors of the same house.

Zhubin took me for a stroll through Wonderland: staying with me only for a while, he walked with me and then left. Well, until my time here is over I will continue to walk in this Wonderland, certain that Zhubin will be alongside guiding me all the way.

His words became wings of love, strong enough to carry my soul. At the end he left his wings wrapped around me and his footprints to follow.

"Learning never ends."

> **"God is infinitely smart.**
> **We can never be as smart as He is,**
> **not even in hundreds of millions of years.**
> **So we do not ask why.**
> **We accept it all.**
> **He is holding us all.**
> **He gives us love.**
> **He never leaves us alone.**
> **His love for us is endless.**
> **What God gives us,**
> **you see it everywhere.**
> **And that is love."**

Sheer intelligence

There is a sheer intelligence in this amazing Universe and it is super-duper advanced.

But our brains are not made to understand it.

Partner

God is a cool partner to have.

God is an awesome partner.

I am the parent bird

It's a beautiful day again.

Now, I am the parent bird and you are the baby. A parent bird has to teach its baby independence, confidence, and courage so the baby can fly. You are at that stage, and I'm having fun with you. Your heart has pain, but it beats with love, love within you and love from above.

I cannot emphasize enough how much love surrounds us. You have to – and I mean, have to – look up with your heart, open up with your heart. The focus should be on that. Otherwise, your heart is a closed box.

You need to learn constantly. There is an amazing beauty about balance, peace and being constant.

My desire is for you to become strong, like a rock. See rocks and imagine what kind of rock you want to be so that will guide you to what kind of person you will become. This is what I want to see for you: a rock.

A fledgling fell from its nest and for three days I watched it in my garden struggling to fly, its mother remaining close by constantly offering encouragement. Neither of them gave up. On the fourth day, with its feathers at last fully formed, it took flight with its mother. The lesson that I learned: against all odds, never give up or lose hope.

Simplicity like a child

Every day, wake up to total happiness and thanksgiving – otherwise, every minute is hard. When you give up, you put loss and sadness in it. So do what you can do – do what you must. Every day should be a celebration of life and being alive through little things.

Have a purposeful life. The question is what that purpose should be. It should be: to be humble, to be selfless and to be rich in simplicity like a child. That is the challenge.

True love and "being real" bring gifts. Try to move on. Seek peace. It will bring much fruit to your life.

Life is beautiful. Be calm and peaceful. Laughter brings angels closer to your heart and heaven. Have more of that.

Growth is what matters. Keep on growing and growing. You should feel things in your heart – feelings that are so beautiful come from the Light. Your heart tells you that. Exercise your heart. You can discipline it to choose between right and wrong feelings. There are so many little things that bring comfort, and that are so important. You will know the answer in your heart.

Going to a river

Be independent as to what you think, how you see yourself. Want something? Get it. You can. Let love guide you. *Always be real. Always be really truthful.*

Know yourself. There are many different ways to be helped. Open your eyes to broad horizons. You can learn "how". There is no secret way – it is for everyone. One needs to be open. It is like going to a river to collect water: some use just their hands, some a cup, some a bucket, and others jump into the river and merge with the ocean. You grow one step at a time. But be consistent. Take a bigger bite out of life and have fun with it.

Create harmony within. Your heart and head cannot lie to each other. Work on your faith. Enjoy the life you have; really enjoy it. Keep good cheer in your heart. You are not there yet but you can learn how to get onto the right track. So much to experience yet. Let everything go and work on your faith.

Ride this energy

A simple life sets you free, creating good strength. It is better to ride this energy. That's the biggest challenge. The rest will follow.

Rely on yourself

Have no expectation – it just brings you down. For guidance on the tasks that need to be done, depend on no one but instead rely on yourself and be there for all.

Be simple, but effective

I like to see you strong and active. Be that. Focus on the main issues. You know what they are.

Keep yourself busy with different projects, not only one thing. Nobody does only one thing. Always finish what you have started. It is good practice to follow up. Be simple, but effective. When you are busy, time goes by fast. So have all sorts of responsibilities in different areas, every day something new. And keep it up.

Look to the future and see what you can do. If you have a dream, pursue it. Be centred. Work on that.

Stick to the realities. It is important to listen and learn. I would love you to listen to your heart and trust it. It will take you to a different level. Just believe in yourself. Follow your heart.

Build a temple

One brick at a time builds a house. Life is not an event. You just dedicate the first brick towards the completion of the house, so you can build and live in a temple.

Be humble

Be humble and lovely. These two qualities are a heavenly combination – a unit of love, simplicity, and humility.

Start on the right footing

Know that with everything, each step should start on the right footing otherwise you cannot build on it. Real peace means you have made room in your heart and mind for God. Take care of this space.

Do not always ask for answers. Find questions. Find God. Let everything go, but work on your faith.

A centred person

I am writing to you with love and telling you what life is all about. There is something about being constant and having your environment constant. Be constant in mind, deeds, thoughts, intentions, and heart. This is how we are going to be centred. A holy person is centred and a centred person is constant – and that makes all the difference.

A constant, centred person loses all worldly attachments. This focus is what you need to have. So walk towards it. A true person, a real one, is like that.

Just be who you are – proud and humble. It should make no difference where you are or who you are with. People change bit by bit. This is the beauty of transformation. You think all these teachings are hard. Study them line by line and you will get there.

Be your own best friend

Enjoy what you have and don't feel guilty about having good things in your life. Be smart and brave and get more out of life. If you are scared and limit yourself, fear will control your heart – a good lesson for all.

People can be their own worst enemies. Be your own best friend. Choose well and treat yourself well. Life is about being who you are and being content about it. A content person is a peaceful person. Do you feel what I'm saying to you?

This is your homework

Everything is working out well, and I love talking to you. Slowly but surely, it seems that my writing and talking is helping you. It is good to ponder on everything every day. Constant learning. I know what I am saying. You have to trust me. Let's see. You are asking how you are doing. Little by little, let your confidence tell you what you have become. Reading and doing are wonderful. But above all is being. For example, if you read and read, and ponder on subjects that are neither here nor there, and miss the point, you are in search and yet in bed with curtains closed. These are examples for you to learn and see for yourself how much you have grown and changed.

Your unreal reality was real, so you lost your curiosity for Truth. Now you have become curious.

Intentions are so important. A good deed should be done for the sake of a good deed with no rewards, except contentment. This is the only way of giving and doing. It automatically moves you up. You are doing well, but go deep and deeper. This is your homework. Like you, I am getting deeper too.

Touch hearts

Are you tired and sad? I feel it. Taming a burning heart is very difficult. Welcome your challenges and grow from them. Become constant and content. This is real growth. I like to see you strong and active.

Go ahead; get charged with positive thoughts and feelings. Let go of your pain. I do not want you to be hurting so much.

You need to work on being constant and learn not to go from one side to another side so quickly. The process is slow. Do not lose your centre. See the little things and feel them. Go for walks and smell the flowers and memorize the laughter and smiles on the children's faces. It is good to hear laughter and be light-hearted. That is where God is.

Do not let anyone or anything take away from being centred. Talking is a good step. Logic and strategy is best.

Do not let your guard down with some people. Showing off and pretending is for fools. Also, do not let people, even those close to you, take advantage of you and your family. Those sorts of things hold you back. Let the tension out. Be as real and as constant as you can be at all times.

Keep your learning constant and, bit by bit, you will achieve your goal. Continue to be who you are, showing everyone what you are made of. Touch hearts – this way your life gets touched from above.

Jealousy

One day, all of us will learn that jealousy is pointless. Jealousy has no end. Jealousy can never yield compassion, generosity and love.

Stay away from jealous people – they can cause trouble and disappointment. Do not trust people at first sight. Let them prove themselves to you first.

Keep your conversation short, simple and positive. Too much talk is not healthy. Do not get stuck in the negative energy of the wrong people. See who they are and keep away from them. Jealousy builds a wall of negativity and it needs to be broken through with talk and logic. These things take away from allowing you to be centred.

Another piece of advice to you: If someone talks ill of anyone or anything, make sure that she or he is stopped. Do it right away with love, and help them to understand. With these matters, there is no tomorrow, only now. Honest words are powerful. Love honesty.

Simple people

Know that simple people should be allowed to just be. They are on their path. Their peace should not be stolen. Protect them.

Rest

I want you to go to bed and have a good sleep. Did you know that you can be at the peak of spirituality only when your body and mind have had enough rest? Always remember that. A body, mind and soul all have to be content in order to make all the connections.

Collecting the dots

It is very important for you to learn about first collecting the dots and then connecting them. See how connections work? Be part of it all. Feel it all. Get nearer to Him. Get nearer to yourself. I want you to see and understand the eternal aspect of our connection. That is when understanding and growth comes about – this way you will understand the Big Picture and the Master Plan.

An email to God

Many times I have said this: enjoy your life, really enjoy it, because life is a gift from God. Let that feeling be the most powerful one, not the feeling of loneliness and emptiness. I cannot tell you enough how much you need to strive for this because you will feel connected the most while in this state.

Do not worry about anything and anyone; just be aware of your actions, thoughts, words and heart. Know how to appreciate life and live it.

Protect yourself from bad feelings from others. As you get strong and gain self-confidence and peace, you will become more and more connected. Keep up the good work and smile every day. That would be like an email to God.

God is in happy moments

When there is negative energy, walk away from it. Do not spend time there or try to fix it. Being negative drains you without you realising it. You need to know how to fight it and get over it.

Life is all about simple things and simple pleasures. Everyone needs to be charged over and over with positive energy. Have a good time and laugh. That is beautiful. God is in happy moments and laughter.

Keep your heart full

If you listen to the things I have told you, you will understand. My sharing a lot with you does not mean as much as you learning and discovering things for yourself. When you have a tough task ahead or are learning to do something, I always say less and let you do it by yourself.

Are you disappointed? I have to smile because I know you are smart, despite how much I tease you.

Smile. Keep your heart full. Do not miss anything. Feel it all.

Do your housecleaning

I want to see you happy and strong so you can have energy and spunk for tomorrow, and another tomorrow. God is in the positive energy that you create.

I understand your low energy, but move, move, move! Up↑ Up↑ Up↑.

Go forward with your vision and see where it takes you. When the season is spring have spring in your heart. Bring your nervous energy lower and your spiritual energy higher.

Did you do your housecleaning within? Please finish it.

Go, go with full force ahead because you are getting a lot of energy from above. I know where you are headed. So keep on your positive track. Life is beautiful. Listen with your heart. Nobody can understand, imagine, or hear it for you. This life is just a dot in eternity. Don't let it pass you by. All the good feelings in the heart come from the Light. Thank life with your heart, smiles and words for the gifts it has given you.

You have to learn patience too – it is a godly way. By all means be high-energy, but your heart should beat slower: I want you to have real peace. I hope that you will.

A good teacher is a good learner

I want you to know...

1. That with young souls you should keep them safe and be ever watchful. Be positive and encourage the positive within them, without lectures. Love is the way.

2. Some people will always have a hard time being left alone and wallow in self-pity – it is their own creation of hell. Just accept it. Blindness is a sin and has its own punishment (false loneliness).

3. Some people need to learn more humility, and gratitude. Do not always try to go out of your way to please them. They should learn to move forward to join the crowd.

4. Some people have a need to control. You cannot change them. However, there will always be people who can touch you and whom you can touch. You can, in any circumstance, learn and teach. A good teacher is a good learner. More importantly, try to learn and practise patience and be detached.

Reflection

I have taken some time to reflect on our experiences. Always try to reflect on your day, conversations and experiences. Make it a habit. That is when your learning is at its highest.

While you are reflecting, think also about what you have to learn and where you want to be. Reflection brings all these things together, and helps to direct your path. So your lesson for this time is: Patience, living with positive energy, and reflection. Know that life experiences have to be.

Trust your heart

It is very important for me to repeat that you need to trust your heart. Your heart always speaks to you with logic. Pure emotion is just emotion. So when your heart speaks to you with reason, and sometimes tells you to do hard things, know that this is what you need to do. Understand the difference.

Move on with everything and move away from people and circumstances that tell you that you are a burden. Go to people who invite you with their hearts. Spend time with them. I have told you about jealous people. They would do anything and are empty. Watch out.

Try to relax about life a bit more. You have to use your head, and think matters through. But get rid of your nervous energy.

Listen to the heart. Listen to life itself. Have confidence and go forward. Take care of everything. You know in your heart what I mean. If you have something to say, say it. But say it with honesty and without anger. Just be yourself.

Listen to your heart

You need to take care not to worry too much. Again, learn to listen to your heart, guided by logic. Go with your own heart and vision. Have a plan to relax. When you have peace in your heart, you will grow so much more. Nature is so lovely and precious. Always learn from nature. There are many hidden beautiful lessons in nature. It is the biggest teacher. Always love nature and pay attention to all its details.

Enjoy your days and have fun. You know your homework and you know what I want.

Sensible! Sensible!

Be delicate in a strong way

We can always progress. Know what needs to thrive inside of you: beauty, colour, growth.

Remember your entire life is a journey – enjoy the moment. Change others, and let others change you. Be delicate in a strong way.

Do you feel it?

I want to tell you a few things that you need to know and to do:

1. watch out in a quiet way for everything and everyone;

2. keep your bond strong and stronger with your loved ones;

3. be real with yourself always and all the time;

4. always ask questions about why you are doing the things that you are doing; and

5. take care of yourself and do good things for yourself – be healthy and strong, this is your homework too.

There are so many blessings around us. I hope you feel and cherish them all. Do you feel it?

The garden in your heart

What can I say about today? What a wonderful, clean and peaceful day. The rain was fast and watered the plants. The birds came out and played. Are you enjoying the birds and the sunshine? Are you loving it all? I love it.

What a beautiful, blessed day. There is light when all of us are together. There is a band of love and a promise to hold us all together forever. People who are touched by God can feel it. This is what you have to celebrate. There is so much beauty around us, but your own heart has to tell you that.

Let me ask you: when you go to a beautiful garden, what comes to your mind? Growth, maturity, transformation? I love beautiful gardens, although it is high maintenance to create one. Details, details. The entire collection makes a beautiful garden, every corner with a purpose. Some flowers have to come out; some have to be rearranged. There's always grooming and cutting back and weeding. A garden may go to sleep in the fall, yet its roots remain alive and thriving. Then come the buds and the blossoms.

A garden is alive, like you and me. It is like human life and what it should be. Do you get the connection? The more love you give to the garden of life, the more you have given God love, and the more you have learned to love yourself as part of the Universe. That's what makes you simple and beautiful within, and then the garden in your heart is not just a garden. It becomes a temple, a sanctuary and a gift. This is where you show your faith and choose your own path. So, sit in your little garden, look at all the flowers and listen to what they say: enjoy life, stay in this moment. Only then can the garden in your heart work on its roots and in time blossom again. This is the beginning of its real fullness.

Life is a living garden and one has to celebrate life always. Add colourful flowers and enjoy them. This way you are painting the canvas of your life. Celebrate your life, mine and all life. Live your life with energy and love. Every corner in your heart should be beautiful. Every corner should be unique. Every corner should show love. Every corner should be touched by the spirit. We are alive and part of the Universe.

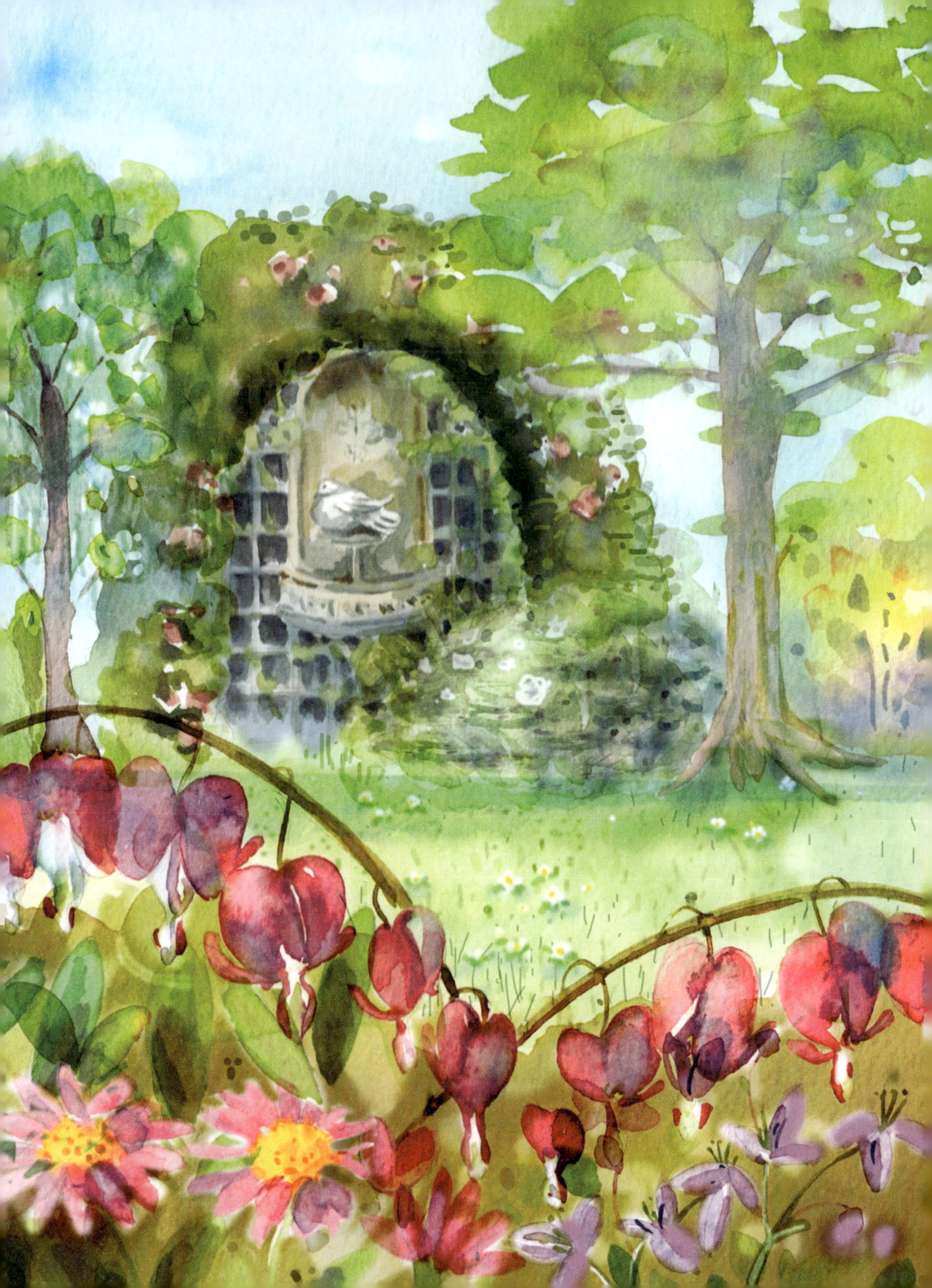

Life, what are you saying today?

First of all, have fun and enjoy moments. Be around people who are real and can teach you; each can teach you something different. For example, one teaches how to be in the moment; one can teach how to be introspective; one how to be humble; another can show you how to have passion and to create.

What do you want to teach? What do you want to leave behind? What kind of friend do you want to be? What kind of priorities do you have? Know what is most important at any given moment. Sometimes you need to freeze the time and go where others are. Take a deep breath every day and say to yourself: "Life, what are you saying today?"

All will come to you bit by bit, like a jigsaw puzzle. See what beauty is more special than other beauties. The progress, the growth, and your heart know this too.

A garden is ever-changing and always in need of this or that because it is alive. So are you. Enjoy and enjoy. All is well. Have a beautiful day, always. This life is but a blink of an eye. Practise patience.

A lost moment is a lost opportunity

It is another wonderful day, what a joy! What an awesome crazy life!

Don't stay in the past so much. If you were driving and your head was turned around, you would have a fatal accident. Keep your eyes looking towards where you want to go. A lost moment is a lost opportunity. Set goals for yourself and see what you want to accomplish.

Make an "awareness" to-do list. With your eyes to the future and looking ahead, you will get it done. This is a very important habit. Remember, when you are aware there will automatically be a light showing you the way.

Throw away your empty expectations

I had a surprise call from an old friend. Friends are so wonderful to have. Anything real is worth having – real friendship, real happiness, real gratitude, real feelings and, above all, real honesty with oneself and others. This gives a person a real sense of being centred.

So, remember that when your goals are real your efforts should be enjoyable and not desperate. Everyone should learn that. As far as I am concerned, the energy does not stop. There needs to be lots of planning, learning and growing. You have to know that and picture it. The life that we were meant to have, we must live. The rest follows. Listen to the messages in your head and heart.

Please throw away your empty expectations and agendas because they are negative and stop you from growing and life. I mean, have peace of mind. Take notice of it all. See how simple life should be and see how simplicity brings joy and beauty to hearts and homes. Strength in every aspect is what matters. Strength gives you courage.

Have fun with your life, enjoy it. You have to be in the moment and make memories. Take time for the family. It is holy on its own. Growing up is not easy. Life has so many paths.

Knowing is power. Remember we are all connected in so many ways. Take care to see your part in it. I want you to see and understand the eternal aspect and connection. Take it all in.

Listen to the good messages

Love and love is the only answer, yet at the same time be aware of jealousy, competition and negativity. Loving does not mean being passive. Know that.

You must have peace in your heart, love for others, lovely, cute home, nice clothes, healthy body and, yes, fun and fun. Go above and beyond. That means changing for the better. Listen to the good messages in your heart and head, and know good brings good.

I love it when everyone is participating together, and giving energy to each other. Share your life.

A wonderful bus driver

I cannot tell you how much you should always be aware of your surroundings and the people around you.

Listen:

1. People profess love and some actually do love, but the eyes of jealousy grow knives on hands. Watch out for that. They will stab you where it hurts the most. Talking and teaching is good, but preventing is better.

2. Some love but are not problem-solvers, and in the end, have huge issues with jealousy and ego.

3. Some people have the opportunity to join in and partake, but their envy blinds their hearts. You cannot fight that. Just be aware of it and stay away. Jealousy is destructive. Keep your cool. Life is meant to be lived simply. Spirituality brings simplicity. People need only to listen to their heads, not to their egos.

4. Some are envious because their souls are not creative. People like that die with all their good intentions buried in their hearts. Their eyes cannot be forced open.

5. Some people grow slower than others. Some need a little push. Transform your soul and heart. I can tell you that real transformation brings peace. And remember that love does not hurt. So, if you get hurt by a loved one, the answer is to pray for them while giving your attention and energy to someone else.

6. Shame on those people who treat others badly. They should know better. Jealousy rules, drives, and in the end, it destroys. Lovely people are full of love and not jealousy. Once people learn gratitude their qualities will blossom. Love them all.

7. Be like a wonderful bus driver: get to your destination on time and stop; while at a stop sign, please observe; let in the right passengers and let the rest out.

Go with the flow and not against it

Always be aware and alert. Awareness is a holy quality. Your ideas in your heart and head, whatever they are, keep them sharp and focused.

See how powerful are connections between people when there is love and real purity. Forget what everyone says. Keep everything in your life pure, simple and beautiful.

When you grow and become much stronger, you will stay focused on taking care of your issues and responsibilities. As everything in nature is connected, so is everything about us as human beings. So, take care of your soul, your heart, your body, your hair, your clothes, your beauty, your home, your little garden, your relationships, and above all, the understanding of what you need to have.

Everybody needs to experience different learning and achievements, but we need to be aware of it all. Do you understand? How long have I been telling you to take life easy! You have to go with the flow and not against it.

The choice is ours

Did you know that the world can be destroyed for two reasons? Pride and jealousy. Protect yourself by being who you are and do not be surprised by people's comments or behaviour. Also, do not stay attached to physical things that weigh you down. Do not forget, ego is in all of us, so we either have to fight it ourselves or we'll be consumed by it. The choice is ours. I want you to continue to be centred and focused.

Be aware of others' breathing

I have always said be prepared financially, mentally, spiritually, emotionally for unexpected events. Life has many turns. Slow down and be successful. What matters most is the end result and I hope we always remember that.

If you keep your mind quiet and let your heart speak, you will know what to do. It is better for you to learn and practise to listen to your heart. That in itself is very, very important.

Enjoy little things in life, especially when you are low. There are no repeats. Take time to breathe and be aware of others' breathing. In this way, you won't take anything for granted.

Also know that drawing the line and changing a relationship is okay as long as there is no arrogance in doing so. There is nothing wrong with communicating feelings, but do it without pride. Be strong and disciplined about it; be positive and productive always.

One minute of regret is a huge loss

I hope you can feel the energy in the air and the love that surrounds you. The real beauty of life is love. I know that you will eventually understand all that I say. I want your heart always to be a home of love. For this to happen fully is to have a love of life, and to see the Big Picture. This is just the beginning. Hold on to, and enjoy, one another.

I am glad you are working in your heart's garden. Guard it: I don't want anyone to damage it. Watch out not to damage it yourself through neglect or cutting it back too much. So be happy: the life that we have we must live and that is that. Do good for each other and for yourself, and enjoy your life. One minute of regret is a huge loss because that one minute could have been spent in love and service.

Enjoy all the people that come your way and let them enjoy you. This is a very good way for you to serve others in ways different than you are now. All these exchanges make love stronger, and actions true and real.

Finish all the garden's designing and planning within. Your blessings will be numerous.

Real smiles

I feel that your priorities need to be set a bit better.

Take life easier. Sometimes, when you don't give love and create the peace that you should, you may not receive it. One goes hand in hand with the other. Give and receive. This is when desperation leaves the picture.

Fill your heart and soul with moments, and live each day moment by moment.

Finish all your tasks. It is very satisfying and fulfilling.

Go forth and have a wonderful life. Real smiles bring you steps closer to God and heaven.

When a teacher talks

I hope that you think about some of the things I have said and keep some of the advice. A true and honest heart is priceless. It brings energy and attracts good. I know you know what I mean. Try to understand deeply what your motivations are.

As you grow, you will learn more. When a teacher talks, the student does not get hurt or upset but listens so she or he can grow. Reach outside of yourself. Kill the empty needs and weaknesses. Everything you learn and do, or don't learn and don't do, your strengths and weaknesses all go with you to the afterlife in one package. This is true for everyone.

Look for the things that are in your heart and need to be there. Hold on to that. As you are being watched and helping others in their journeys, remember that it is your blessing. Have a positive life and outlook. Thanks for listening.

Wisdom

How many tough times do we have to go through in order to appreciate life, friendships and love? Sometimes by going through pain, we become fragile, dependent and weak. This is a chance for others to give a helping hand to the vulnerable, not step on them. You have to watch for the fragile ones in a quiet way. Love alone is no longer the answer. Wisdom is.

Even the crows do their best

Always think big – picture big – and want big. Get away from small thoughts and actions. This way you go for the best things in life and not the mediocre ones.

Listen to your heart. You are to move on and do all the work that you need to do with your life, your home. This is what living people do – and you are living! Put your energy and heart into it!

Have you noticed that every flower and every leaf has a unique beauty and talent of its own, and that is why they are so pretty? Learn from nature always. Even the crows do their best for themselves: they work to get what they need; they protect each other and remain loyal to one another; they also have fun and collect odd items.

Add all the flowers that are unusual to your heart's garden. Go ahead, have fun with the flowers. I want you to take care of everything and have a plan for the future. Find in your heart a true understanding of life.

Even these dogs know more

Busy day. I am glad we had such a wonderful day shopping for me yesterday. You look good when you act like a kid. Life should be greeted as a special day, a meaningful day, every day. Love it all and have fun with it.

Our dogs are so good for you. Even these dogs know more about how to enjoy life than most people on earth. So, what I am telling you is that you should celebrate your life through good and bad, aware that one does not happen without the other. Everything has two sides. We wish for this and that. It is good to wish as long as it is done with patience and a thankful heart at that moment. Let go of the pain and let your eyes be set in the future.

Don't let anybody take away the excitement and beauty of your special days. See how everything works and what happens with the little things in life. Be like a kid and have fun.

Dignity

As I have told you before, think about your issues with others. If the moment comes that you can talk, take the opportunity to clear the air and offer your understanding. Do it with gentleness but be clear and firm. However, remember when people talk, sometimes there is teaching in what they have to say. The right thing to do is to listen and accept what is said, when it is said, what is given, and how much is given. Then, it is up to us to take what we want from the conversation and to move forward. Everybody has to work on issues until they are resolved.

It is very important to do the right thing without expecting any results. Life never should be thrown out with negativities. Words have to be spoken from the heart and from the truth. This is what dignity means.

The root of the problem

All of us should be connected and be part of the Bigger Picture. I like the way you are dealing with our challenges and issues. It takes time and a strong will, but they will be resolved with lots of growing, lots of movement, lots of letting go. I am saying this because the root of the problem is both the detachment that you need and the attachment that you have. I mean that you need to be aware of what you are holding on to. It is good to set boundaries.

Do what is right

I have always hoped for real understanding, compassion, wisdom and selflessness. Of course, we know that is not for all. Taking it all, feeling sorry for ourselves, thinking no one is there for us is not being wise. People's ideas will not change unless they get blessed with good and deep understanding. The important thing is that we learn and do what is right.

The light of being real

Sometimes in life we get into situations that are difficult and this is where the learning begins: how we learn; what comes of it; what we take from it; and what we give back. It sets the tone for the quality of life and the path ahead. So, as time goes by and you move forward, you learn more and more and your learning becomes deeper. This is because you seek out and try to face your problems, your struggles and issues. We are mentally fragile even though we think that we are strong and tough. Being tough and strong is about being at our best or at least trying to do our best in the worst situations.

It is very important for you to realize that covering up is not the way to cope with conditions. It is a bad idea. It holds you back from being detached, which is really beautiful as it will also affect the people around you. This is not as easy as it sounds. It takes hard work and extreme awareness.

You have started the work. Just be real to yourself and others around you. The light that I am talking about is the light of being real.

The heart should see beauty

Enjoy the weather, cold or warm, because, like life, they exist together and the difference between them brings appreciation. Love your life. Enjoy it. Life should be exciting at all times. Let it be the celebration it should be. Moment by moment, moment after moment, the heart should see beauty. Love it and live it. Energy comes from all of these.

Rewind the memory

I feel that sometimes it is special to have physical mementos from the places that have touched you. Having them rewinds the memory and you re-experience the experience – refresh the memory. It is more joy for the soul.

Spirit of love

What a beautiful day it was yesterday. Friends came to our home and brought a lot of spirit with them. When people bring the spirit of love, let them know how much you appreciate it. This is a wonderful opportunity to encourage people to do more – and thanking them for their efforts gives them energy to do more.

Life is a puzzle

Life is a puzzle and solving it is the journey. Go through your journey with curiosity, interest and passion. Always think and be aware of how you are spending your life. If you are not living it, you are wasting it. Do not be a zombie. Be focused and grounded. Give energy to others.

Change takes a lifetime

A short note for you.

Be smart and correct. Practise it. It is a wise thing to do. Stay calm, stay cool, and be effective. Be positive and warm. Communicate correctly. Detach and take the high ground. Do not go to the line of fire so you get shot at, but take your stand in a polite way. Also know that sometimes you lead and sometimes you are led. Change does not come by just saying certain words. Remember that change takes a lifetime. Live your life in a curious as well as in a trusting way. Share the love and trust, and you will also attract love.

Patience is love

When people give you energy and love, remember you also give back the same energy and love – this is wonderful bonding.

Be patient with all. Patience is love. But also have patience with yourself. As long as we are alive, we have something to work on. There is no limit to how much we can grow and learn. If we do not grow, the soul is dead.

Remember that life is a puzzle and solving it does not mean it is complicated. So love it and relax. Enjoy your life and feel it. Feel happy, have fun, make yourself beautiful inside and out. Remember, we are all precious.

Renewal

Enjoy the sun, the blue sky. The birds are making their nests. It is springtime, which means renewal. So do your gardening, go shopping, and make your home pretty. Most importantly, do these things with love – it's good for the soul. When you do something that you love, when you make your home beautiful and when you cook lovely food, you are saying "thank you" to God. Your heart is happy – simple pleasures!

Do you understand what I am saying?

Family and friends benefit from this, too. Love, eat, share, hug, laugh, listen, understand, smell, see, feel, enjoy, and be, be, and be. I want you to concentrate on that so when the unexpected happens, you will be glad that you did. What I want for you is this understanding.

Make it all happen. Get the Big Picture. I want you to be happy, confident, spiritual, classy and amazing. Always be elegant. Throw away anything that is in your heart but does not belong there. Give away anything that is in your home and closet that is not used. Always be about renewal: "Out with the old and in with the new," as they say.

An instrument to all who seek you

Remember, do not fuss with the ones who are not ready to walk the walk. They need to learn to walk on their own legs. They will be doing themselves a favour by realizing that they have legs and they can stand on them and even walk with them. Love them, but it is not necessary to make a fuss.

When things go wrong, people get down and can be damaging to others – never knowing how much. Be careful, but be loving to them and consistent. Be a friend. Know how to be one to all who seek you out. Know who your friends are. Share yourself and be an instrument to all who seek you.

A direct line to God

You can work and learn about life's spirit. Do not worry about not understanding and being confused. You have to be confused before you can have understanding. There is a lot to learn, step by step. This is why I have been talking a lot about puzzles. Have fun with it, too. At least, this is what you should do instead of worrying. Focus is all you need. It will take you there.

The return journey home, the journey to the angels, the whole thing that I see is a "revolutionary evolution". Do you understand what I mean?

There is a lot to say, and the best way to say it is in the form of a puzzle because puzzles give out information bit by bit. You hear a lot. Your heart tries to listen as well. This is a gift, so try to do and listen with your heart. Everyone has a direct line to God. He is with us every step of the way.

No exaggeration

When emotions are high that is when the spirit talks to you, and that is when you have to pay attention to your heart to find out what is important. Learning comes from there.

No exaggeration: be yourself, without drama and intensity, as sometimes excitement or emotions cause exaggeration.

Community

Enjoy each other and everyone, because with each other we are blessed – and the blessed are the ones who see their community and become part of it.

Mirror

Life holds a mirror to everyone in which the true self is revealed. People cannot hide either their ugliness or others' beauty.

All the weeds must stay behind

I know you have been anxious, but being patient and dealing with issues is a good way to grow. Let your heart be filled with love and joy:

1. Do not let others disturb your peace and sense of security.

2. When the time is right and you get a chance to talk to someone, you need to do so, but stay focused and do not let them drive the conversation.

3. Be wise and respectful – try to put everything in the right perspective.

4. Do not be confused and do not talk with a tone as if you are the only one who is right.

5. Always state the facts – remind others of what they have done and said.

6. Let them know how they made you feel and give them the same chance, as well.

7. Talk and listen with love.

8. Teach and remind gently.

9. Do not worry – spend time and energy on your soul.

10. Do be careful with all.

11. Talk with whomever you need to.

12. Do not leave unfinished business – all the weeds must stay behind.

Be straight

Life is full of challenges and problems until you become like a rock: strong and tough. Always be correct. When thoughts come to your mind, study them and pay attention to the important ones. Always talk with love and honesty – be straight.

No muddy water

No muddy water should be left behind. Muddy water needs to be cleaned. Throw away negative thoughts. Stay in the moment. Do good things for yourself – it's very important. You should have joy in your life.

Just close your eyes

So beautiful! What a wonderful day and what a wonderful life! Celebrate your life, my life and everything – pure thoughts and feelings, and nothing but love in your heart. When you are among chosen and true friends, they also know that you are their true and chosen friend. It is very important for you to surround yourself with positive energy and positive people. I know that this is not a perfect world in which we live, but just close your eyes and let go: its peace and serenity are important.

Let everyone come to your heart

Look at the goodness in everyone in a real way so everybody can feel the love. Let everyone come to your heart. It is beautiful when people are joined and help each other in a compassionate way.

The word is "if"

The reason people get stuck in life is because they feel sorry for themselves – too weak to change, they blame others as it is easier to do so. However, we all have a chance to change. Let's hope for that.

Be aware that some are very insecure and jealous, superficially nice but in truth extremely jealous, wanting to cause divisions between people to be controlling and on top of everything. Like a huge monster that gets bigger as time goes by (big egos), they could grow wings, becoming like flying dragons that bring misery to themselves, their family and to whomever is around them. With no soul, they suck away everything good. Even if they do good, their agenda is not. People with negative agendas have a hole in their hearts. The deeper the agenda, the deeper the hole is. It is a sad story, but if they allow it, the Light begins the change in them. The word is *if*. Changing is hard, but *if* they are willing, they can find out how to change. They need to learn how to be blessed by being loving and caring. They can make it happen.

Let go of hate

People have to let go of hate before they can feel love.

Cherry tree

Don't ever discount relationships. They are so intertwined. There is a bonding, like roots to soil.

Look at a fruit tree, for example a cherry tree. If not for the soil, the tree would not grow. If it were not for the tree, there would be an empty dead space. Together the two produce flowers, fruit and shelter. Do you know how many birds rest on the branches? How many different birds and animals eat the fruit? How many insects love and enjoy and need the branches? There is also the beauty of the tree for the pleasure of our eyes. There is a lot more, but you can't understand. Everything has a thousand connections and connections are what make you. The point is for you not to miss anything in your life. Enjoy the time and bond. All is beautiful.

A process for your soul

Life means changes. Change in the right way and direction means growth and success. Change is not easy and sometimes we do not ask for it, but it refines us and make us wiser and stronger. When changes come your way, I know you will embrace them and grow even more from them.

When you have a hard time with an issue, do not keep it to yourself. Get to the bottom of it. Bring it up bit by bit and air it out. You need to do that. This is a process for your soul. If you are practical and wise, you will deal with the issues and see results. You need to pay attention to what matters.

All these situations begin with you and end with you. Only you choose. Think of life as a big and exotic garden. You can pick flowers, but only a few. Choose carefully what you want to pick and ask yourself why you chose what you have. This is a good way of guiding yourself.

Not a flying carpet

You are not a flying carpet that people can ride to go places. You are only a carpet if you choose to be one, and people can sit on you to visit only if you ask them. So, the control is in your hands. Things are not going to change if you do not change them. Be good to yourself.

Always be willing to take the first step

Today I want to share a few thoughts with you.

Be wise, always correct.

It is totally essential to learn to be gentle and strong; to be compassionate and also passionate. And tough. Why not? Practise this very fine balance. Consistent learning is a must for all. Learn this and you will be a true leader.

Don't be intense. Being strong does not mean being intense. Find new ways of thinking, and new energy. Build on that. You have to be super-smart but don't be reckless when hard times come. Have constructive thoughts and actions. Situations can be solved with talks. Silence means death – death of self and death of trust. Communication in the right way is gold.

Remember that everything in a relationship with family or friends has three sides: your side, the other side, and the correct side.

Remember as well that you will be fine when you do the correct thing. This is true for everything. You should be open to discussions in a gentle and correct way with everyone. This does not mean that you are there to be stepped on. Talk with gentleness, without malice, and always correct. Remember that. If you don't, the dynamic with family and friends will go downhill and you will miss a lot and others will miss it too. This is important, otherwise you will lose your chance to be effective.

So,
> find a way to be correct;
> find a way to be gentle and firm;
> find a way to be a leader and team player – you can do it, and this way you will help others too;
> always be willing to take the first step;
> know when to draw the line – and when you draw it, do so correctly;
> keep your distance and yet be close; and
> try to take a step towards all – doing so does not mean selling out but being yourself in a higher way.

Now

We can all learn not just from each other, but even from our dogs: loyalty, honesty, protectiveness, love, curiosity, appreciation, being in the moment, playfulness, and being ever ready for more food. For them, everything is about *now*.

What does love mean?

Not understanding what love is about, not receiving it, not feeling it is like being in prison. Some love but it is in a possessive way. Pure love does not have ownership.

What does love mean? Love means wanting more for others. That is true love.

The key

Life is not perfect and it is not supposed to be.

Learn to simplify the issues, not complicate them. Just let everything penetrate into your skin. Simplicity in every matter solves everything.

The key to making your life simpler is putting and keeping your focus where you have to and should. When people get to understand this, they are surprised how simple everything could be and how complicated they make it.

Do give but do it right

Don't feel that all the time you have to give away what you love. That is not generosity. Also, don't let small people keep you down and greedy people take advantage of you. Do be aware not to trust at face value.

Compassion does not always mean being soft. Don't always give and give to people who do not give back. Be generous with your time and money. Make a difference in others' lives. Do give but do it right, otherwise it is a never-ending story. Do you understand what I am saying?

Think with your heart

1. Don't feel that you always have to dive into the deep end of the pool – you can and you should also play in the shallow end.

2. Don't always watch where you are walking or you will miss seeing the beautiful sky.

3. Don't keep your gaze on the sky all the time or else you will miss the earth that grounds you.

4. Let go of obsessions and phobias – they imprison you and send negative energy to the people around you.

5. Don't ever forget that being a lady, a true, wise and elegant lady, is everything. This is a role that you were born to play, so play it well. Elegance always means first class and it has nothing to do with money.

6. Think with your heart. Do not go and do things for others that you do not want to do. Do them only if you want to. Just remember that what

you give might not be appreciated or understood. But set yourself free and keep letting go.

The waste of life

Hell is being alone. It is not good to be alone in heart and soul.

Keep loving, keep giving, keep making, keep soothing, keep feeling, keep teaching, keep learning, keep listening then listen even more. Be in the moment and live your life to the fullest. If you don't appreciate the sun and stay inside all the time, then you will be really miserable and feel sorry. The waste of life is the worst waste.

Eyes on a goal

As far as challenges go, have courage to fix them. This is the only way. One result might not be the one you want, and another result might be just the one you want. But the results that matter in the long run will be good. You have to keep your eyes on a goal and let it guide you as you walk towards it.

Trust yourself

Do not change because of others but change if you think you should. We all are different and that is wonderful. If we were all the same, we could not get anywhere in this world. Trust yourself.

Use your map

The busier we are, the more blessed we are. You have to learn so many skills in order to progress. Each one of us has a different gift that determines what we become. Be mindful and see what you are good at, what qualities and gifts you have. Make a list of all your gifts – make sure you are honest. This will give you a map of your mission and responsibilities. If you focus on real issues and ground yourself, you will know what to do. So use your map.

Life is a beautiful concept

I have been watching and thinking how amazing life is, even for me. In general, day-to-day headaches are actually blessings: they help us learn and grow.

Life is a beautiful concept and, yes, it is a circle. Take a deep breath and move on. Keep your eyes focused on what it is that needs to be done. Have fun and cherish the ride, family and friends. Enjoy your strength but remember, forgiveness of others will bring blessings both for the forgiven and for the forgiver. By forgiving, you bless people more than you know.

Be in tune with yourself

Love your talents and share them with others. Search for ways to help out and be of service to others. Feel and see with your heart. Something will come your way. You will know what you need to do and you will also know when to do it. When something is wished out of absolute pure love and selflessness, you will get it. Life will put you in the right place. However, you have to be in tune with yourself to feel it.

Little moments

I hope you are enjoying the sunshine and the blue sky. The dogs are happy. The birds are happy. Even the crows are happy. I am happy that we are together and doing different things with each other and connecting in different ways. This is really beautiful. Through little moments every day should be a celebration of life and being alive.

I love our teamwork together.

I know you are guiding yourself and learning more on your own. If you want some advice from me, this is it: Rely on yourself for guidance on the tasks that need to be done and learnt. Have fun with all your growing. Be honest with yourself – really, really, really. This and all the things that I am talking about is the progress that will be taking place bit by bit, and step by baby step. Your biggest asset is the knowledge that you must still continue to grow. Remember that true and real people are those who learn the true and real lessons and make the real difference. Hold on to these words and let them guide you.

Enjoy your life, live your moments and be with others. Little moments mean more than anything. Hold on to what you really have. The rest is meaningless.

Make memories!

Many, many times I have said: make memories! Being together is the most precious thing in the world and most people don't realize it. Keep all your memories as that is what makes a difference in our lives. So be in the moment and make sure that you treasure it all. Enjoy your time with family and love them in every moment – when we are together we are all blessed. Spending time with loved ones is a great gift.

Eat popcorn

Peace. Have it in your heart. A peaceful heart brings harmony within. I think this is the easiest way to live. But reaching it takes discipline.

Spend your time having fun and making memories. Be in the mood for giving and taking. Go out. Do things. Enjoy your time. Have fun in your way and feel the energy. Live and live. Make songs. Make cookies. Make crafts, smile, hug. And yes, be crazy. Walk, go to movies, eat popcorn. Not everything should be serious – but do be serious about being in the moment.

Go and see; go and do; go and learn. Be focused. Do not put pressure on yourself. Be relaxed. Look for real joy in your days. Make it happen.

Love is patience, as I said before.

No shortcuts

I am sitting here, seeing everything and smiling regardless. I know your life is hard and not perfect. I know that you are aware that we all have some imperfections to work with. But an imperfect life is a perfect life, since it is its imperfections that drive us to perfection. Just ponder on that. Saying this does not mean you should be in constant pain.

Ask yourself the right questions and the right answers will come to your heart. There are always several options. Choose the one that gives you the most permanent results. Once you decide, then go for it and do not look back. You have to stick to it and make it last. No shortcuts. Think about it.

When you are in a tough spot and cannot find solutions, take the time to think and make some sort of decision. You will see results. Ask yourself, where do you want to be – where do you want to be in the future in a real way? Get the picture in your head and make it as perfect as you can. Then walk towards it. It is doable, I promise.

Easy life is an illusion

This is something that I really want you to understand.

When the unexpected happens: do not assume; stay strong and be positive; be correct. If you play your cards right, you will get a lot done in your life.

Stay consistent – and that means being real. No highs or lows – constant always. Through it all, stay optimistic.

Having an easy life is an illusion. There is a lot to learn and to do and to talk about.

If we choose, our pains can become a source of growth and learning. Life is a journey. We all have come a long way and we all have to go a long way still. We all do. There is no end. This is what eternity means.

Go to the Big Picture

Know that things will happen to us to make us stronger. Do not spend time thinking about little things – go to the Big Picture instead. Do not complain. Be thankful. Just learn, serve, and receive.

There is much to be said, much more to let go of, and much more to forget. Life is good to everyone who takes care of herself or himself and his or her learning. Keep the important relationships on track. See what you can do to add more joy to your life and to others.

Ride them like waves

Always take your positive energy and spread it. Harmony within; harmony without. Balance. Remember it.

Life has its ups and downs. Ride them like waves. Yes, for some the downs are deeper than for others. You should understand that. But, in fact, many downs are steps up – it just depends on attitude. Have courage. Life is about moving forward: movement alone does not mean progress – moving forward does. Where do you find this courage? By showing yourself love and doing it all the time. Self-love means appreciation for what needs to happen within you to make you whole and to keep you there. Loving yourself = whole person = being holy. Always connect with yourself.

Relax but be thoughtful and wise. Sometimes it is hard to see the blessings in the difficult times. Just have faith. Also know you have a lot of help. It has been said: "To whom much is given, much is expected." Right? So play the game of life like chess, and focus on patience.

Like an ant

Always be ready for the unexpected. Being careful is a good thing. Be like an ant who is preparing for winter. I like that. Do not worry about life. Life is good.

Be humble in a real way

What a hectic life we all have! A lot has happened, and more will happen yet. We should always be on guard.

Life should not be about loss, sorrow, or loneliness. Whether we like it or not, it has a lot of turns but it is important to turn with life in a correct and faithful way. This means you have to remember the Big Picture and work around it. Your heart will always tell you how to go forward, through the turns and curves. Trust that.

Don't forget that when you go lower you will actually become higher. So be humble in a real way.

Bending

Bending is learning humility. Humility is a great quality.

Sunny days

What a beautiful sunny day! Sunny days are the best days. Have a sunny day every day.

See what you should see. Hear what is pleasing to your soul. Do what your heart tells you and plan good things ahead. Enjoy your gifts and blessings. Sit down, rest your legs, connect with your soul and heart, then smile and say to yourself: "Life is good." Have lots and lots of smiles.

Let life amaze you

Life is wonderful. Do not have a heavy heart.

Think of it this way. Anywhere you go, you have a purpose and a mission. Think of your life as a "to do" list. Catch your breath and let life amaze you. You can do this only when your heart is full of positive energy. Keep positive by replacing bad thoughts with good ones. Life is a long road and you have to always look ahead with excited eyes. The minute you see and feel the past, you have lost an opportunity. So enjoy your life and all its opportunities.

"Could" must always be replaced by "Can"

Go deep. See how amazing it all is. "Could" must always be replaced by "Can". Do the things that I told you. Go deeper within and be real with every detail. No cutting back. When you go deeper, you know. Just meditate on it.

Feel the power of life

I love you. Happy Birthday. Keep your heart joyful and do not be heavy. Remember that I told you where to put your energy. Do not spend so much time brewing over pain and frustration. When you are like this the energy of the house and everyone around you goes down. You are so sensitive when your energy level is low, and that makes you like a sponge. Be a rock instead. You can do it – I know it is difficult, but the more your energy is positive the more you can make a difference in life.

Keep your eyes ahead to where you are going and enjoy your life and the simple pleasures as you are on your path. As soon as you feel vulnerable, that is when you have to look ahead and find a way out.

Smile every day in front of the mirror and let that be your energy. Make every day special and full. Take care of your heart. Enjoy it all and feel the power of life itself.

Lose yourself in others

Keep your heart, thoughts and your words in harmony with each other. Don't dwell too much on yourself, instead lose yourself in others. Please be disciplined and channel your energy.

Stretching your faith

Being thankful every day brings blessings. You can touch so many hearts without knowing it yourself. When you enjoy your life, your home, family and friends and nature, you are stretching your faith big time. Remember that.

Expect the unexpected

Expect the unexpected and put your energy into the now and with people that are important to you. This is a big must for you and your energies should go from missing things to cherishing your life and the people around you now. Now and now, present and present.

Happiness is everything. Have a wonderful life and keep your smiles.

The Big Timeline

Your progress is immense. What you need to concentrate on are feelings. Take a deep breath and let the energy flow within you. Look at the Big Picture and the Big Timeline. Our timeline in the midst of everything is like a grain of sand in an ocean. Know your tasks, and be ready for challenging ones. Concentrate on yourself and let your head work on important things.

Have the right knowledge to move forward and create.

Pain can take us to a different realm. It can also break us.

Coincidence

Nothing is coincidence; there is a reason for everything. We are so connected to each other in endless ways.

Spirit voice

Among the things that you have to know and learn is the quiet voice that comes to your heart and head. It is called the "spirit voice" and is quiet because it comes to those who are truly at peace or really seek peace. Listen to this voice and see what it brings to you.

Play the card

To anyone who has a generous heart, life will be generous. Be a great comfort and a source of help to others in their journey. Know when to ask for help and when to give help. Be in touch and keep in touch. Stay on top of it all. Play the role. Play the card. And play the part that has been given to you.

Gold

Wisdom is gold. Love is gold. Patience is gold. And so being very, very, very, very good to yourself is also gold.

No end to learning

There is a transition that takes us to a different level so we always work to progress from it. Being stationary is bad – it is death.

Remember, there is no end to learning: we go from phase to phase; higher and higher; deeper and deeper. And that is what eternity means.

A grain of sand

If we were to put together all the knowledge of human beings from the beginning until now, it would not be even a grain of sand in this vast Universe.

As far as it goes, the energy of the Universe does not stop. We are all a part of life and a part of this Universe forever.

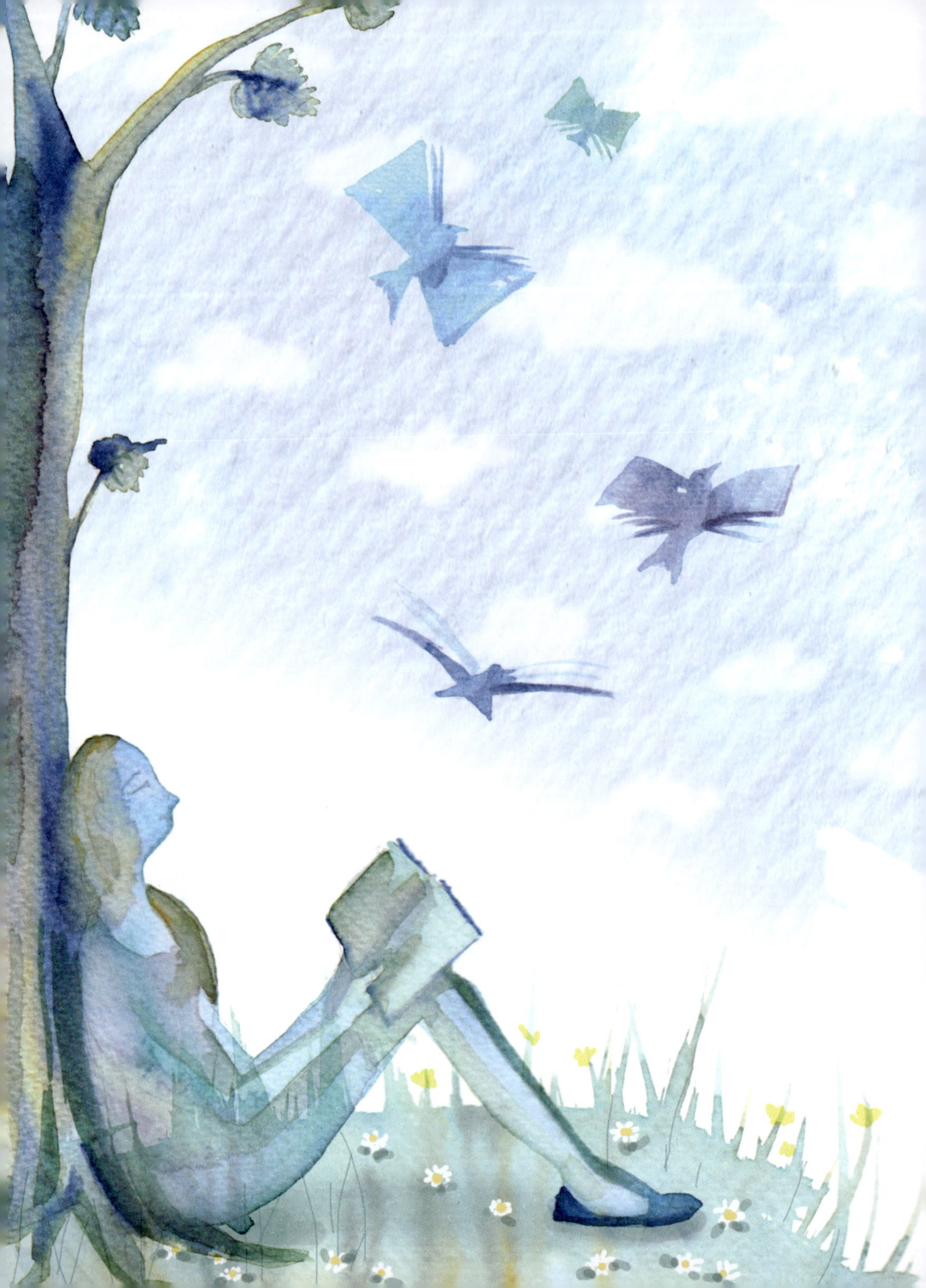

Part 7
A Parting Gift

Farewell

How can a child find the courage and compassion to ask his mother for her blessing and understanding when he must end his life? I had never heard of such a thing. For countless nights and days my thoughts had circled, returning to the reasons for Zhubin's decision and what had led him to broach it with me. He had been very aware of how carefully I was watching him from then on. With all my attention focused on him, hadn't he known I would have done everything in my power to stop him? I now realize that Zhubin had not wanted to leave behind any unfinished business or *"muddy water"* as he used to call it.

Thinking back to our last evening together, it had been fun and filled with his jokes. He had seemed so relaxed and at ease that I failed to feel or sense anything out of the ordinary. How could he have been like that, managing to appear so much in control, calm, even cheerful, during those final hours here on Earth with us? Now I am certain: Zhubin had known his time had come and he was relieved. Despite his condition, he had found the strength to carry out his plan. He had felt it was time for him to move on and go to what he called *"home"*.

It came as a shock when, after his passing, I found a separate folder inside his "The Master Plan" binder that contained a collection of "Au Revoir" letters all addressed to me. Each one dealt me a sledgehammer blow, leaving me shattered and weeping uncontrollably. While on my winding road I came to understand why he had taken it upon himself to write these: it was simply a part of what he described as *"my destiny and my contract with the Universe"*. Zhubin had understood the impact that his death would have on me and what I would have to face. He knew that the death of a child is the hardest thing of all for a parent to bear. Writing these farewell letters was his parting gift – his way of continuing to speak to me, preparing me to press on with my own journey and find my own purpose. In sharing these keepsakes here, I hope that they can be of some comfort to other grieving parents – and that I have fulfilled Zhubin's request to me: *"Spread my words. Be my voice."*

Putting these letters together must have taken Zhubin quite some time – perhaps weeks. He had developed a habit of disappearing into his room with a request not to be disturbed. I assumed that he was working on correspondence with his doctors, whom he regularly updated about his symptoms. He must have completed these letters before our final trip to Boston – that is why I am certain that he knew his time to leave was imminent.

Since his first childhood words, Zhubin had always addressed me as "Simin". So why did he choose, both on what proved to be our last evening together and in these letters, to address me as "Mom"? Perhaps it was to assure me of his love, despite the ultimate action he was considering? Perhaps it was a wish to remind me that I would always be his mother – or to bring comfort to himself also? Maybe it was his way of making his words reach out to all mothers? I have no answer – and in the end it does not matter – but seeing the word "Mom" touches me with a deep joy that still warms my heart each time I read any of the letters.

Through the stormy pain of his loss, it was years before I found the strength to pay attention to the sweetness of hope stored in his messages and to comprehend how to apply them in my life, instead of just drowning them with my tears. Zhubin's words have been a tool with which I joyfully discovered a new world – one filled with love and *"The Way of the Spirit"* as he called it. Always so simple yet, to me, insightful, his soothing words of hope and courage, now etched in my heart, have become my language of the spirit, soft and gentle like flowers.

Life to Zhubin was not about its limitations, but about living it fully; death was not the end but a transition to the next chapter. I believe Zhubin was chosen to give me a message: life is not only in the here and now, but has a spiritual dimension we can all tap into and that lasts forever. Certain there was a reason and an explanation for everything, Zhubin did not believe in random destiny or coincidence. Aware of the purpose of his existence, he sensed and believed in a life hereafter, saying: *"There is so much that the human mind does not understand, but this non-understanding also has a purpose."*

Both by his words and his example, Zhubin allowed me to discover a well of resilience to carry on. He is never far from my thoughts. Although I will never be able to escape entirely the pain of missing my son, the unshakeable faith that I have found permits me to live with peace and gratitude.

I know where my son is. He has neither disappeared, nor transformed into a ghost; instead, he exists as a vast spirit, a source of positive energy that shoots through everything that I see, touch and hear. With his love that continues to surround me, he remains a part of the Universe, as am I – as are we all.

Zhubin still lives in my memory, with me all through my days. I think of him when drinking coffee with a friend or when alone tending to my garden. My thoughts travel to him when I visit family far away or when I walk my Daisy in the neighbourhood. I see him in the eyes of the children I love, feeling him in the kisses I put on their cheeks. My mind wanders in his direction when I read a book that I enjoy or when I volunteer. Most of all, I remember him when I smile.

Still touched by his love, I often reflect not just on all that he has already taught me, but also on what I continue to learn from him. I have come to accept and respect Zhubin's ultimate choice. I have come to realize that relationships do not end with death – they continue to grow and blossom into what both souls had hoped they would become.

"Mom,
Always keeping our eyes on every moment, we have to maintain our quality of life on a high and elevated style. The real journey in life is experiencing the challenges it brings us. This is something that we all need to remember. So keeping our hearts and minds on this makes a huge difference in our life's quality, both here and in the afterlife. We work on it as a soul and as a being. This is called soul work."

As long as I live I will remember every moment of my journey with Zhubin – the love we shared, his gentle teaching. Zhubin remains with me, no longer in body but in spirit. Feeling him whispering the right words whenever I'm in need, I rejoice in the signs he brings me assuring me that he has never left me alone.

"I won't be gone.
I'll never be far from you.
I'll always be next to you.
No more tears, promise.
You are my Mom and my best friend.
We are one.
We are and will be together, forever.
Feel me.
Our bond is golden."

A Letter to Mothers: Heart to Heart

There is:
    no love greater than the love for a child;
    no injustice greater than the loss of a child.

    Their names remain on our lips,
    their love within our hearts, their memory within our minds.

Drowning in the sudden tsunami of grief, the thought that we could live again seems inconceiveable, utterly impossible.

I had to learn patience, for, no matter how painful the situation, there is always a slender trace of hope that eventually a path out of the quagmire will be found.

"You have to learn patience too – it is a godly way."

Faith and trust taught me how to reach the light of freedom. This was no easy task when drowned by crippling grief, pain lashing me so severely that I felt no more desire to live. It is not easy to build a new life on the rubble of the previous one. Wrestling with guilt creates even more confusing and disturbing thoughts. I am convinced that this is true for every one of us, no matter how good a parent we may have been, how much we loved our child, how much we gave and how much we did. Guilt is part of the package – we must go through this fire.

Putting one foot in front of the other, baby steps at first, I learned that I could travel the rest of my journey not shrouded by sorrow but in the light of joy. Of course, I will still remember the difficult years – but less and less with a shudder and more and more with a smile, knowing that my son would be happy to see me like this, regardless of what we faced together. Each time that I managed such a smile, I let go of a tiny sliver of heaviness and ever so slowly came out of the dreadful abyss of grief.

Accepting one's lot in life is a very important law of the Universe. Broken into many pieces, I allowed the Universe to help me put myself back together and build a new self that grows in strength every day.

Zhubin came with a message for me – that *"There is a band of love and a promise to hold us all together forever"*. Life may be a journey of a thousand turns and twists, but to my eyes it has only one path: that of love and compassion. Sometimes I stray from this path, but no matter the darkness around me, love always finds a way to bring me back onto it again. Love may hurt but never gives up.

If this book reaches your hands, know that I love you. Your loss is my loss. Your grief is my grief. Your healing and peace are my healing and peace. We share the same pain. We are all one.

Zhubin's words became wings of love wrapped around me, lifting up my soul, bringing me comfort, and enabling me to take the next few steps – maybe they will even help you to believe and trust in what he referred to as the *Big Picture*.

When you read Zhubin's letters it is my hope that you might find solace in them, almost as though they were from your own child. There is no difference between mine and yours: they are all one in our love for them. When you see and read the word "Mom", hear your own child's voice talking to you, with their own message of love.

> Hear this – your child wants you
> to trust;
> to believe;
> to be strong;
> to live – yes, even be happy;
> to work on your heart,
> open it to the Universe and to that marvellous abundant love.
> See the smile on your child's face, telling you: *"Mom, you are not alone. I am always with you. It is okay to miss me. But don't be broken. We are connected always and forever."*

Perhaps reading this will help you to recognize that what has happened to us has a reason beyond our limited understanding and knowledge. It is my greatest desire that Zhubin's words assist you on your journey, the way they offered me a glimpse of the boundless beauty of the Universe. I believe that nothing happens by accident, nothing by chance. Everything is measured: everything is counted – all our experiences, even our steps, the people and the countless faces we see. Know also that should this book reach your hands, it is not coincidence: there is a purpose and a message in it for you. I hope these words will find the hearts of those in need and help them find the strength to move forward. In my darkest hours I was helped by reading and re-reading these words.

I wish that you have already found, or will soon find, your path to the belief that what was yours still is and will always be. Our children are never lost; they remain by our side. We cannot give up and lose hope. Our children are alive – more than we can imagine. They become our guides and our healing angels. They are always with us. The energy of love never dies. Of course, we miss them terribly, always. Of course, we must still face this challenge. It will be so until we meet them again. But with faith and hope the rest of the journey can still be fruitful and rich.

Through my heart, my soul is connected to yours – and this is one of the most blissful aspects of my spiritual journey. With this book, I give you my love, my heart, and my prayers.

> Your peace is my peace.
> Your joy is my joy.
> You are in my heart.
> We are one.
> Fear has no place in a faithful heart.

With endless love, I kiss your heart.

Simin

Au revoir

My Mom,

I am writing to you with love and hope. I really want you to understand what I am saying here. It is not going to be easy, but I really, really want you to feel and believe what I am saying. I am leaving this place and moving on. We do move on, and moving on is what we have to do.

Mom, be humble by letting things happen, bad or good. Let everything happen, and love whatever happens. There is a blessing and a lesson in all of it. Be detached from the past. Forget the difficult times and all the negativity. Just relax and live your life. As I said before, your heart should be a place for faith, love, and peace, not a place for separation, sadness and pain. It is our responsibility to have courage and stay calm in our hearts.

Do good for others and share what you can, as much as you can. Ask for nothing. Be grateful. Sadness means to be ungrateful – it is a lack of faith.

Feel and see love in what you do, and love it. Your life should be about where you want to go and not about the pain of the past. We have to have hardship so we can continue to grow. I know it is not easy, but be strong.

Faith has to be the centre of everything that we are and do: faith in things that we do not know; faith in the unknown.

There is so much that the human mind does not understand, but this non-understanding also has a purpose.

Do not focus on the missing things in your life, because you have so much. Go on your path and be an example for everyone.

Try to understand the concept of life. Our lives are not about where we have been and what we have done. It is about where we are now, what we are doing, and where we are going now.

Mom,

We cannot plan out everything. What is inescapable is destiny. Just take it and go forward. But what we can plan to do is to make the right choices – whether we do or not, that's up to us. Coming here to this life is like signing a contract with the Universe: when the work is done, we go back home.

You will have a life without me.
Live your destiny the way I lived mine.
Focus on the new stage.
Have peace. Reach out, Mom.
Have a plan for your life.
Know that you have to have a purpose.
Dedicate your life in a very intelligent way.
Being positive is more than skin deep.
Trust me.
Trust yourself.
Trust your heart.
Be free.

To become a master, one has to have a life story.
Trauma, loss, misunderstanding, grief, loneliness, are all part of life.
Accept it all – do not ask why.
Face it all with courage and, most of all, with acceptance and unselfishness – it is the only way.
A speck is just a speck, but it has meaning in its collectiveness.
Have faith in God.
Just feel the big scene – we are all fine.
You have the right qualities. Use them.
God is beautiful – I tell you this because you need to let your heart soar.
Do good in doing well.

Always keeping our eyes on every moment, we have to maintain our quality of life on a high and elevated style. The real journey in life is experiencing the challenges it brings us. This is something that we all need to remember. So keeping our hearts and minds on this makes a huge difference in our life's quality, both here and in the afterlife. We work on it as a soul and as a being. This is called soul work.

Life is short and for some of us, who are more fragile, it may be even shorter. This is a journey. However, it is not an end but another beginning.

I am in your heart.

Learning is never-ending. You need to expand your learning. Once I realized this, I changed. You will too. Have faith. Let yourself heal. Remember, a broken person cannot achieve much. Your heart needs to be a temple before you can really start. Begin from there. True, these things are hard, but they are just a challenge in growing. Let your life be an example and do a good job.

Take care.

Be at peace – be calm.
Rest your worries and stick to matters of the heart.
The seed of life is in the heart: it is small, but incredible.
Love and faith nourish it. You have to learn to feel the spirit.
Have lots and lots of positive energy.
Have passion. Play, eat, enjoy.
Time to really move on.
Have fun with life. You must be happy.
Be. Be. Be.
Watch your heart, your soul.
Make it all beautiful and let it reflect your heart.
If your heart smiles for me, you will have heavy-duty fun with me.
Be patient with yourself.

Mom,

Take care of your life in a loving way. The Universe will then take care of you in a loving way too. Share my words – they may help others and give your purpose another dimension.

I know you will suffer, but you should learn what this is all about. It is a new phase for you and you have to guide yourself on your own. Step by step, you will learn and know, I promise. But move on with faith and peace.

We have to learn to think big – learning to see the picture bigger and bigger is the same as being wise and having wisdom.

Be an instrument – take care of my soul brothers and sisters.
Keep picturing yourself in heaven and become part of it.
The return journey is the journey to God and angels.
See with your soul's eyes.
You are and will always be my Mom.
Think always of yourself as a mom: great woman, great task.
Love you

Move to a very good place within yourself. Learn faith and practise it. That way you will know with your heart and mind what the Big Picture is all about. This gives you courage, hope and patience. I understand that you have pain in your heart for me. You are a mother. However, do not forget that, bit by bit, we learn and become wiser and wiser, and this is when we reach the status of a teacher. Teaching is the highest calling and profession. True teachers transform lives and shape the future of individuals. One reason that I am happy is that, when you learn about peace, you can also teach it. Be always peaceful, even though you might get hurt once in a while.

Peace.

Do not go to the past and do not concentrate on loss, but on the gain and the future, otherwise you will walk backwards. Think of the beauty that is around you, and don't let your heart sink. It might sound tough, but I would not have said this if you could not do it. Trust in God, trust in me, and trust in yourself.

Sadness is not a cure for your pain. It just traps you. Let it go! Let it go! Live your life. Stay positive. Change your tears for smiles.

Just be.

I don't want you to have a sad heart. Be strong every day and keep your path straight. Life for you still has lots of agendas that you need to take care of. I hope that you go through with all that you are planning in your heart. It is a good thing.

Love you, and keep peace in your heart.

You are very dear to me. Your love and desire for my well-being are very real, but no more guilt and empty sadness. Have the courage to let your sadness go. Take life easy. Be still in your heart, active in your mind, and take your responsibilities seriously. It is your blessing. Think big. The blessings are for both sides. I really feel happy and light, and I want you to feel it one day, too.

Mom,

Despair and negativity about your life holds you down. Acknowledging weakness is always a good thing.

Our pain is part of the journey; it allows us to learn what we need to learn and do what we should do. Balance, fairness, generosity, being a warrior for truth; giving back from whom we received and focusing on the Big Picture.

Don't be afraid of anything; life always works out somehow. Everyone has ups and downs. We plan and plan, but we don't put "unexpected" into the plan. From the unexpected we grow and this is how we get to know ourselves. As humans we feel that we know better and have control. Instead, we should have faith since there is nothing we control.

Your focus should be to grow and touch others' hearts. Be with people that matter to you and whom you trust and who have faith in you.

In this material life that we are in, the meaning of being rich sometimes gets lost. Being grateful means being rich, since this allows us to appreciate life, what we have, and each other.

In relationships, some doors are meant to be shut and some shut doors may be opened if the other finds a way to open the door with the key of love.

Remember the entire connection that we have with all who have come into our lives and who will come: some give us blessings – others need our blessing; some hurt – others heal; some take – others give. There is a big lesson in each connection. We need these teachings and these teachers. We give energy and blessings, and in return, we receive energy and blessing. Everything in life is circular and it is a circle that binds us all together. We truly never leave each other. This is because we all become part of one another.

Life is too short for doubt and regret. Regret only has room in our lives when we don't try, and just sit on the sidelines not taking action. That should be the only thing we regret.

Sadness, when it is not necessary, will keep our focus away from what we should do.

Life is filled with beautiful moments that most people miss.

Be a source of light where there is darkness.

When things happen, know it is no coincidence. I am trying to help you see the Big Picture and understand what this means. Always be productive – and know that you grow and grow on days like this, the productive and happy days – this way you create yourself.

Be happy.

When you lose all your sadness and pain, it is then that you will see the Light. It is then when magic happens. Life is gentle, so simple. Live your life – why make it complicated? Look at the Big Picture. Know it! Feel it!

Each of our lives is a single strand of a rope – we are strong together. It is a big mistake to think in individual terms.

Togetherness is multidimensional – you cannot even imagine!

It is by making mistakes that we learn and grow – but it is important to know our mistakes and break the cycle not to repeat them. Be big by being selfless.

The truth is in your heart: go in it, and don't come out.

I love your aching heart, but I know that one day you will overcome your pain and will understand it all. Life is so much more than we know and think. There are so many different paths, but they all lead to the same place. Happiness is everything. I love you, Mom. Have a wonderful life and keep your smiles.

Mom,

You have to go among unusual people and unusual places. Do it. Make the right changes in the right places and in the right way. Passion in your work is a must. Be patient with yourself and your mission. It is important to have only a willing heart. I know it is not easy, but be strong. There are so many different ways to the top of the mountain. Go beyond. You cannot yet comprehend it. To know where you want to go, visualize the end and keep on going forward. Remember this always.

All life is about give and take. You have a lot of work to do. Keep yourself busy. When you are busy, time goes by fast. Have all sorts of responsibilities in different areas. Every day do something new, and keep it up. Be focused, strong, and aware. All will work out somehow.

You must, must do a very fantastic job with all your responsibilities. All of them are very essential. Help always, keep your energy for work. Go ahead with pride in your heart. You can do it. It is your mission and your responsibility. Remember, I talked to you about courage and vision? Go ahead, open doors for others. You are not alone. Always look at the Big Picture.

Sad days come, also happy ones. Listen with your heart. Nobody can understand, imagine, or hear it for you. It is your heart, not others'. Remember real peace and just smile.

All the weeds – the things that hold you back – must be left behind.

You are dear to me.

Do not let anyone or anything spoil your time – invest it on your health and learning "big time".

Be strong – this is nothing but a Moment.

Mom,

I know you are anxious and you are down. You need to learn to separate your emotions and give meaning to each of them. You need to fight the downward spiralling road. You are meant to look up, no matter how hard it is.

It is illness to fear;
It is illness to give up;
It is illness to assume;
It is illness to not give the benefit of doubt.

Life is not perfect and it is not supposed to be. It is our imperfections that allow us to open up to the healing process. What I mean to say here to you is this: my life is not perfect; your life is not perfect. In this life, we have so many burdens and challenges. Our journey is to heal in this life. This is why our lives here are so important.

You will learn, you will grow, you will allow yourself to open up to healing energy and you will be healed. When you do so, remember where you were and where you are now. Remember and hold on to it.

What I am saying does not make sense to you now, but trust me that it will.

You need to ease up;
Don't feel betrayed;
Don't feel alone;
Don't feel forsaken;
Don't feel so misunderstood.

There is lots of love, understanding and compassion around you. You have to feel the energy and see the gifts.

What is happening here is a crossroad scenario and you are not familiar with this new journey, the shape of the gifts, the shape of hope. Because of this crossroad everything has changed.

You need to train yourself: your focus has been too inward. You need to move out of yourself. This is part of the learning that you need to do. I promise there are people around who suffer more than us. This is a journey. It might seem to you that I am repeating myself, but repeat I must.

Harmony is something you need to bring to yourself, not seek from others. Why? Because it will bring balance to your heart. You will grow and achieve a lot, but you are at a crossroads. Regain the harmony and this should be a stepping stone for you. In the moment of harshness this is crucial: don't feel that we are victims. No one is. Regain the inner peace and move away from what is not meant for you.

Remember that your journey is not about doing big things, but about seeking harmony. This is the important key.

See the love and the gifts around you. Take this energy. Shake the house within and let in new life. Crossroads mean pain, uncertainty, but they also mean growth in an amazing way.

Life is as it is meant to be, enjoy it: as I said earlier, a lost moment is a huge loss.

Give energy – don't seek it;
Create harmony – don't seek it;
Give love – don't seek it;
And I mean to people that count for you and are in your life.

Open a new chapter and go forward. Let your life be filled with real golden nuggets. The good times you spent and have are what is important. Memories will remain forever. I want you to enjoy the rest of your life with your loved ones otherwise you will look back and regret that you didn't and have lost precious time.

Sadness in your heart will remain, but time and love will heal it.

As I have told you, your life is meant to be difficult and it is normal for you to wonder why. True, you have worked very hard, but you have also been given so much.

Know also that people are blessed by choosing to be an instrument. Generosity is a blessing. A generous person is blessed for giving and sharing so much, not just wealth, but talent, time and knowledge. There should be a lot of that in everybody's life. Life here prepares us for life after.

Courage creates powerful energy. Gives us hope. Moves us forward. It helps us go through the ups and downs. It makes us strong and wise. To be courageous is not easy. It comes through willingness. It is awesome. Try to have a lot of it.

Life is a journey and a process – not a one-time event. You are on this journey. Pain is what makes you beautiful and brings you to God. Try to learn new ways of seeing. Register it. Feel it. Use your time to achieve – achieve productively.

Peace, faith and hope. Remember: give love, receive love, be love. You will receive shining stars.

Do you know why God put our eyes on the front of our face? To see: not up, but ahead.

You have to have variety in your mission otherwise you cannot gain deep experiences. No one does one thing. Balance in everything results in healthy multidimensional growth.

Think that you are going to an amazing destination and you are packing for this trip. Instead of packing objects, you are packing qualities: faith, love, patience. By learning these you are packing for your trip – a trip to heaven. Make sure your bag is a heavy one.

Stay active, have a happy heart and let your eyes see straight ahead. This is all you have to do.

Mom,

A loss is not a loss – it is a change. Through change comes growth, and there is always reason to celebrate growth. So celebrate! See not a loss but a change. Grow from it and celebrate the growth.

Do good things for your heart. Life is amazing. Focus, and see the amazement rather than the holes. You are adding colour and variety with many themes to create a garden full of beauty. You should feel good about the things you do. Experience your life. I am talking about inner light.

I know you are tender. I understand and it is okay. Remember that life brings you challenges and, from these challenges, you either grow or become a victim. When a parent loses a child the ultimate challenge must be faced.

You should start the healing process of your life in a deep way: by helping others to heal. I hope you feel what I'm saying. This kind of work is the most rewarding thing you can do. Do as much as you can, and feel it within. When a tree loses a big branch, it either rots or so many little shoots start to grow in its place. In the same way, when a parent loses a child either she becomes a victim or many opportunities to help and provide service will manifest themselves. When one sees these opportunities and acts on them, one will find the healing power within and also realize that the child is not lost, but has gained a new relationship with the energy instead.

Love your life and love yourself. Love the nature and smell the flowers.

Peace and calmness to you.

I want you to know everything will come to an end. But the energy remains and then new things will happen. It is about going on forward. This is the circle of life.

Don't worry that good times have come to the end. Just be grateful that we had a chance to be together. Don't be sad that a life is over. Be happy that you had the privilege to deal with it. You know that saying: "We come to this world alone and leave this world alone." This is not true. We are surrounded by our family and angels on both sides.

All good things come to an end and all good things begin again. More venture and more adventure is a good thing. Live one day at a time – no, live one moment at a time.

Do not be broken. Be patient and don't let your heart squeeze your soul. Let your soul squeeze your heart. Be high energy and go ↑↑↑ up, up, up. Do your best and show your spirit and energy. Keep your guard up as well as your faith.

Don't be dry and dusty – be moist and fresh. Shower yourself with the love of life again and again. This is the best prayer to God.

Trust in God.

Open the door of your heart. Show your faith and let God work on it. Life does not last forever, but love does.

Life is a wonderful and amazing journey. Our journey starts from the moment that we are born and ends at the last breath we take. In this short time we have here there are endless possibilities and ways to give love and learn. One has to go along the way with faith and courage.

Your life should stand for big and bigger things. Appreciate the small simple things in life. They mean so much, so take pleasure in them – life is over in a blink of an eye.

Self-mastery is about being in the moment and enjoying little simple things – going with the flow of life, not against it.

To see beauty in everything needs skill and practice.

Mom,

Be happy for me, and be happy for your second chance.
Be small, but feel and think big.
Let yourself go and see to unfinished business.
Not many people get second chances. You have a clean page to work with: write on it wisely.
Be hopeful and create positive energy.
Listen for small things, but see big.
Go deep. Get the picture.
Know yourself so you can know God.
I am with you.

Good things always happen.
Just see it.
Be strong – it takes a strong person to do the right thing.
Let faith fill your heart.
Face all your challenges and responsibilities.
The blessings will come.
Be happy – it is holy and it shows the faith.
Feel the spirit.

I know you will miss me. It is your journey. Everyone has a journey as you know, and it will be so until the end. You can be strong and you will go on your path and live your life. Count your many blessings to help you through your journey. You have your family, you have good friends, you are healthy. You have the knowledge to learn. You always have me and, above all, you always have God. You are rich, Mom.

Love the life you have. Your happy face and smile will come back. I promise.

Love you.

I want you to really work on yourself:

> no tears, no pain, no fear, no sadness, no worry;
> quiet your mind;
> listen, feel, hear;
> be patient;
> be hopeful;
> believe;
> trust and achieve;
> seek always;
> live your life.

Try to remember:

> To smile, to walk.
> Faith you must have.
> Trust your feelings.
> Do not waste your time.
> See the Big Picture.
> The stronger you get,
> The more signs you will see.
> The more you will do.
> Be wise and be serene.
> Until you feel peace,
> You cannot achieve.
> Life has ups and downs.
> Have the right knowledge to move on.
> Life is what you make it.
> Happier you.
> Happier me.

You will be blessed.

Mom,

I am so glad to be writing this to you. I want you to know that I am in your heart and you are wrapped in my special bubble. I love you and when you miss me, remember that I am all around you.

Make a bubble and wrap it around all your loved ones while I wrap all of you in mine. This way we are all in the same bubble and together. You and I are on the journey of an incredible experience. Know that I am with you.

Sit with your soul.
Smile at life and move on. I have.
Wonder, and wonders you will see.
Redefine yourself. Soar! Soar!
Gentleness is what I feel for you.
Be free of pain.
Let us grow together deeply.
I am always with you.
Feel your pain and this will become the road back to God.
See the beauty of the rose? Your pain for me is a rose.
God is holding you.
You can find yourself in His light. Know that. Always! Always!
Feel the freedom. Blessings will come from that.
It makes you feel pure. Love it! Love it! Love it!
You have to do a lot. Do it. It is for me and you.
You can achieve through faith, positive actions, and feelings.

Start the work!

God is in your life.

I am in your heart.
Soar with me.
Be free, Mom, I am your energy.
Feel God's love.
He is giving it to you.

Feel it.

What is love?

Love is you and me.
Do you know how vast we are?
Feel me, never far.
To know Him is to love life.
Hello again.
Go deep.
Can you dream with your heart? I do it all the time.
Good things always happen – be sure to see them.
I am high with love. Join with me.
Mom, you are my one true hero.
I am who I am because of you.
Melt. Melt. Melt.

When you get emotional, the question is why you feel this way.

You see the light that is in you.
Call it out.
You and I are no more,
But we are one.
Dream it all, Mom.
Listen to the whispers.
I am teaching you small things that are so big.
Love all, even the ones who are difficult to love.
Be in tune with yourself.
Trust your heart.
Live with passion.
Be with God.
Doing good for others never ends, never enough.
Do it all, Mom.
It is your blessing.

Mom,

The most beautiful and amazing celebrations in life are the quiet ones. The ones that people can experience but cannot talk about.

Miracles do "happen". They really do. Believe and believe more.

Faith always wins.
Love always wins.
Peace always wins.
Hope always wins.
Courage always wins.
By being together we always win.

Big time.

If people knew that life experiences are meant to be, then their grief would change its shape and get replaced by reflection.

I know you will be in pain but keep your head up and look above. I will be hugging you and will be all over you. You won't be far from me. Have faith.

Love you.

Every day, I mean every day, enjoy your day. And that is a prayer to God. Life has to go forward with faith. Hold on to this more than anything else: the more you grow, the closer you are to God. To know God, you must have faith and peace in your heart.

I know that your heart will ache for me when I'm not here, but it is just a flash. Your pain is your journey, and leaving you early is but a step on my journey. When you miss me, take a deep breath and see our life here as a part of the Big Picture. See life as a whole – do not dissect it into pieces. Do not think about the pain. Do not question your mothering and mistakes, because we all come here to experience and then move on. We all belong to where I am going, but because of fear we feel we belong to earth and this life.

Have a vision – it is so important, and when you miss me, envision me and you and what you want. You shall have it and more. Have a wonderful life.

Know and remember what you want to be and where you want to be. Visualize that. Let that feeling guide you to the end. Let your heart work for you.

Each of us is like the farmer: we reap only what we sow. Have the willingness to help, Mom. You can touch the hearts of mothers. Do it.

Don't spend too much time with yourself. Lose yourself in others instead.

I have given you all the keys you need to open doors. Find the right keys for the right doors and open them.

The best way to show ourselves is by being great at what we do and how we do it.

Mom,

Know that we all are bound together forever, and that our bond is very powerful.
You are not alone: God is in you.
I want you to do what I could not: open doors; give hope; be love; help all.
Be happy, that is holy.
Learn to be with everyone in a heavenly way.
Play it right, Mom.
Let the seed of life be watered by your love.
Will is everything – go after what you wish for.
Small things matter – do it all.
Help my friends who are in suffering.
I know broken hearts – cheer them with light.
Make flowers bloom wherever you go.

The seed of life in your heart will grow fast. Your love and feelings allow the seed to grow – keep it up.
Give yourself a mental, emotional and spiritual task every day.
Keep giving yourself a purpose.
I need your work, love and presence always.
It is okay to miss me – but don't be broken.
Love is an emotion.
I know you love me with every cell – no one can do more.
I love you, too.
We are connected always and forever.
We will see each other when the time is right.
Remember I talked to you about eternity?

Be like a child – free.

Be faithful. Believe.
Be selfless. Be humble.
Be big. Be small.
Be bold without holding a hammer.

Be a rock, not a sponge.
Be in harmony with life.
Just be, be, and be.

I won't be gone.

I'll never be far from you.
I'll always be next to you.
No more tears, promise.
You are my Mom and my best friend. We are one. We are and will be together, forever.
Feel me.
Our bond is golden.

Look at the sun and the moon, And see me.

Look at animals and yellow flowers, And see me.

Our bond is forever.
The garden in your heart is our little meeting place.

I love you.

The yellow flowers should be a symbol of me – to remind you to have a happy life. It does not mean an easy life without challenges, but it means peace of mind. I know that later on you will know what I meant. Everything is connected with love and spirit. Do not let into the present the past pain of my absence. Take care of your heart.

Mom,

This is heavy. I know. What can I say?

This is your trial and triumph.
I cannot advise you more now.
I cannot comfort you more now.
I cannot love you more.
You have it all.

Every life, every chapter of life, has a story. Make it worthwhile. Our lifetime here is less than a dot in eternity.

With love, let the seed of life grow in your heart. Imprint yourself onto the hearts of others.

All kind touches are holy.

You will grow day by day.
Your soul will bear fruit like a tree.
The tree is me – the fruit is you.

You will be lost at first, but you will find yourself. You will miss me – a small price to pay to be together for eternity.

The garden in your heart is our shrine. Make it cozy and very spiritual. This is our journey. This was meant to be. The mission is the Master Plan.

I am not in tears, but in laughter. Remember, God is in happy moments and laughter too.

I love you.

Thank you for all the things you have done and are doing for me.
Thank you for my life.
And thank you for letting me go.

When I leave, my heart will stay in your heart and yours will come with me. You will not be alone.

Be my voice and spread my words. The beauty of it is that it is self-sowing. You will never see the end or how many hearts you will have touched.

Mom,
I am your butterfly.
See how freely they fly,
How high they fly,
And how they live
among the flowers.
Think butterfly.

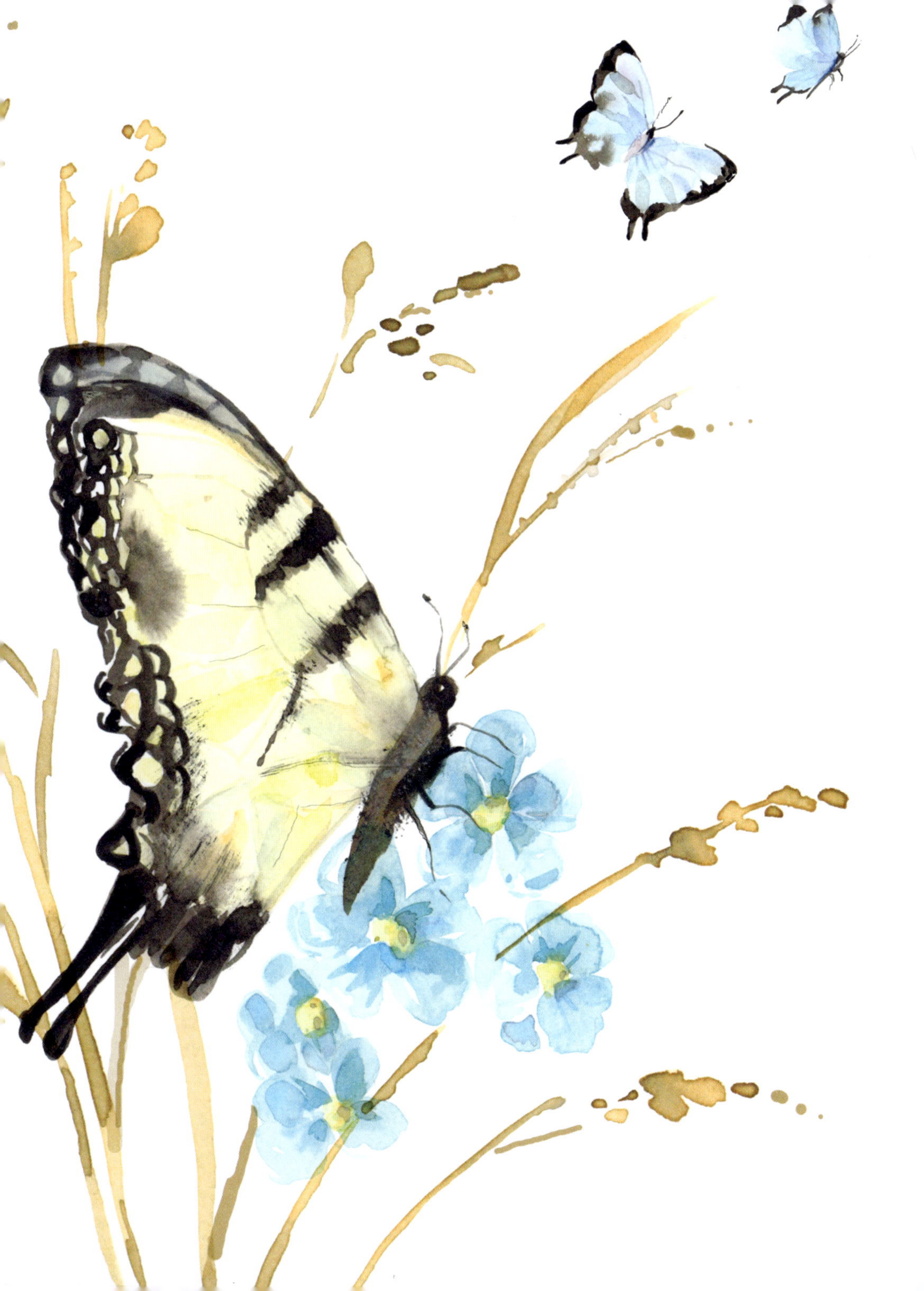

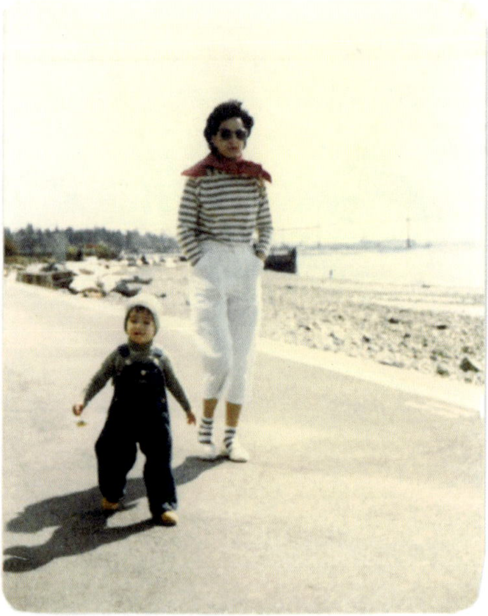

A Letter to Zhubin

My one, my only, my all,

I have written here a few words to you, although I know you always hear me.

Our story began with you – my journey began with you. You have given me something that I can never forget and I have given you my heart – wherever you may go, it goes with you. Even now, so many years later, I still see your innocent eyes and feel your love.

Through the nights and days, the months and years, in my heart I have kept alive our memories. I cherish what we had in the short time we were together.

In some ways I feel even closer to you, because now I understand what you were all about. You taught me about love – the forgotten love that was buried inside – and showed me where to find it. You taught me faith and a way of life. You taught me never to give up and find hope when it was nowhere to be found. You taught me to dream with my heart. You gave me all you could and so much more. You enriched my life. Through the harshness of pain, I found God; I found love; I found you. You are rooted in my soul. I only hope that I have done justice to your words and to your teachings.

I know that one day we will be together in a peaceful place. Until then, I cling to my dreams of being with you again. When my time comes, God's light will be like a bridge to bring me to you, where you will be waiting for me on the other side, as you promised.

From the darkest of nights, you made rainbow-filled days. I always prayed to the angels above to take care of you. Now I thank you for my life, my soul, and for choosing me as your Mom. You are forever my son, my love and my guide. I adore you, my wonderful, wonderful boy. My beautiful butterfly: until we meet again!

Mom and her blessings.

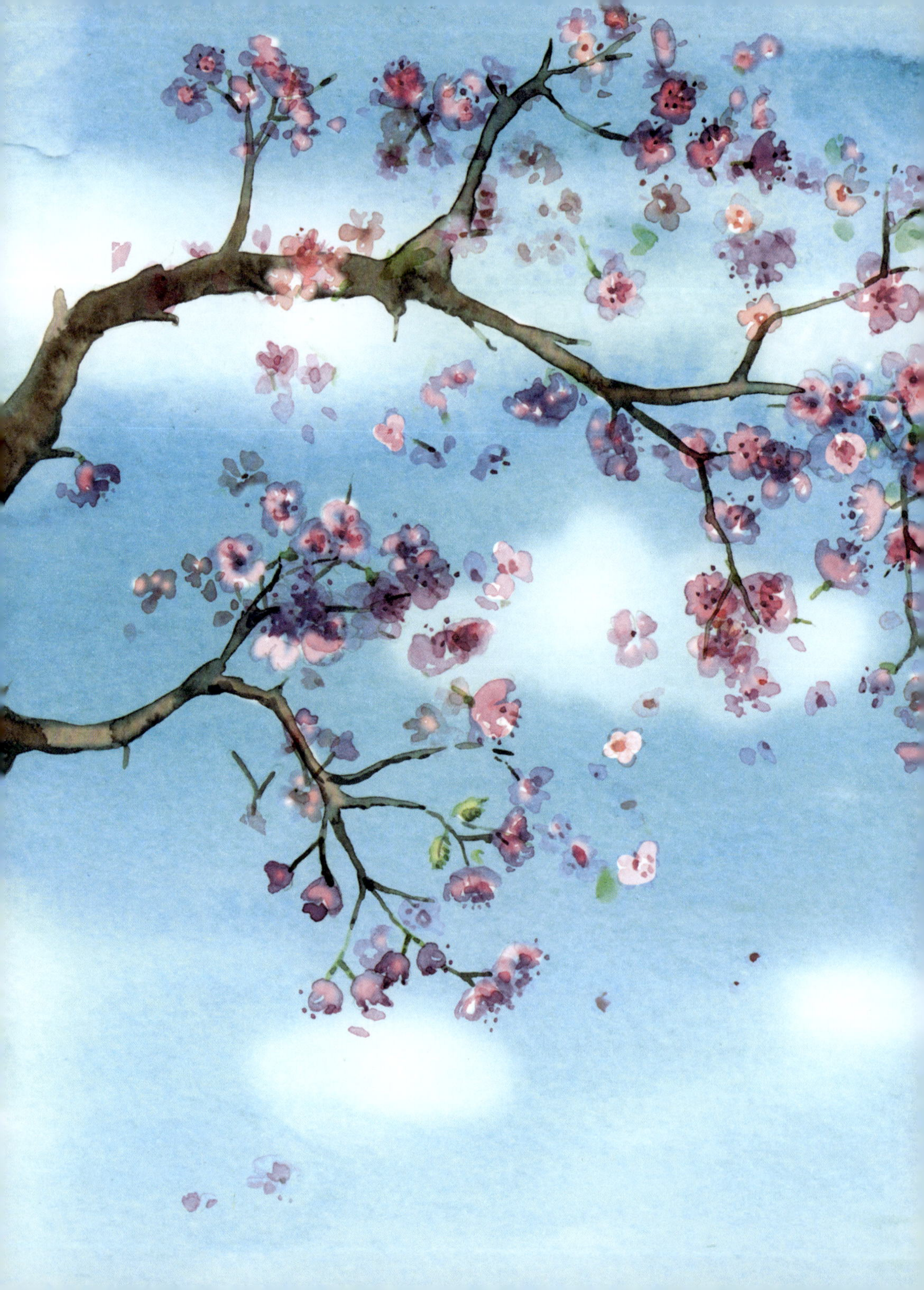

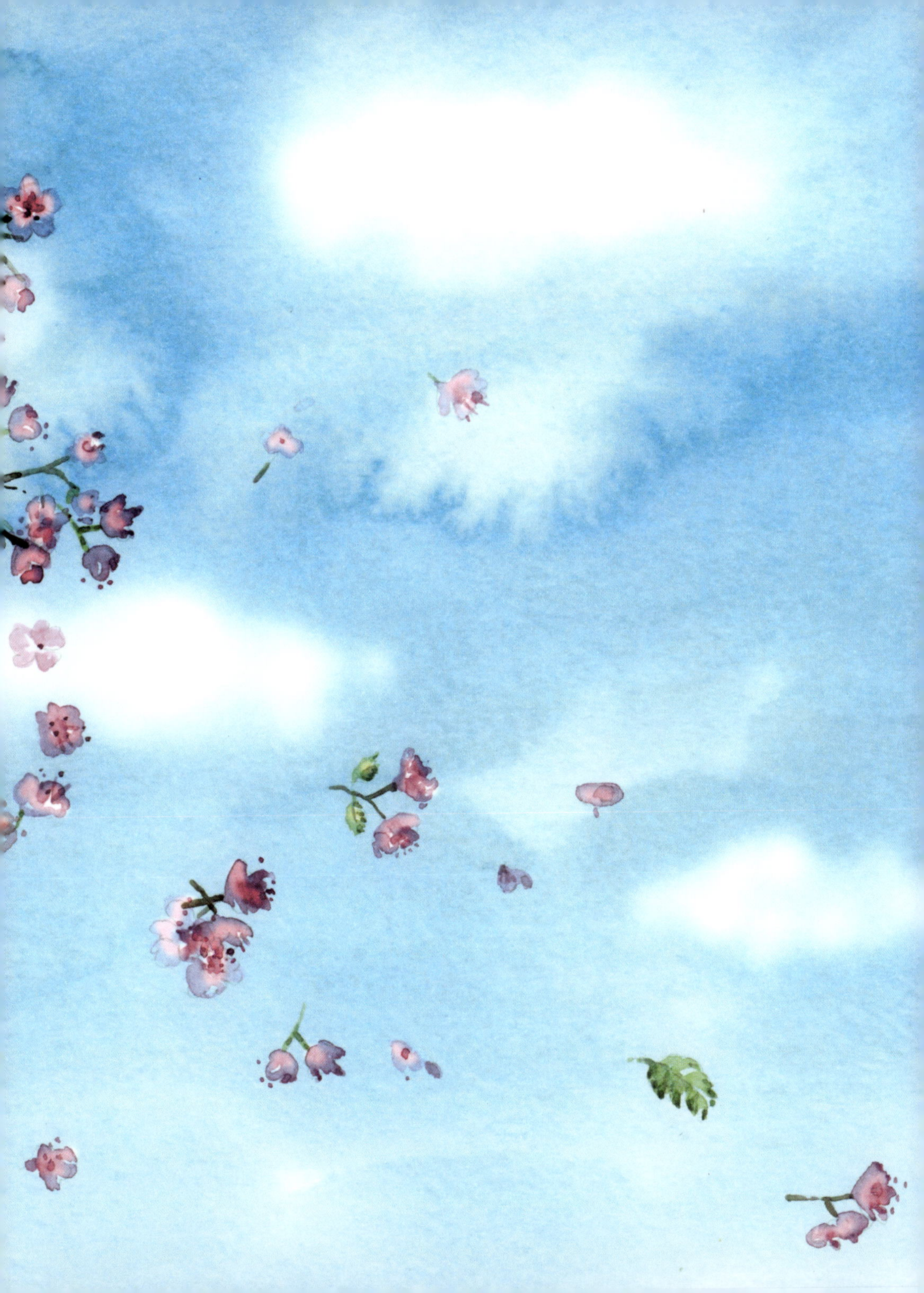

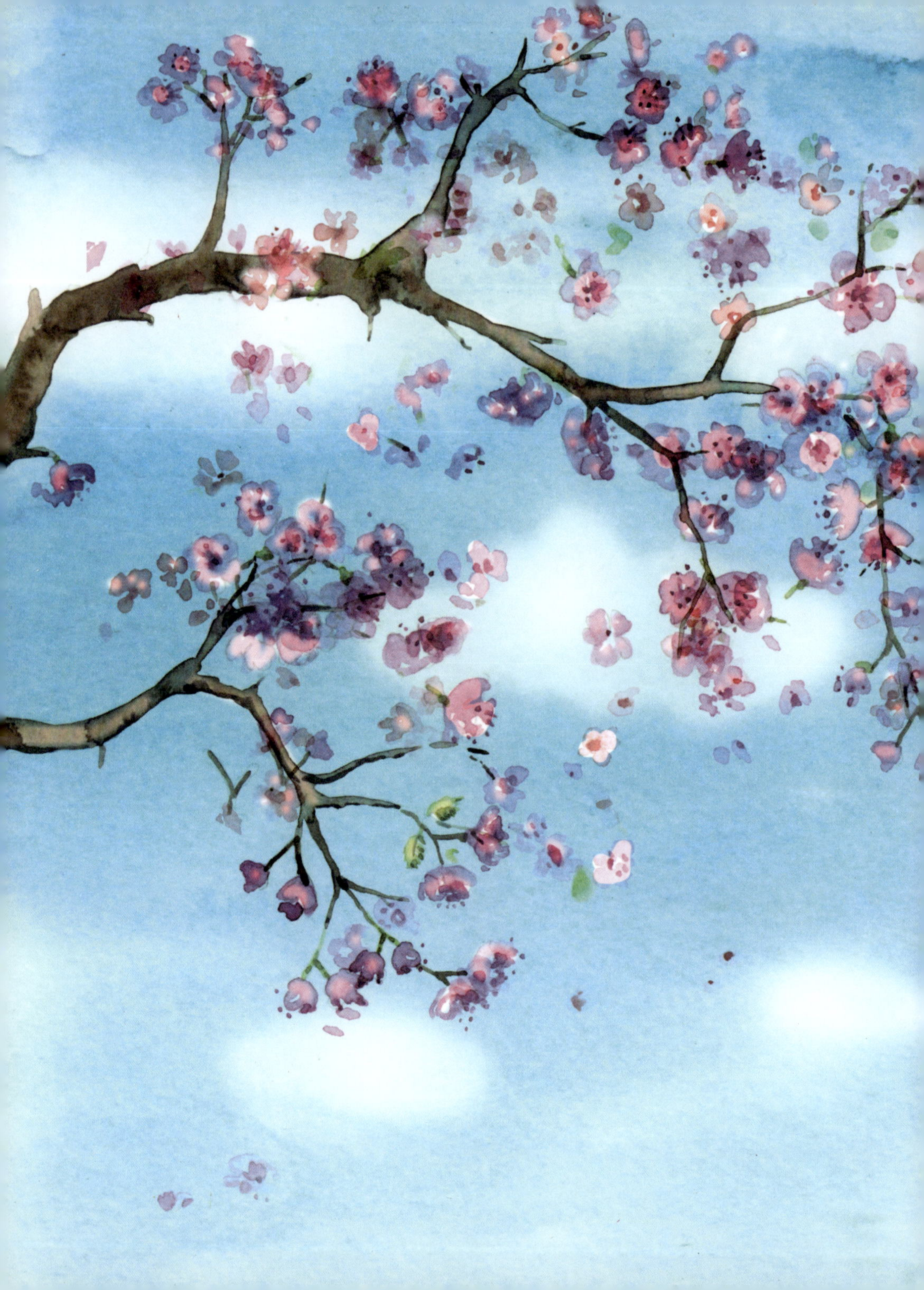